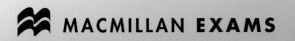

MACMILLAN EXAMS

DIRECT TO FCE

Student's Book

Roy Norris and Lynda Edwards

MACMILLAN

Contents Map

Writing	Use of English	Listening	Speaking
Email (FCE Part 1)	Multiple-choice cloze (FCE Part 1) Transformations (FCE Part 4) Open cloze (FCE Part 2)	Sentence completion (FCE Part 2)	Personal questions (FCE Part 1)
Articles (FCE Part 2)	Transformations (FCE Part 4) Word formation (FCE Part 3)	Multiple matching (FCE Part 3) Multiple choice (FCE Part 4)	Talking about photos (FCE Part 2)
Reviews (FCE Part 2)	Transformations (FCE Part 4) Open cloze (FCE Part 2) Multiple-choice cloze (FCE Part 1)	Multiple matching (FCE Part 3) Multiple choice (FCE Part 1)	Collaborative task (FCE Part 3) Further discussion (FCE Part 4)
Letter (FCE Part 1)	Open cloze (FCE Part 2) Word formation (FCE Part 3)	Sentence completion (FCE Part 2)	Collaborative task (FCE Part 3) Talking about photos (FCE Part 2)
Story (FCE Part 2) Letter of application (FCE Part 2)	Word formation (FCE Part 3) Transformations (FCE Part 4)	Multiple matching (FCE Part 3) Multiple choice (FCE Part 1)	Talking about photos (FCE Part 2) Collaborative task (FCE Part 3) Further discussion (FCE part 4)
Essay (FCE Part 2) Email (FCE Part 1) Review (FCE Part 2) Letter of application (FCE Part 2)	Multiple-choice cloze (FCE Part 1) Open cloze (FCE Part 2)	Multiple choice (FCE Part 4)	Collaborative task (FCE Part 3)
Review (FCE Part 2) Story (FCE Part 2)	Open cloze (FCE Part 2) Transformations (FCE Part 4) Word formation (FCE Part 3)	Multiple choice (FCE Part 1) Sentence completion (FCE Part 2)	Survival
Letter (FCE Part 1) Essay (FCE Part 2) Report (FCE Part 2)	Transformations (FCE Part 4) Multiple-choice cloze (FCE Part 1)	Multiple choice (FCE Part 4) Multiple matching (FCE Part 3)	Talking about photos (FCE Part 2)
Set Books (FCE Part 2) Informal letters (FCE Part 2)	Open cloze (FCE Part 2)	Sentence completion (FCE Part 2)	Collaborative task (FCE Part 3)
Email (FCE Part 1) Article (FCE Part 2) Review (FCE Part 2)	Multiple-choice cloze (FCE Part 1) Transformations (FCE Part 4) Word formation (FCE Part 3)	Multiple matching (FCE Part 3) Multiple choice (FCE Part 1) Multiple choice (FCE Part 4)	Collaborative task (FCE Part 3) Further discussion (FCE Part 4) Talking about photos (FCE Part 2)

Answer key

Page 161

Introduction

Direct to FCE is a preparation course for students wishing to take the Cambridge ESOL First Certificate in English examination, equivalent to level B2 in the Council of Europe's Common European Framework. The course is designed to improve your overall language level and help you develop the skills which are required for the FCE exam. The Student's Book comprises ten units, providing a range of interesting topics to stimulate discussion.

In this book you will find regular **Help** boxes, which give advice on how to approach the various task types in the five papers of the FCE exam. There are also **Remember** boxes, which provide reminders of the main points of this advice. Reading, writing, listening and speaking **skills** are given comprehensive coverage in each unit, and to help you further with writing, there is a **Writing Bank** at the end of the book. This includes an example question and model answer for all the different writing types in the Writing paper, highlighting the most important features of each one. The Writing Bank also includes Useful language sections and further writing tasks for you to do.

In order to help you increase your word store, there are two or more **Vocabulary** sections in each unit. In these sections, particular emphasis is placed on collocations, pairs or groups of words that are often found together, and

these are highlighted for you to record in your vocabulary notebooks. In units 2, 4, 5, 7 and 9 there are sections focusing on different aspects of **Word formation**, which are designed to build your vocabulary and prepare you for the Word formation task in Paper 3 of the FCE exam.

There are also two or more **Language focus** sections in each unit, aimed at revising and extending your knowledge of the main grammatical structures you are expected to be able to use at this level. Each section refers you to the relevant part of the **Grammar reference** on the website, but only after you have first been given the chance to show what you already know about the structures being dealt with.

At the end of each unit there is a two-page **Review** section. This contains exercises which provide specific practice in the vocabulary and structures from the same unit, and, in some cases, earlier units. The Review section also includes Writing and Use of English tasks, which offer more general practice in Papers 2 and 3 of the FCE exam.

Accompanying the course is a **Website,** which has four computer-based tests which can be done in practice mode and in test mode. There are also downloadable workbook-like materials for each unit in the Student's Book. The Grammar Reference section is available as a downloadable pdf together with the Listening Scripts.

The First Certificate in English examination

The FCE examination consists of five papers, each of which is worth 20% of the total marks. To obtain a passing grade (A, B or C) a candidate must achieve a total score of at least 60%. The final grade is based on the combined scores from all five papers, so a low score in one paper does not necessarily mean you will obtain a failing grade (D or E).

Paper 1 Reading (1 hour)

This paper has three parts, with reading texts taken from a variety of sources. There are two marks for each correct answer in Parts 1 and 2, and one mark for each correct answer in Part 3.

Part & task type	Number of questions	What you have to do
1 Multiple choice	8	Decide on the best answer from a choice of four.
2 Gapped text	7	Replace sentences which have been removed from a text.
3 Multiple matching	15	Match questions or 'prompts' to the correct text or part of a text.

Paper 2 Writing (1 hour 20 minutes)

This paper has two parts. There is one Part 1 question, which must be answered by all candidates in 120 – 150 words. In Part 2 you choose one question from four and write 120-180 words. Each question has an equal number of marks.

Part & task type	Number of questions	What you have to do
1 Letter or email	1 (compulsory)	Write a letter or an email in response to a given situation. Prompts are provided in the form of written input material such as an email, a letter or an advertisement.
2 From the following: article, essay, letter, report, review, story	4 (choose one)	Write your answer according to the task instructions. The last of the four questions has two options, each based on one of the two optional set reading texts.

Paper 3 Use of English (45 minutes)

This paper has four parts, with a total of 42 questions testing grammar and vocabulary. There is one mark for each correct answer in Parts 1, 2 and 3, and up to two marks for each answer in Part 4.

Part & task type	Number of questions	What you have to do
1 Multiple-choice cloze	12	There is a text with 12 gaps. For each gap, decide on the best answer from a choice of four. The main focus is on vocabulary.
2 Open cloze	12	There is a text with 12 gaps. Complete each gap with one word. The main focus is on grammar.
3 Word formation	10	There is a text with 10 gaps. Complete each gap with the correct form of a given word. The main focus is on vocabulary.
4 Key word transformations	8	Complete a gapped sentence with two to five words, one of which you are given. The completed sentence must have the same meaning as the lead-in sentence. The focus is on vocabulary and grammar.

Paper 4 Listening (approximately 40 minutes)

This paper has four parts with a total of 30 questions. Each part contains one or more recorded text, which is heard twice. Recordings may be monologues, such as speeches, lectures or announcements, or they may be conversations, radio interviews or discussions. You are tested on your ability to understand, for example, opinions, attitudes, specific information, gist or detail. There is one mark for each correct answer.

Part & task type	Number of questions	What you have to do
1 Multiple choice	8	Listen to eight short unrelated extracts, and answer one three-option multiple-choice question for each.
2 Sentence completion	10	Listen to one or more speakers for approximately 3 minutes and complete gaps in sentences with words or phrases from the recording.
3 Multiple matching	5	Listen to five short related monologues and match each speaker to the correct option.
4 Multiple choice	7	Listen to one or more speakers for approximately 3 minutes and answer seven three-option multiple-choice questions.

Paper 5 Speaking (14 minutes)

This paper has four parts. There are usually two candidates and two examiners, one of whom conducts the test and assesses, while the other assesses but does not take an active part in the test. You are given marks for range and correct use.

Part & task type	Time	What you have to do
1 Personal questions	3 minutes	Respond to questions from the interviewer with information about yourself.
2 Long turn	4 minutes	Talk about two photographs for one minute, and comment briefly on the other candidate's photographs.
3 Collaborative task	3 minutes	You are given visual material and have to speak with the other candidate about it in order to complete a task.
4 Discussion	4 minutes	Take part in a discussion which is related to the topic of Part 3.

A

B

C

D

Vocabulary: Influences

1 🗨 These pictures show different influences in our lives. Discuss these questions with a partner.

1 How can these people and things influence us?

2 Are these influences good or bad? Why?

2 a Use the verbs in the box to complete the phrases in 1–5.

| admire | ~~copy~~ | ~~talk~~ | ~~have~~ |
| ~~do~~ | ~~look~~ | ~~shape~~ | ~~encourage~~ |

1 My kids think he's perfect – he **can** _do_ **no wrong**! Obviously he's going to _have_ **a very big influence on** their lives.

2 I really _admire_ parents who spend a lot of quality time with their children. And if they _encourage_ them **to** read, they open up a whole world of fantasy and adventure.

3 When I was very young my best friend could _talk_ me **into doing** anything she wanted. She was very persuasive!

4 Some people believe everything they read and this can really _shape_ their **opinions**. It's quite dangerous really.

5 This guy is a role model for a lot of youngsters. The kids _look_ **up to** him and _copy_ **his every move**! He needs to understand the responsibility he has.

b Match the comments to the pictures. One comment can not be matched to a picture.

3 🗨 Discuss these questions with your partner.

1 Which teacher has had the biggest influence on you?

2 Which celebrity today do you think is a good role model?

FCE Reading Part 3: Multiple matching

1 🗨 Work in pairs. You are going to read a magazine article in which four people have written about the person who has influenced them the most. Look at the people (**A–D**). What influence do you think they had?

2 Now look at the questions and read the text carefully to answer them. For questions **1–15**, choose from the people A–D. The people may be chosen more than once.

Which person who is described

gave <u>advice</u> to the writer at a time when he/she was <u>not at all receptive</u>?	1	D
is one of <u>many</u> people who have been <u>important</u> to the writer?	2	A
<u>always</u> remained <u>calm</u>?	3	B
was easier to talk to than a <u>relative</u>?	4	D
was <u>unselfish</u> with their time?	5	B
passed on their free-time interests to the writer?	6	B
changed the way a lot of people thought?	7	C
encouraged the writer to get help from others?	8	D
stopped people laughing at the writer?	9	C
influenced the writer's peers as well as the writer?	10	A
influenced the writer more than he/she first realised?	11	B
was the reason for the writer changing career?	12	D
was continually imitated by the writer?	13	B
only knew the writer for a short time?	14	A
achieved results by not giving up?	15	D

got

Help

- Read the question and <u>underline</u> key words, as in 1–3.
- Read section A and answer any questions you can. <u>Underline</u> the relevant part of the text.
- Do the same for sections B–D.

PEOPLE WHO HAVE INFLUENCED US

You tell us about the person who has most influenced you in your life.

A My French teacher

Choosing just one person who has had a major influence on my life is practically impossible! There have been people at all stages of my life who I have both admired and been motivated by for different reasons. However, if I have to mention just one it would have to be my French teacher at secondary school. After all, it's because of her that I took a particular career path and ended up where I am today. Her passion and enthusiasm for the subject touched everyone in the class and I knew from the very first moment she started teaching that languages were going to figure somewhere in my life. It's quite scary really, to see how significant a teacher's influence can be. He or she can bring a subject alive for the students – or totally kill it off! Miss Winters was with us only for a term but a lot of her passion for languages rubbed off on me and for that I will always be grateful.

B My big sister

Inevitably, I have to say - my older sister, Ruby. I say 'inevitably' because from the moment I could walk I absolutely worshipped her! She was my idol. As far as I was concerned Ruby was perfect and I used to copy her every move. Her favourite colour was my favourite colour - her favourite food was mine too. Even into our teenage years I followed her taste in clothes, music, and boys! Now, looking back I think what I admire most about her was her patience with me. I must have been a complete pain but she never lost her temper. She gave up a lot of her time to help me with school work and she would regularly sit down with me and talk through any problems I had. Back then I copied her because I thought she was beautiful and clever and I wanted to be just like her but now I understand that in fact her influence also went a lot deeper. I hope I've developed into a caring, patient person and if so, then I certainly learned it from her.

C A character in a film

Without doubt, the person who has had the greatest influence on my life wasn't a real living person at all - but a character in a film! I was a very shy ten year old boy when I first saw Billy Elliot on the big screen. I had always wanted to dance but had never been allowed to. It was my sister who went to the ballet classes and me who tried to copy her steps in our living room. The kids at school knew I wanted to dance too - and I came in for so much teasing it used to really upset me. Where I came from, boys just didn't do dancing - like Billy Elliot! I still had this deep desire to dance - but I'd been covering it up for a long time. Then I saw the film. It gave me the confidence to ask for dancing classes and it also altered everyone else's perception of boy dancers. There was no more teasing or making fun of me. I stayed at the dancing school until I left full-time education and now dancing is my career. I often wonder how many other lives Billy Elliot is responsible for changing.

D My best friend

When you get into real trouble and think there's no way out, the last person you want to talk to is your family. You feel that you've let them all down. I'd got into a bad state. I was into drugs and I was going round with the wrong people when my best friend realised what was happening and persuaded me to get out. It can't have been easy - I wasn't listening to anyone at the time. But he stayed with it and refused to abandon me. And in the end he talked me into getting counselling and the people I spoke to really helped me turn my life around. Without him my life would have been completely different - I might not even be here at all. Boyd helped me see life in a different way and because of him I gave up my job in insurance and retrained to be a counsellor so that I could help other young people.

---

3 a Complete each gap with the correct form of a verb from the text. The letters in brackets refer to the paragraphs in which the verbs can be found.

1 If you carry on spending money like that, you'll end up bankrupt. (A)

2 I hope some of your good luck will rub off on me! (A)

3 I look back on my childhood with great fondness: it was a happy time for me. (B)

4 Jack and Katy had a big argument but they talked through their problems and now things are fine again. (B)

5 Abby was trying to cover up her feelings but I knew she was very upset. (C)

6 Ben's exam marks were poor and his parents felt he had let them **down**. (D)

7 My friend has given **up** his well-paid job to work with problem teenagers. (D)

b 💬 Discuss the meanings of the phrasal verbs with your partner. Then check your ideas on pages 158–159.

4 💬 Do you know any people who have been influenced in the same ways as the writers of the article?

Language focus: Past tenses

1 Without referring to the reading text on page 7, complete each gap in these extracts with the correct verb form. Then check your answers in the text.

1 It's because of her that I _took_ a particular career path. (Text A)

2 I _had_ always _wanted_ to dance but _had_ never _been_ allowed to. (Text C)

3 I _was going_ round with the wrong people. (Text D)

4 I still had this deep desire to dance but I _had been covering_ it up for a long time. (Text C)

2 a Match the verb forms you wrote in extracts 1–4 in exercise 1 to a past tense a–d below.

a past perfect simple   b past simple
c past continuous   d past perfect continuous

b Complete these rules with the correct past tense.

1 The _d_ is used to refer to how long the action went on for before something else happened.

2 The _c_ is used to refer to an action in progress at a particular time in the past.

3 The _b_ is used to refer to an action was completed in the past.

4 The _a_ is used to refer to something that was true, or an action that was completed before another action in the past.

Read more about past tenses in the Grammar Reference.

3 Complete each gap with the correct past form of the verb in brackets.

1 The film really _affected_ (affect) me. I _was having_ (have) nightmares about it for days afterwards.

2 The teacher _walked_ (walk) through the door just as Marc _was imitating_ (imitate) her!

3 I'm sure I _passed_ (pass) my driving test first time because my dad _encouraged_ (encourage) me to practise every day.

4 Jackie _had_ (have) a red face at lunchtime because she _had been exercising_ (exercise) all morning.

5 When I _was_ (be) a child I always _looked up to_ (look up to) my older cousin.

6 My friend _wanted_ (want) a biscuit after dinner but I _had eaten_ (eat) them all.

4 a Complete these sentences so they are true for you.

1 Last week I .... several times.
2 Last night I didn't .... because ....
3 Yesterday, I was .... when ....
4 Last weekend I .... while ....
5 I once .... for several hours.

b Work in pairs. Discuss your sentences.

Speaking and vocabulary: The weather

1 a Work in pairs. Describe the weather in the photograph. Where do you think it was taken? How do you think the people in the picture are feeling?

b Discuss what you think happened before and after the picture was taken. Use the different tenses you looked at in the language focus section.

c What is your favourite kind of weather? Why?

2 'Collocations' are words that often go together. For sentences 1–8, underline the correct word in *italics* that often goes with the word in bold.

1 A really *heavy/large* **downpour** stopped the tennis match.
2 During the night **temperatures** can *cut/drop* to minus ten degrees.
3 It was quite uncomfortable because the **humidity** was very *tall/high*.
4 The weather forecasters say that we're in for a *strong/hard* **winter** this year.
5 We couldn't continue the walk because it started **blowing** a *wind/gale*.
6 A lot of elderly people were taken to hospital during the **heat** *wave/storm* last summer.
7 We had a **cold** *spell/session* in March and all my plants died.
8 There was a *slim/light* **breeze** that kept the temperatures on the beach down.

3 Tell your partner about the last time you experienced the different weather conditions in exercise 2.

FCE Use of English Part 1: Multiple-choice cloze

1 Read the title of the article below from a magazine. What do you think it's about? Read the text, ignoring the gaps, to check your answers.

2 Read the text again and decide which answer (**A**, **B**, **C** or **D**) best fits each gap. There is an example at the beginning (**0**).

Before you do the exercise, read the information in the Help box on page 126.

Slaves to the weather?

It's a fact that blue skies tend to lift the spirits and (**0**) .... the world seem a better place. It's also true that overcast rainy days can make us feel gloomy and depressed. Or is it? It may (**1**) .... as a surprise to some of us to learn that there is, in fact, no hard evidence to (**2**) .... the theory that the weather plays an important part in influencing our moods.

A recent internet survey in Germany, which involved (**3**) .... more than a thousand people questions over a (**4**) .... of eighteen months, came (**5**) .... the conclusion that apart from a small number of people who suffer from SAD (Seasonal Affective Disorder), a real problem where doctors (**6**) .... depression to the weather, most of us are not really influenced by the weather at all. Apparently we believe that weather can influence our mood simply because we have always been told it can. The survey even claims that (**7**) .... experts believe that all SAD sufferers feel depressed in the darker winter months, there are in fact some who suffer depression in the summer and (**8**) .... in the winter!

For many people, however, these findings do not reflect their own (**9**) .... Surely people tend to smile more when the sun is shining? Don't we (**10**) .... low when it's dark and rainy and less keen to get up and do things? There are even some psychologists who relate excessive heat to a (**11**) .... in the crime rate because high temperatures can make people more irritable and aggressive. One thing is true – people do love to talk about the weather, (**12**) .... in the UK, and they are going to be talking about this survey for quite a while!

0	**A** get	**B** let	**C** <u>make</u>	**D** do
1	**A** arrive	**B** make	**C** come	**D** find
2	**A** reveal	**B** support	**C** allow	**D** base
3	**A** asking	**B** reporting	**C** discussing	**D** questioning
4	**A** season	**B** period	**C** length	**D** date
5	**A** to	**B** at	**C** for	**D** with
6	**A** put	**B** link	**C** cause	**D** add
7	**A** although	**B** however	**C** when	**D** despite
8	**A** look forward	**B** run down	**C** cheer up	**D** take off
9	**A** experience	**B** history	**C** actions	**D** habits
10	**A** take	**B** think	**C** feel	**D** sense
11	**A** rise	**B** lift	**C** progression	**D** height
12	**A** very	**B** remarkably	**C** especially	**D** often

3 a Work in pairs. Do you agree or disagree with the points made in the article?

b Write a short comment to post on the magazine's website, expressing your views about the article.

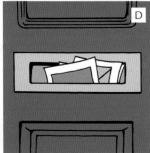

Speaking and reading: The influence of advertising

1 Match these words to the pictures.

> billboard   junk mail   commercial   jingle   cold calling   poster
>
> Advert

2 💬 Discuss the following questions with a partner.

1 Do the methods shown in the pictures persuade you to buy more? Why/Why not?

2 Can you sing a famous jingle?

3 What sort of companies advertise by cold calling?

4 'You get what you pay for!' What do you think this saying means? Do you agree?

5 What was the last thing you bought because of an advertisement? Are you glad you bought it? Why/Why not?

3 Read five people's online comments about advertising. Match the writers **1–5** to their points of view (**A–E**). <u>Underline</u> those words in the comments which help you make your decisions.

1 The writer gets irritated about this way of advertising. *B*

2 The writer prefers a recommendation when making a decision about what to buy. *A*

3 The writer thinks that complicated adverts aren't very memorable. *C*

4 The writer worries about the safety aspect of these adverts. *E*

5 The writer says it's possible to avoid receiving this form of advertising. *D*

A   The problem is that there is so much choice these days. We're continually bombarded with adverts telling us why our lives will change if we buy one particular product! I don't know about you but I just tune out when the adverts are on. If I want something new I usually ask a friend who knows more about it than I do!

Posted by: <u>Jones12</u> on February 13, 2011 9.30am

B   Something I absolutely hate is cold calling! Sometimes I rush to answer the phone because I think it's something important only to find that it's someone wanting me to buy double glazing or change my electricity supplier! I get really ratty with them!

Posted by: <u>Retired</u> on February 14, 2011 2.51am

C   It's crazy but some of the most stupid adverts sell the most products! If it's simple with a catchy jingle and an obvious message, it often sticks in people's minds and they remember it when they're out shopping. Sometimes you can't get them out of your head and that's a pain! But at least you remember it. All these clever adverts where you can't really tell what's being advertised – I'm sure they can't be very successful.

Posted by: <u>Executive</u> on February 14, 2011 8.15pm

D   Most people never even look at it. I always put it in the bin. There are ways of asking to go on a list so that you don't get junk mail but it's quite difficult I think. I pity the postmen quite honestly – they're the ones who have to carry it round all the houses. Does anyone really read it?

Posted by: <u>London10</u> on February 15, 2011 8.20am

E   I think billboards can be quite effective but in some places there are just too many and you drive past without really looking at them at all. They can be quite dangerous too if you think about it! If it's a really stunning or shocking picture it can make you lose concentration! But I must admit it can be a quick, direct way to get a message across.

Posted by: <u>Eloise</u> on February 15, 2011 10.42pm

4 💬 Work in pairs. Decide which of the speakers you agree with and which you disagree with. Give reasons.

FCE Listening Part 2: Sentence completion

1 a Look at the picture for 10 seconds. Then cover it and write down what you remember about it.

b Compare what you remember with a partner. Do you remember the same things?

2 💬 You are going to listen to an interview about product placement.

> *product placement* **noun** the use of a company's product in a film or television show as a way of advertising the product

What do you think are the advantages and disadvantages of product placement for:
- the advertiser
- the viewer

3 🎧 1.1 Listen to the interview. How many of the points you mentioned in exercise 2 did the speaker talk about?

4 🎧 1.1 Listen to the interview again. For questions 1–10, complete the sentences.

It might be product placement if you see an actor eating a [chocolate bar] **1** .

It isn't new to see product placement in [films] **2** .

One popular type of product that we often see on the screen is [soft] **3** drinks.

Products are often positioned in a special way to make the [name] **4** visible.

The professor says that one car was specially built for the film 'I, [Robot] **5** .

A famous USA TV show that has product placement is [American] **6** Idol.

In other types of programmes it's better if the product is not the [Center of Attention] **7** .

Some people are worried that the quality of the programmes will [get worse] **8** .

Technology helps people to avoid having to watch the [commercial] **9** .

At the moment product placement is not allowed on children's TV or [The news] **10** .

5 💬 Work in small groups. Choose a TV show you all know. Imagine you have been told to place the following products into the programme. Discuss how you would do it as subtly as possible. Where would the products appear and what would the characters say?

An internet server   A brand of crisps   A mobile phone   A designer handbag   Trainers

Help

- Read the sentences. Think about the type of information you are looking for: is it a name, an action, part of an example etc? Decide also what type of word will fit grammatically: is it, for example, a noun, a verb or an adjective?
- You will hear the exact words in the recording that you need for the answer but the other words in the sentences may not be exactly the same.
- Your answer should be no more than three words.
- When you have completed the task read through the sentences carefully to make sure they make sense.

Language focus: Present perfect simple and continuous

Present perfect simple

1 a The present perfect links past and present time. Look at each extract **1–4** from the listening on page 11 and answer these questions.

1 *You've probably seen it over and over again.*
Is the speaker talking about the exact time that you saw it?

2 *Think of some films you've seen this year.*
Is the time period finished yet?

3 *The USA is way ahead of Europe ... they've had product placement in TV shows for quite a while.*
Does the USA still have product placement in TV shows?

4 *Now that the European Parliament has made [product placement] legal, ...*
What is the possible effect of the European Parliament's action? Check your ideas in the listening script on page 150 and complete the sentence.

b Match uses **a–d** below to an extract **1–4.**

a To talk about a recent event with a result or relevance to the present.

b To talk about an event or events that occurred at some time before the present. The exact time is either not known or not important.

c To talk about something that happened before the present. The time period is unfinished.

d To talk about something that started in the past and still continues in the present.

2 Here are some more examples of the present perfect simple. Match sentences **1–6** to uses **a–d** in exercise 1.

1 I've seen a lot of TV shows from America with product placement.

2 I've done my assignment so I'm free now!

3 Lars has been on holiday for three weeks! When's he due back?

4 I haven't received any emails today but I've written loads.

5 I've had a cold since the beginning of the week. It's really getting me down.

6 The company has cancelled the contract with the supermodel, so we won't see her face on their products any more.

3 These time words and phrases are often used with the present perfect simple. Complete each gap with a word or phrase from the box. There may be more than one possible answer.

> already   never   since 2009   ever
> just   yet   so far this month
> this morning

1 They've received fifteen complaints .... and it's only the 5th!

2 He's always asking me to do things that I've .... done!

3 The book has been out of print ....

4 I've .... watched American Idol and I don't intend to!

5 Although we bought the software on Tuesday we haven't installed it .... but we hope to do it at the weekend.

6 Have you .... complained about a TV show?

www Read more about the present perfect simple in the Grammar Reference.

Present perfect continuous

1 Sentences **1–3** all contain the present perfect continuous. Decide which sentence talks about:

a an activity that finished recently?

b a series of repeated actions in the recent past?

c an activity that is still continuing now?

1 We've been driving for three hours - are we nearly there?

2 I think it's been raining – the pavements are wet.

3 I've been going to the cinema a lot lately.

www Read more about the present perfect continuous in the Grammar Reference.

2 <u>Underline</u> the correct alternative in italics to complete the dialogue. Explain why you chose these forms.

A: **(1)** *Have you seen/Did you see* the new TV ad for Coca Cola yet?

B: You mean the one they've been showing before and after the evening news? People at work **(2)** *have talked/have been talking* about it for days.

A: I can understand why. It's amazing! There **(3)** *have even been/were even* articles about it in the newspaper over the last few days. Apparently it's one of the most effective ads ever!

B: Yes. It's certainly affected me! **(4)** *I've been drinking/I drank* much more coke recently than I normally do. In fact over the last two days I have **(5)** *drunk/been drinking* all the cans in the fridge, and they usually last me at least a week.

A: Well, it hasn't had the same effect on me! I still don't like coke! But I must admit **(6)** *I was/I've been* a lot thirstier recently. It's a very clever campaign. The last one **(7)** *wasn't/hasn't been* nearly so good.

B: Really? I think they've always **(8)** *been having/ had* great adverts. Good to watch and very effective. But it's a bit scary to think that we're so easily influenced!

3 💬 Discuss these questions with a partner.

1 Have you been doing anything too much recently? What?

2 Is there anything you haven't been paying enough attention to recently? What?

3 Have you been texting someone a lot recently? Who?

4 Have you been watching any TV programmes a lot recently? Which ones?

5 Have you been going anywhere a lot in the last few weeks? Where?

FCE Speaking Part 1: Personal questions

1 For **1–3**, circle **a** or **b**. Then read the Help box.

In Part 1 of the Speaking test you have to:

1 **a** talk about yourself
b talk about your partner

2 **a** give a short personal history
b answer direct questions

3 **a** give short answers
b extend your answer with one or two sentences

2 💬 Ask and answer these questions with a partner. Extend your answers, eg. for question 1 *I come from France. I was born and brought up in Paris but now I live in Toulouse.*

1 Where are you from?

2 How long have you lived here?

3 What do you like about living here?

4 What interesting things have you done recently?

3 💬 After asking some simple questions about where you come from the examiner will ask you one or two questions about different subjects. These will still be about you, people you know, your experiences and your ideas.

With a partner, take it in turns to ask and answer these questions about people in your family.

FAMILY

1 Who do you admire most in your family? Why?

2 Who in your family did you use to get on best with when you were young? Why?

3 Who do you think you are most similar to in your family? Why?

4 💬 Work in pairs. Student A turn to page 126. Student B turn to page 129. Follow the instructions.

Help

- Don't memorize whole sentences about yourself. Your language should sound natural.

- Always extend an answer if you can. Never simply say 'yes' or 'no'

- However, do not summarize your whole life story. Make sure your answers are relevant to the questions you are asked.

FCE Writing Part 1: Email

1 Read the following Part 1 task and answer this question:

What mobile phone would you recommend to Tessa?

Your English-speaking friend, Tessa, has lost her mobile phone. Read Tessa's email and the notes you have made. Then write an email to Tessa, using **all** your notes.

Sympathize

From: Tessa

Sent: 2nd March

Subject: Lost my phone

Great to get your email and I'm glad to hear that you've been working so hard! Did you get your essay finished on time? I'm afraid I missed the deadline and I had to ask for extra time.

No – say why

The reason I haven't called you recently is that I've lost my mobile phone! I know, typical me – left it on the train while I was coming home late one night! Bet you've never done that! Anyway, obviously I need to get a new one. I'm so confused by all these advertisements for mobile phones and networks – I just don't know which one to go for. What would you suggest? Money's not a problem really as I've just got paid for my summer job. Let me know what you think.

Yes, I have – say when

Thanks

Tessa

Recommend .

2 Read Tessa's email again and answer these questions.

- Is Tessa's email written in a formal or informal style?
- What style would you use for your reply to Tessa? Why?

3 <u>Underline</u> examples of the following features of:
   a informal punctuation e.g. *exclamation mark*
   b contractions e.g. *I'm*
   c missing words e.g. *(I) left it …*
   d informal words and phrases e.g. *great, typical me*

4 ◯ Work in pairs. Discuss how you could develop each of the four handwritten notes in a reply to Tessa's email and write down your ideas.

5 Now read the following student answer. Does the writer, Maria, include any of the ideas you mentioned in exercise 4?

Hi Tessa,

Thanks for your email. Actually, I didn't get my assignment in on time either! My computer crashed while I was writing up my conclusion. I lost all my work so I had to do it all again! I was really fed up as I'd put in a lot of work.

I wondered why you hadn't called me. Poor you! It's impossible to be without a phone these days, isn't it? I lost mine once – I'd only had it a week. I left it in a supermarket at the check out while I was packing up the shopping! I know what you mean about the adverts. There are so many and they all promise different things. Personally, I'd go for the new Nokia. I've got one and I think it's brilliant. It's not that pricy either. But don't lose it this time!

Call me when you've got it and we'll meet up.

Love

Maria

6 Work in pairs. Take it in turns to choose an item you have lost or broken and ask your partner for a recommendation for a replacement. Use the expressions in the Useful Language box.

e.g. A *Can you recommend a good dictionary? I've lost mine and I need a new one.*

B *I'd go for the Macmillan English Dictionary. It's very ...*

Useful language

Asking for a recommendation:

I've lost my ... . What do you suggest/recommend I get?

Can you suggest/recommend a good ... ? I need a new ... . Any ideas?

Recommending:

I'd go for ...

I'd suggest/recommend the ...

The ... is really good.

If you ask me, the best ... is the ...

There are no two ways about it. I'd get the ...

7 Answer the following Part 1 task.

You have received an email from your English-speaking friend Johnny who is going to buy a new computer. Read Johnny's email and the notes you have made. Then write a reply to Johnny, using all your notes. Write **120–150** words.

> *Yes – give details*
>
> *Tell her*
>
> *Recommend*
>
> *Yes – say what and why you bought it*

From: Johnny

Sent: 4th May

Subject: Help!

Ages since I heard from you! What have you been doing? Life's good here – lots of sunshine. It hasn't rained for over a month! So, we've been going down the beach a lot. But school starts soon – unfortunately! Are you back at school yet?

Talking about school, I've got some good news. Dad has finally agreed to get me a laptop! Trouble is I have no idea which one to get. There have been a lot of adverts for Dell laptops recently – and then there's Apple Macs too. Help! You're the expert and I really trust your judgement. Can you recommend a good one that doesn't cost the earth?

And while we're on the subject of spending money – have you bought anything interesting recently?

Write soon

Johnny.

Help

- Make sure you write something about each handwritten note, otherwise you will lose marks. Develop each one in the same way that Maria does in her email on page 14.
- Remember to use features of informal writing as in exercise 3.
- Organize your email into paragraphs.
- Always refer to the received email: *Good to hear from you/Thanks for your email/Lovely to get your email etc.*, and end with a suitable comment: *Let me know what you think/Write soon/Let's meet up soon/Give me a ring/All the best etc.*
- Use linking words to join ideas.

  *My computer crashed **while** I was writing up my conclusion .*

  Find other examples of linking words in Maria's email.
- See pages 140–141 for more information on writing informal letters and emails.

Review

For questions 1–8, complete the second sentence so that it has a similar meaning to the first sentence, using the word given. **Do not change the word given.** You must use between **two** and **five** words, including the word given. Here is an example (**0**).

Example:

0 When did you buy that dictionary?

HAD

How long ...HAVE YOU HAD............................that dictionary?

1 I haven't watched TV for at least three weeks!

LAST

It's at least three weeks ...*Since I last watched*... TV.

2 The last time I went to France was three years ago.

FOR

I have ...*not been to France for*... three years.

3 I met Gary when we were at university together.

KNOWN

I ...*have known Gary since*... we were at university together.

4 We were playing football just now and we are really dirty.

BEEN

We are really dirty because ...*have just been playing*... football.

5 I've never eaten a better meal than this.

EVER

This is the ...*beast meal I've ever*... eaten.

6 Who was your opponent in that tennis match I saw you play yesterday?

PLAYING

Who ...*were you playing*... against in that tennis match I saw yesterday?

7 I didn't feel very well this morning and I don't feel any better now.

FEELING

I ...*have been feeling*... ill all day.

8 This is my first visit to the USA.

NEVER

I ...*have never visited*... the USA before.

Language focus

<u>Underline</u> the correct word in *italics*.

I (**1**) *was coming/came* home from school this afternoon on the bus when I (**2**) *noticed/had noticed* a notebook on the floor under the seat in front of me. I (**3**) *was picking/picked* it up and (**4**) *was realising/realised* that it (**5**) *was belonging/belonged* to Olga, a friend of mine. She (**6**) *was writing/had written* her name on the inside cover. I (**7**) *phoned/had phoned* her straight away. She (**8**) *was walking/walked* her dog in the park so I (**9**) *went/had gone* to meet her and give her the book. She was really pleased that I (**10**) *was finding/had found* it. She (**11**) *worried/'d been worrying* about it for hours because it (**12**) *was having/had* all her notes for the exam in it. Apparently, she (**13**) *was dropping/'d dropped* it on the bus at lunchtime. How lucky that I (**14**) *was choosing/had chosen* that seat on the bus!

FCE Use of English Part 2: Open cloze

Read the text below and think of the word which best fits each gap. Use only one word in each gap. There is an example at the beginning (0).

Ronnie Scott's

Ronnie Scott's, the famous jazz club in London, **(0)** has _JUST_ celebrated its fiftieth anniversary. It was opened by Ronnie Scott and his friend Pete King after they had **(1)** _been_ to New York on a trip. **(2)** _The_ jazz scene there had had an enormous influence **(3)** _on_ them and they decided to create something similar in London. It **(4)** _was_ immediately a great success. But even then Ronnie had absolutely **(5)** _no_ idea that it would end **(6)** _up_ as the world renowned institution that it now is. Over the last fifty years many of the best jazz artists in the world **(7)** _have_ played at Ronnie Scott's and have been a source **(8)** _of_ inspiration to a whole generation of young musicians. **(9)** _Since_ its debut the club has always had a lot of members **(10)** _and_ even poor economic conditions haven't had a negative effect on **(11)** _its_ popularity. Although Ronnie himself died a long time **(12)** _ago_ his legacy remains and music lovers from all walks of life continue to keep the spirit of jazz alive at Ronnie Scott's.

Vocabulary

1 Complete each gap with a word from the box.

back	for	off	up (x 2)
down	into		

1 Most children look _up_ to an elder brother or sister.

2 When I was ill I had to let _down_ a lot of people at work because I just couldn't finish the reports on time.

3 It was hard to get to the next level of the computer game but I didn't give _up_ !

4 I wish I'd gone _for_ the chicken – the fish has made me feel quite ill.

5 Dan talked me _into_ going to the cinema with him but I didn't really enjoy the film.

6 When I look _back_ I can see that I've done some really silly things over the years.

7 Pete's obsession with computers has rubbed _off_ on his younger brother and he's going to study computer science at university.

2 Complete each gap with the correct words. You are given the first letter.

1 There was a heavy d_ownpour_ just as we were leaving college this afternoon and we all got really wet.

2 We've been going through a bit of a cold s_nap_ recently and we've had to turn up the heating.

3 Do you remember the h_eat_ wave two summers ago, when we weren't allowed to wash our cars or water our gardens?

4 During the day the humidity was very h_igh_ and there wasn't even a light b_reeze_ to make it bearable.

5 We had a very hard winter and the temperatures regularly d_ropped_ to below zero.

Writing practice

Look at the reading text on page 7 again. Write a short paragraph for the magazine about the person who has most influenced you in your life. Say how the person has influenced you and what you have learned from him or her.

Unit 2 Success!

Vocabulary and speaking: Success

1 🗨 Read the quotations about success and discuss the following questions with your partner. Give reasons for your opinions.

What is each quotation trying to say?

Do you agree or disagree with it?

Which is your favourite?

> You've achieved success in your field when you don't know whether what you're doing is work or play. **Warren Beatty**

> The only place where success comes before work is a dictionary. **Vidal Sassoon**

> Success usually comes to those who are too busy to be looking for it. **Henry David Thoreau**

> I have failed many times, and that's why I am a success. **Michael Jordan**

> If at first you don't succeed, try, try again. **Proverb**

> Success isn't permanent and failure isn't fatal. **Mike Ditka**

> All you need in this life is ignorance and confidence; then success is sure. **Mark Twain**

2 <u>Underline</u> the correct word in *italics* to form common phrases with the words in **bold**.

1 I always study hard and usually *get/turn/do* **well in exams**.

2 It's still a man's world in my country and very few women *get/make/go* **it to the top of their profession**.

3 I don't think I would *be/go/get* **a success as a** teacher – I don't have enough patience.

4 We used to be told that the only way to *work/succeed/get* **on in life** was to have a good education, but that's just not true nowadays.

5 **Things are** *going/doing/turning* **well for me** at the moment: life is good!

6 I'll probably stop working when I have *filled/achieved/succeeded* **my ambition to** become rich and famous.

7 If there's a problem or things don't *go/pass/result* **according to plan**, I don't worry because I'm always confident that everything will *put/turn/give* **out right in the end**.

8 I *got/had/did* **it**! I finished the exercise and *got/worked/made* **them all right**!

3 Discuss with your partner how true the sentences in exercise 2 are for you or your country.

FCE Listening Part 3: Multiple matching

Help

- On the recording you will not hear exactly the same words that appear in sentences A–F. Before you listen, it is helpful, therefore, to predict possible ways in which the speakers will express the ideas in the sentences. As you read through A–F, think of different ways of saying each one.

  e.g. A It was a long time before I was successful, I needed to wait many years, I wasn't successful straight away

- You will hear all five speakers once, with a short pause between each one, then the whole recording is played again. Listen both times very carefully to what each speaker says before making your final decision.

1 🎧 1.1–1.6 You will hear five different people talking about success. For questions 1–5, choose from the list (A–F) what each speaker says. Use the letters only once. There is one extra letter which you do not need to use.

A I had to be patient for success to come.

B I enjoy the wealth associated with success.

C I listened to the advice of other experts.

D A successful person is someone who accomplishes their goals.

E A combination of factors is required to become successful.

F You need to have confidence in your own ability.

Speaker 1	C	1
Speaker 2	F	2
Speaker 3	D	3
Speaker 4	A	4
Speaker 5	E	5

2 Check your answers by reading the listening script on page 150. <u>Underline</u> the parts of each extract which guide you to the correct answers. The first one has been done for you.

3 Speaker 1 says: *They earn a lot of money and some of them have a very high opinion of themselves and their abilities.*

The mention of 'money' and 'a very high opinion of themselves' may have caused you to choose, incorrectly, either **B** or **F** as your answer. These are examples of **distractors**: language or information in the script that may cause you to choose an incorrect answer.

Look at the listening script again and identify the distractors for Speakers 2–5.

FCE Speaking Part 2: Talking about photos

1 🗨 Look at the photographs below. They show people who have succeeded in something.

Student A: Compare the photographs and say how you think the people are feeling.

How are the people feeling?

Student B: When your partner has finished, answer the following question.
How do you normally celebrate a success?

2 🗨 Now change roles.

Student A: Compare the photographs and say how difficult you think it was for the people to achieve success.

How difficult was it for the people to achieve success?

Student B: When your partner has finished, answer the following question.
Which of the two people had to work harder to achieve success?

Help

Student A

- Do not give detailed descriptions of each photo. Instead, comment on the similarities (*Both photos show …*) and differences (*In the first photo … whereas in the second one …*), before moving on to the second part of the task.

- The second part of Student A's task, introduced by the words 'and say' is always written as a question above the photos. Refer to this if you forget what you have to do.

Student B

Develop your answer by giving examples of situations or reasons for your opinions.

FCE Reading Part 2: Gapped text

1 💬 Many British children say they want to work in their own sweet shop when they grow up. What was your dream job when you were a young child?

2 The reading text is one of a series of articles entitled 'How I made it'. Read the headline, introduction and first paragraph of the article, and predict what general points the article will mention.

Example:
I think it will say how Michael Parker got the money to start his business.

3 Read the base text (the main text with the gaps) and check the predictions you made in exercise 2. Do not read sentences A–H yet.

The sweet taste of success

Michael Parker, founder of 'A Quarter of' expects to sell £3m of old-fashioned sweets this year, writes Rachel Bridge.

When Michael Parker started his online old-fashioned sweet shop, he had the advantage of one secret ingredient - nostalgia. He got the inspiration for his business, 'A
5 Quarter Of', from memories of the sweet shop at the end of the road where he grew up in Beaconsfield, Buckinghamshire.

Parker did well at school and later went on to study marketing and operational research
10 at **Lancaster University.** `1` **He eventually left there** at the age of 33, to set up a marketing company from his home using savings of £500. He learnt everything he could about the internet and soon found
15 himself work helping firms to improve their position on search-engine sites.

But it was three years later that Parker came up with his winning idea. His brother had told him about **a firm** he had heard about on
20 the radio. `2` Parker said: "I thought if they could get ten orders a day by making people take a fixed selection, maybe I could get ten orders a day letting people choose what they wanted."

25 He designed the website using a free demo disk from a magazine and then went to a local wholesale shop and spent £85 on sweets. `3` **"I thought if it makes me £200 a month it will be an interesting
30 thing to do** and I will have learnt how to do websites for shops, which might come in handy for my marketing business."

And for the first six months it was just that. "I would get an order a day if I was
35 lucky. I would have the sweets in the office with me and at about 3pm I would weigh them out and post them off." `4`

Things did not always go according to plan.
Shortly before Christmas one year, two
40 newspapers wrote **articles** about the firm.
`5` He said: "**We had 5,000 e-mails** and I worked out that if we worked absolutely flat out from 7am in the morning to 11pm at night every day in the run-up to
45 Christmas, we might just be all right. We couldn't answer the phone. We just had a message on it saying, sorry, we are so busy we can't talk to you." In the end, they managed to send out all the orders.

50 Parker has continued to **extend the initial selection of fifty types of sweet**, often influenced by customers asking him to search for their childhood favourites.
`6`

'A Quarter Of' now sells seven hundred
55 different varieties of sweet and **turnover this year is expected to be about £3m.** `7` "I will not compromise. If I think a sweet is not good enough for the site, we won't have it. You can get loads of cheaper versions of
60 sherbet lemons, for example. They probably taste nice but **the only ones that we sell on the website are the ones that I remember.**"

He has this advice for budding entrepreneurs. "Give it a go. So many people have e-mailed
65 me to say they had the idea of starting an online sweet shop but didn't do anything about it. And learn as you go along. If you wait until you have got it absolutely perfect, you will never do it."

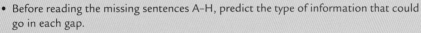

4 Seven sentences have been removed from the article. Choose from the sentences **A–H** the one which fits each gap **(1–7)**. There is one extra sentence which you do not need to use.

Help

- Before reading the missing sentences A–H, predict the type of information that could go in each gap.

  e.g. 1 This will probably mention a job that Parker had between leaving university and starting his marketing company.

- Read the missing sentences and decide where each one should go. When making your choices, make sure you read the information both before and after each gap in the text.

- Some parts of the base text have been highlighted to help you. Underline any words in the missing sentences A–H which help you make your choices. Note that in the FCE exam none of the text is highlighted.

- When you have finished, read through the whole article again with the missing sentences in place to ensure that it makes sense. Check that the extra sentence does not fit into any of the gaps.

A However, after the first half-year Parker hired a PR company to advertise his website and as orders grew he took on staff to help him.

B Parker thinks the secret of his success has been having a strong vision of what he was trying to achieve, namely the sweet shop from his childhood.

C These created so much interest that Parker had to stop taking orders on December 9th.

D Fortunately, Parker succeeded in persuading them to continue production of their more traditional sweets.

E To begin with he imagined it would be a small operation.

F After graduating, he followed no particular career path, working first for a bank, then at Anglian Water and finally for a company that made automatic doors.

G One addition, sweet tobacco, made of coconut strips dusted in chocolate powder, has become the company's bestseller.

H It put together boxes of traditional sweets to send to British people living abroad.

5 Underline the phrasal verbs **1–6** below in the text, then match them to their meanings **a–f**.

1 grow up (line 6)
2 go on + infinitive with *to* (line 8)
3 set up (line 11)
4 come up with (line 17)
5 work out (line 42)
6 take on (sentence A)

a think of an idea or a plan
b start to employ someone
c change from being a child to being an adult
d calculate
e start a business or an organization
f do something after you have finished doing something else

6 Discuss these questions with a partner.

Read the last paragraph of the base text again. Do you think you would be a success as an entrepreneur? Why/Why not?

Do you know any famous entrepreneurs from your country? Why do you think they were successful?

Do you think you can learn to be an entrepreneur or does it depend on your personality?

Language focus: Ability

1 a In the following extracts from the reading text and missing sentences on pages 20 and 21, use the correct form of a word in the box to complete each gap. You may need to write a negative form.

> succeed   manage   can (x2)

*'We (1) .... **answer** the phone. We just had a message on it saying, sorry, we are so busy we (2) .... **talk** to you'. In the end, they (3) .... **to send** out all the orders.* (Line 45)

Fortunately, Parker (4) .... in **persuading** *them to continue production of their more traditional sweets.* (Sentence D)

Check your answers in the text.

b Rewrite all four sentences in exercise 1a using an appropriate form of *be able* and making any necessary changes to the verbs which follow.

Example:

1 We **weren't able to answer** *the phone.*

2 a Read the following sentences and explain why *could* is possible in **1** but not in **2**. Use the words in bold to help you.

1 Apparently, my dad <u>could</u> dance really well **when he was young man**. ✔

2 My dog ran away **last night** but we <u>could</u> find him and bring him home. ✗

b Rewrite sentence 2 in three different ways using *manage*, *succeed* and *be able* instead of *could*.

c Note that although *could* is only possible in sentence 1, *couldn't* is possible in negative versions of both sentences **1** and **2**.

My dad <u>couldn't</u> dance very well when he was a young man. ✔

My dog ran away last night and we <u>couldn't</u> find him. ✔

3 In sentences 1–6, **one** of the three alternatives is **not** correct. **Cross** it out and say why it is not possible.

1 I'd love to *be able to/know how to/can* speak Japanese.

2 I *couldn't/didn't succeed in/didn't manage to* get to sleep until after midnight last night.

3 I've never *been able to/managed to/could* whistle with my fingers in my mouth.

4 I *was unable/was incapable/didn't learn how* to ride a bike until I was about ten.

5 I had problems with the last English homework but I *could/managed to/was able to* finish it in the end.

6 It is *unable/impossible/not possible* for me to lend money to anyone at the moment.

4 💬 Work in pairs. Discuss how true the sentences in exercise 3 are for you.

🌐 Read more about ability in the Grammar Reference.

5 Read the text below, ignoring the gaps. Then complete each gap with **one** word from the ability structures in the Language focus section.

> Perhaps my biggest success was when I appeared in a school play. I was really very shy as a teenager and I didn't think I was (1) _____ of acting on stage in front of an audience. But my drama teacher was convinced I'd be (2) _____ to do it, so I decided to have a go. It was quite a large part, but I (3) _____ to learn my lines without too much effort, and I also had to learn (4) _____ to fight with a sword, which was good fun. On the big night I had butterflies in my stomach, but I (5) _____ in overcoming my nerves and I (6) _____ remember now actually enjoying myself. I think it helped that the stage lights were shining into my eyes so I (7) _____ not see the audience. Unfortunately, my father was (8) _____ to see me perform because he was in hospital, but they filmed it all and he (9) _____ able to see the DVD when he came out. It's (10) _____ for me to watch that DVD now without giving a satisfied smile: I wasn't a brilliant actor, but I did it and I'm proud of myself for agreeing to take part in the play.

6 Write a short text about a time when you had a success. Include some of the ability structures from the Language focus section.

Word formation: Adjectives

1 Write the appropriate adjective form of the words in brackets to complete these extracts from the reading text on pages 20 and 21.

   a But it was three years later that Parker came up with his _winning_ (win) idea.

   b I would get an order a day if I was _lucky_ (luck).

   c It put together boxes of _traditional_ (tradition) sweets to send to British people living abroad.

   d I thought if they could get ten orders a day by making people take a _fixed_ (fix) selection ...

   e I thought if it makes me £200 a month it will be an _interesting_ (interest) thing to do.

   Check your answers in the text.

2 Use the suffixes below to create adjectives from the words in **1–8**. The same suffix is required for all three words in each group. The final word in each group also requires a spelling change. The first one has been done for you.

-able	-al	-ent	-ful	-ing	-ive
-ous	-y				

1	attract	impress	decide
	attractive	_impressive_	_decisive_
2	poison	danger	humour – ous
3	profession	emotion	nature – al
4	wealth	cloud	sun – y
5	care	harm	beauty – ful
6	reason	comfort	rely – able
7	frighten	worry	surprise – ing
8	depend	insist	appear – ent

3 Use the word given at the end of each sentence to form a word that fits in the gap in the same sentence.

Help

Use the words in **bold** to help you choose the correct form of each word. As well as deciding on the correct part of speech (noun, adjective, adverb or verb), you may need to consider, for example, whether an adjective or adverb is required, an adjective is positive or negative, or a noun is singular or plural.

Examples:

   0 **Congratulations** go to Joe Kennedy, **the** _lucky_ **winner** of a digital camera in this month's photographic competition.   **LUCK**

   00 I have some **bad news** I'm afraid. _Unfortunately_ the end-of-term party has had to be cancelled.   **FORTUNATE**

   1 In an effort to keep **fit and** _healthy_ a growing number of retired people are joining gyms.   **HEALTH**

   2 We **enjoyed** the film **but** the seats in the cinema **were really** _uncomfortable_ .   **COMFORT**

   3 The increase in the number of road accidents is a _worrying_ **problem**.   **WORRY**

   4 After completing his round-the-world cycle ride, Jacobs said **he felt** _exhausted_ and was looking forward to sleeping.   **EXHAUST**

   5 The referee stopped the match when **a** _spectator_ **ran** onto the pitch.   **SPECTATE**

   6 The incident **was seen** by nearly **ten million television** _viewers_ .   **VIEW**

   7 **Despite claims** that the drug has **no** _harmful_ **effects**, many patients are **refusing to take it**.   **HARM**

   8 **I had to write my article again**: the teacher said there were **too many** _careless_ **mistakes**.   **CARE**

   9 Footballer Mark Sutton was **arrested** yesterday for **driving** _dangerously_ .   **DANGER**

   10 The **speech** was intended to be _humourous_ **but** I saw **no one laughing**.   **HUMOUR**

FCE Listening Part 4: Multiple choice

1 Work in pairs. Imagine that you want to take part in a sporting activity to raise money for a local charity. Here are some of the activities you are thinking about.

Cycle 100 kilometres

Run a half-marathon

Swim 40 lengths (2 kilometres) of an Olympic-size swimming pool

Play table tennis non-stop for 8 hours

Play basketball in a wheelchair for 4 hours

Talk to each other about what you would find easy or difficult about each activity, then decide which one you would both do together.

2 You will hear an interview with Mark Jacobs, who has just cycled round the world. Read question 1, then look at the shaded part of the script on page 151 and choose the best option (**A**, **B** or **C**). <u>Underline</u> the part(s) of the script where you can find the answer.

1 What motivated Mark to cycle round the world?

A His grandfather encouraged him to do it.

B He was trying to break the world record.

C He wanted to collect money for an organization.

3 Explain why the other options are wrong. Refer to the script.

4 1.7 Read questions **2–7**. Then listen to the recording and choose the best answer (**A, B or C**).

2 What does Mark say about the <u>people</u> who came to <u>welcome</u> him home?

A Some of them were crying.

B Many were surprised by his appearance.

C There were not as many as he had expected.

3 It was important for Mark each morning to

A get up at exactly the same time.

B have a large breakfast.

C phone home.

4 While he was cycling, Mark frequently felt

A fed up.

B lonely.

C tired.

5 Mark says that high winds caused him to

A progress more slowly than planned.

B lose confidence in his cycling ability.

C fall off his bicycle and injure himself.

6 What does Mark say about the technological equipment he took?

A It wasn't very heavy.

B There was too much.

C Some of it was stolen.

7 In some countries he visited, Mark was impressed with

A the quality of the food.

B the generosity of the people.

C the size of the houses.

5 Look at the script on page 151. For questions **2–7** <u>underline</u> the part(s) of the script that gives you the answer and explain why the other options are wrong.

Help

- Read the questions and options. <u>Underline</u> key words in the questions to help focus your attention on the important information when you listen to the recording. Question 2 has been done for you.

- The first time you listen to the interview, put a mark next to the option you think is correct. Listen carefully the second time before making your final decision.

- As with other parts of the listening paper you will hear distractors.

6 a At the end of the recording, the interviewer says:

'After the news summary, we'll be opening up the phone lines for listeners' questions'

Write down four questions that you would ask Mark about his trip.

b Work in pairs.

Student A: You are the interviewer. Ask Mark your four questions, and any others which may be relevant.

Student B: You are Mark. Respond to the interviewer's questions, developing your answers as much as possible.

Now change roles.

Language focus: Comparisons

1 Complete each gap in these sentences from the listening with one word.

1 The record stands at 175 days and it took me quite a lot longer .... that.

2 I wasn't quite .... handsome as when I started out!

3 In fact the wind was by far the .... difficult thing I had to deal with during the whole trip.

4 It seemed as if .... harder I pedalled, ... stronger the wind decided to blow.

5 I got to Australia a .... later than I'd intended.

Check your answers in the script on page 151.

2 Copy and complete the table with the comparative and superlative forms of these adjectives and adverbs.

> fast   wet   white   early   slowly
> gentle   reliable   good   bad   far

Adjective/ Adverb	Comparative	Superlative
fast	*faster*	*the fastest*

3 a Match the structures and examples 1–5 to their functions **a–e**.

1 *a bit/a little/slightly* + comparative + *than*
Alex is **slightly shorter** than Helen.
not quite + *as/so* + adjective/adverb + *as*
Alex is **not quite as tall as** Helen.

2 *(quite) a lot/much/far* + comparative + *than*
The stage show is **far more enjoyable** than the film.
not nearly + *as/so* + adjective/adverb + *as*
The film is**n't nearly as enjoyable as** the stage show.

3 *by far/easily* + superlative
This is **easily the most expensive** campsite we've ever stayed in.

4 *just/nearly* + *as* + adjective/adverb + *as*
I'm **just as old as** Paul.
just/nearly + the same (+ noun) + *as*
I'm **just the same age as** Paul.

5 *the* + comparative, *the* + comparative
The faster you work, **the less time** it will take.

a to show that two changes happen together; the second is often the result of the first.

b to talk about people or things that are the same or almost the same in some way.

c to describe big differences between two people or things.

d to describe small differences between two people or things.

e to emphasize the difference between one person or thing and all the others.

b Read sentences 1–5 in exercise 1 again and match them to functions **a–e** above.

 Read more about Comparisons in the Grammar Reference.

4 a One word in each of these sentences is not correct. Change the incorrect word.

1 Books are many more interesting than films.

2 It's better to try and fail that never try at all.

3 The people in my country are among the friendliest of the world.

4 The more qualifications you have, the easiler you will find a job.

5 The Harry Potter films are by far the most entertaining films that have never been made.

6 Cats are not quiet as sociable as dogs.

7 English is probably the more difficult language of all to learn.

8 Many of the mistakes in this exercise are the same like the ones that I often make.

b Do you agree with sentences 1–8? Tell your partner, giving reasons for your opinions.

Vocabulary: Sport

1 Find the following words from the listening in the photograph on page 24. They are all related to cycling.

handlebars   saddle   pedals   pannier

2 a <u>Underline</u> the word in each group which is not normally associated with the sport in bold. Decide which of the sport(s) mentioned it is usually connected with?

a   football
boots   referee   track   match

b   tennis
racket   net   umpire   pitch

c   basketball
goggles   time out   referee   court

d   athletics
court   field event   meeting
starting blocks

e   golf
course   clubs   vest   tournament

f   swimming
lane   helmet   costume   pool

g   skiing
slope   sticks   slalom   hole

h   skating
Rollerblades™   trunks   rink
knee pads

b Copy the words from 2a, including those you <u>underlined</u>, in their correct groups in your notebook. Organize the words into the following columns. The first one has been done for you.

Sport	Place	Clothes & Equipment	Other words
football	pitch	boots	referee, match

3 For **a–e**, complete each gap with the correct form of one of the words in *italics*. One of the words in each group is not needed.

a   *take part   take place   take over   take up*
Sally has .... **running** in order to keep fit, but also to raise money for charity. She wants to .... **in** the London **marathon**, which usually .... **in April**.

b   *next   runner-up   silver   second*
It wasn't Trenkov's first time as an **Olympic** .... **medallist**: he **came** .... in the same event in Sydney, where he was also the .... in the long jump.

c   *spectators   viewers   public   crowd*
Over twenty three million **television** .... watched American star Serena Williams win the Women's US Open Tennis Final, in addition to the 22,500 .... who filled the Arthur Ashe Stadium. The **home** .... **was** clearly delighted with the result.

d   *beat   win   draw   score*
In last night's Champions League matches, Real Madrid .... FC Zürich 5 – 2, Barcelona .... 0 – 0 with Inter, and FC Sevilla .... 2 – 0 against Romanian opponents Unirea Urziceni.

e   *practise   do   play   go*
I'm sorry, they're not here. Ellie has .... **swimming** and Paul is .... **football**. Well, not a whole game – he said he was going to the park with Steve to .... taking penalties.

4 a   Choose four sports and write a sentence for each one. Include **at least two** words from exercises **1–3** above in each sentence, but do not mention the name of the sport.

Example:
A <u>spectator</u> ran onto the <u>court</u> and began shouting at the <u>umpire</u>.

b 🗣 Read out your sentences to your partner, who will tell you which sports you have written about.

FCE Writing Part 2: Articles

30TH. writing.

1 ⬤ Read the following Part 2 question and tell your partner how

You have seen this announcement in an international magazine:

> **The Importance of Sport**
> *What benefits do you get from doing sport?*
> Write and tell us why taking part in sport is importar
> The best articles will be published in next month's m.

2 Read the model answer on page 127 and compare the benefits th
those you discussed in exercise 1. Then complete the exercises (A
model answer.

3 **a** Read the following Writing Part 2 question.

You see this announcement in your school English-language magazine.

> **Sports competition**
> Your school wants to organise a sports competition for its teachers
> and students. Football, tennis, basketball and swimming have all
> been suggested, but only one will be chosen. Write us an article:
>
> • telling us which one of these ideas you like best for the
>   competition **and** why.
>
> • explaining why you are less keen on the other ideas.

b Tell your partner which sport you would choose and why. Consider, for example, which one would be:

• the easiest to organise.

• the most popular.

• the most enjoyable.

• the best for teachers and students to do together

4 Write your article in **120–180** words. Your article is for the school magazine: you can write in a more formal or informal style, but it must be consistent.

Help

Read the following advice to help you plan your article.

• **Title**: This should give an idea of the article's general content. Write this when you have finished your article.

• **Introduction**: It is important to interest your readers from the start. You can ask a direct question or make a surprising statement. You can also say which sport you like best.

e.g. *Everyone knows how much I love tennis, but it wouldn't be my first choice for the sports competition. I'd go for a basketball tournament …*

or *Can you imagine the fun we'd have beating the teachers in a game of football?*

• **Central paragraph(s)**: Give your reasons. Try to use some of the vocabulary from this unit and structures for comparisons on page 25.

• **Conclusion**: End with a statement or question which summarises your opinions and/or leaves the reader something to think about.

e.g. *Clearly, then, the swimming competition would be the most popular choice. Who could fail to enjoy it?*

• See page 142 for more information on writing articles.

Review

Language focus

Complete each gap with one word.

1 This is probably the .... comfortable room .... the building – it's .... lot colder than any of the other classrooms, and with no natural light it's .... far the darkest.

2 My grandad's .... nearly as old .... you might think. He's got grey hair and wrinkles, but he's about the same age .... Cheryl's dad - perhaps a .... older, but not much.

3 There weren't as .... cars on the road .... we expected, so it wasn't .... a bad journey as last year. In fact, it took us .... than four hours to get there – three hours 50 minutes to be precise.

4 The .... I think about it, ... less I like the idea. Actually, it's probably one of the silliest ideas you've .... had – maybe not .... as silly as your plan to hitchhike to Japan, but almost.

5 They were lovely little cakes. "Eat as .... as you want," they said to us. So we did, and I didn't feel very well after that. Annie felt much .... than me, though, which was strange, because she had .... cakes than anyone else - just two, in fact.

FCE Use of English Part 4: Transformations

For **1–8**, complete the second sentence so that it has a similar meaning to the first sentence, using the word given. **Do not change the word given**. You must use between **two** and **five** words, including the word given. Here is an example **(0)**.

Example:

0 Paul doesn't know how to fry an egg!

INCAPABLE

Paul ....IS INCAPABLE OF FRYING....... an egg!

1 We failed to find a solution to the problem.

SUCCEED

We .... a solution to the problem.

2 I'm sorry but I will not be able to go to the meeting.

IMPOSSIBLE

I'm sorry but it .... to go to the meeting.

3 My younger brother isn't able to look after himself.

CAPABLE

My younger brother is .... after himself

4 My cousin Amy has finally succeeded in getting a job.

MANAGED

My cousin Amy has finally .... a job.

5 Elisa is slightly younger than Lara.

QUITE

Elisa .... as Lara.

6 I have never seen such a dirty beach before!

EVER

This is the .... seen!

7 If you sleep a lot, you'll feel better.

LONGER

The .... you'll feel.

8 There are fewer students in the class than there were last week.

AS

There .... in the class as there were last week.

FCE Use of English Part 3: Word formation

1 Read the text below. Use the word given in capitals at the end of some of the lines to form a word that fits in the gap **in the same line**. There is an example at the beginning **(0)**.

<table>
<tr><td rowspan="2">**Help**</td><td>
<ul>
<li>Read the whole text through first to see what it is about.</li>
<li>Decide whether the word you need is a noun, adjective, adverb or verb. In the example (0), the gap is preceded by an article (*a*) and followed by a noun (*success story*), so we know an adjective is required. For some gaps you may need a negative or a plural.</li>
<li>Make sure you read the whole sentence, not just the line, when deciding on your answer. Be particularly careful when you answer number 6 below.</li>
<li>You may need to:
add a suffix: eg. *EQUIP* → *equip**ment***
add a prefix: eg. *COURAGE* → ***en**courage*
make a change in the middle of a word: *STRONG* → *stre**ng**th*
make more than one change: *USUAL* → ***un**usual**ly***</li>
<li>Check your spelling. An incorrectly spelled word will receive no marks at all in the First Certificate examination.</li>
</ul>
</td></tr>
</table>

A Success Story

The popular family board game Scrabble™ is a
(0) R̲E̲M̲A̲R̲K̲A̲B̲L̲E̲. success story. Over 100 million sets **REMARK**
have been sold in 29 **(1)** .... languages and in 121 **DIFFER**
countries around the world, making it **(2)** .... the **EASY**
world's best-selling word game. It began life in 1931 during
the Great Depression, when, like so many other Americans,
architect Alfred Butts found himself without **(3)** .... **EMPLOY**
His passion for words led him to devise a game he called
Lexico, in which players' scores were determined by the
(4) .... of the words they formed. The board was **LONG**
only incorporated in 1938, when Butts changed the name
to Criss-Crosswords. Some of the **(5)** .... features **ORIGIN**
still appear in today's game, including the values of the
letters, which remain **(6)** .... However, neither **CHANGE**
Lexico nor Criss-Crosswords was commercially
(7) .... and Butts went back to being an architect. **SUCCEED**
Then, in 1948, James Brunot, one of the few **(8)** .... of **OWN**
a Criss-Crosswords game, bought the manufacturing rights,
simplified the rules and came up with the new name of
Scrabble. In the first year of **(9)** .... , just 2251 sets were **PRODUCE**
sold, losing Brunot money. In 1952, however, the Chairman
of Macy's department store played Scrabble on holiday and
was **(10)** .... to find that his own Games Department **SURPRISE**
did not sell it. This was soon put right, sales increased and
Scrabble went on to become a worldwide success.

Vocabulary: Fakes

1 💬 Read the dictionary definition of *fake* and discuss the question below with a partner.

> **fake adj** made to look like something real in order to trick people.

What might be fake about each of these pictures?

2 Underline the correct word in *italics* to complete these extracts from a magazine article titled 'Deception Today'.

A

Phishing is becoming an increasing problem these days and it's important that people aren't **fooled (1)** *at/into* giving out sensitive information online. It's very easy to be **(2)** *taken/made* **in** by **fake websites** that look exactly like the real thing! We have to be very careful and **(3)** *look/check* **out** anything that we think is suspicious.

B

Apparently in some countries it's actually against the law to buy fake designer goods, not only to sell them. Sometimes it's difficult to **(4)** *tell/say* **the difference** between what's **(5)** *imitation/unreal* and what's **(6)** *actual/genuine* but the price is usually **a dead giveaway**!

C

A lot of people have **(7)** *fallen/gone* **for** the 'You've won a competition!' **scam** recently and lost a lot of money. It's often someone on the phone and they **make (8)** *for/out* that you're a winner but of course you need to let them have bank details or send insurance money in advance. The problem is that these people are **(9)** *coming/giving* **up with** new ways to **con us out of** money all the time.

D

These days we tend to think that **(10)** *forgery/imitation* is related more to **(11)** *cloning/impersonating* credit cards rather than printing false bank notes. This is probably because bank notes now have a lot of **safeguards** and it's getting more and more difficult to copy them. However it does still happen so we need to be **(12) on our** *security/guard*, particularly with the higher value notes.

E

The trouble is that a lot of people don't see it as actually **(13)** *cheating/falsifying* – more 'researching' – but the fact is that a lot of word for word **(14)** *copying/imitating* goes on in students' assignments. Easy access to articles and papers on the internet is to blame and there are a lot of people out there whose job is just to produce assignments on demand for a fee! Teachers often can't **(15)** *tell/read* whether the work is original or not!

3 Work in pairs. Give some examples of 1–6 below.
1. Ways students can cheat.
2. Things you can buy that are fake.
3. Things that can be cloned.
4. Scams people fall for.
5. Safeguards on the internet.
6. Things that can be forged.

4 💬 Have you ever bought a fake or fallen for a scam?

FCE Listening Part 3: Multiple matching

1 💬 Work in pairs. Read the extract below from a magazine article about airbrushing. Then answer this question.

How can airbrushing change a picture?

It's a natural instinct to believe that a photograph doesn't lie. Until recently, our eyes have accepted that everything they see is true. However, we now know that this is not always the case. Most of us are aware of how photos can be touched up and it can be fun to do ourselves. But when we aren't aware of it - in magazine photos, for example - many people feel cheated. The now common practice of airbrushing makes a lot of people angry.

2 🎧 1.8–1.12 You will hear five different people giving their opinions about airbrushing. For questions 1–5 choose from the list (A–F) what each person thinks about airbrushing. Use the letters only once. There is one extra letter which you do not need to use.

A It can be dangerous.

B It's done in response to a demand.

C It's acceptable because people are aware of it.

D It's something celebrities have a right to.

E It encourages people to become healthier.

F It's fine if it doesn't go too far.

Speaker 1		1
Speaker 2		2
Speaker 3		3
Speaker 4		4
Speaker 5		5

3 Look at the listening script on page 152 and underline the information that helps you choose the right answers.

Vocabulary: Appearance

1 Complete each sentence with a word from the box that means the opposite of the word in **bold**.

thick	narrow	straight	clear	wrinkled	slim	dull	full

1 Her complexion isn't **spotty** now, it's ....

2 My gran's face used to be really **smooth** but these days it's quite ....

3 Harry was quite **tubby** but since he's been on the diet he's got very ....

4 Jan's parents spent a lot of money at the orthodontist and her **crooked** teeth are now very .... !

5 Hair transplants can make **thinning** hair ....

6 You know you can have injections to make **thin** lips look ....

7 I'm going to have cosmetic surgery to change my nose. It's quite **broad** and I'd like it to be ....

8 When you're not well your eyes often change from **bright** and **sparkly** to ....

2 Match each pair of adjectives 1–5 to the part of the body they describe a–e.

1 crooked/rotten   a complexion

2 piercing/almond-shaped b teeth

3 pale/freckled   c nose

4 shoulder-length/highlighted d eyes

5 hooked/long   e hair

3 💬 Why do people often want cosmetic surgery to change their appearance?

Language focus: Modals of speculation and deduction

1 Read this dialogue between two people looking at a photograph in a magazine. Then <u>underline</u> the modal verbs and the infinitive forms which follow them. The first one has been done for you.

A: *That <u>can't be</u> her real hair. She had it cut really short for her last film.*

B: *I agree. It must be a wig. It can't have grown that quickly.*

A: *But, you know, it could be her own hair with extensions.*

B: *That's true. I hadn't thought of that.*

A: *And she must have had some dental work. Her teeth used to be crooked, don't you remember?*

B: *Another thing - she must be wearing coloured contact lenses! I thought her eyes were brown!*

2 **a** Decide which modal verbs are used in the dialogue to express ideas **a–c**.

a I think this is possible.

b I'm sure this is the case.

c I'm sure this is not the case.

Which two modal verbs can be used in place of *could* in the dialogue with the same meaning?

b Which of the following infinitive forms are used in the dialogue to refer to 1–3 at the top of the next column?

- simple infinitive (eg *be*)
- continuous infinitive (eg *be wearing*)
- perfect infinitive (eg *have grown*)

1 past situations

2 present actions

3 present states

 Read more about modals of speculation and deduction in the Grammar Reference.

3 Each of the following sentences contains one mistake. Correct the mistakes.

1 Jack mustn't have gone to work because his car is still outside.

2 This can't have been Winchester already, can it? It hasn't taken us very long to get here.

3 I'm not sure where Ken is. Try the library – he can be there.

4 I didn't hear Chloe say she was getting married. I must have been done something else when she told you.

5 You seem certain that this painting is a fake, but it could not be – it's hard to tell.

4 Work in pairs. Write three replies and reasons for each of these questions 1–3.

Example:

Are Ben and Sarah back from holiday yet?

They must be back, there's a light on.

They can't be back, their car isn't there.

They might be back, Ben said they were going to try to get an earlier flight.

1 Do you think Lucy passed her exam?

2 Did your mum go shopping today?

3 Does Fred live near the college?

Vocabulary: Expressions with *take*

1 Match each question beginning 1–6 to an appropriate ending **a–f**.

1 Do you **take your time** getting ready in the morning, or

2 Do you **take** your parents **for granted,** or

3 Would you **take the risk of** not revising for the FCE exam,

4 Should examiners **take into account** things like illness or tiredness

5 Would you **take offence** if someone said you should do more exercise, or

6 Do you readily **take advice** from your parents, or

a if you don't do very well in an exam?

b knowing that there is a danger of failing it?

c do you do everything in a hurry?

d would you thank them for their advice?

e do you usually ignore what they say to you?

f do you show them your appreciation for what they do for you?

2 🗨 Discuss each of the questions in exercise 1. Give reasons and examples.

3 🗨 Copy each of the sentences into your vocabulary notebook. <u>Underline</u> the expressions with *take* and note down the equivalent expression in your language.

FCE Use of English Part 4: Transformations

For questions **1–8**, complete the second sentence so that it has a similar meaning to the first sentence, using the word given. **Do not change the word given**. You must use between **two** and **five** words, including the word given. The sentences contain language from units 1, 2 and 3. Here is an example (**0**).

0 Pete can't have gone shopping this morning because there's nothing in the fridge.

   SURE

   I am ....<u>SURE PETE DIDN'T GO</u>........ shopping this morning because there's nothing in the fridge.

Help

- In a transformation you may have to make grammatical and/or lexical changes.
- <u>Underline</u> the part of the first sentence that is not mentioned in the second. It is this part that you will have to think about.
- The key word might be part of an idiom, a phrasal verb or an expression. It might relate to a particular grammatical point or it could be a synonym or an antonym of a word in the first sentence.
- When you rewrite the sentence pay attention to the correct use of verb patterns, prepositions, negatives, conjunctions etc.
- Always keep to the word limit.

1 Helen and Fran were on the same college course so <u>it's possible they met then</u>.
   MIGHT
   Helen and Fran .... they were on the same college course.

2 He's asleep already so I'm sure he was tired.
   MUST
   He .... he's asleep already.

3 I know that Phil has the ability to pass the exam.
   CAPABLE
   I know that Phil .... the exam.

4 To me both pictures look the same.
   DIFFERENCE
   I can't .... the two pictures.

5 First we did the shopping and then we cooked a meal.
   DONE
   After we .... we cooked a meal.

6 It's possible that Kate forgot to turn off the cooker when she left the house.
   REMEMBERED
   Kate .... turn off the cooker when she left the house.

7 Phil might have given your phone number to Brad at the party.
   POSSIBILITY
   There's .... your phone number to Brad at the party.

8 You need to consider the cost of the taxi when planning the journey.
   ACCOUNT
   You should .... the cost of the taxi when planning the journey.

FCE Reading Part 1: Multiple choice

1 Do you recognise the film poster? Have you seen the film? Did you enjoy it? Why/Why not?

2 a What type of film is *Up*? Think of one recent example of the other types of film in the box below and tell your partner what you know about them.

> thriller   adventure film   romance   comedy   horror film   animation film
> science fiction film   psychological drama   period drama

b What other types of films can you think of?

3 Work in pairs. Do you know the names of any famous film companies? What sort of films do they make? What do you know about *Pixar*?

4 Read the article quickly. Is it mainly about *Pixar* or *Up*?

UP WITH PIXAR

It started with a drawing: an old man with a green face fixed in an angry scowl. His little eyes squinted sideways, and his left hand gripped an enormous bunch of coloured balloons covered in slogans like 'love' and 'joy'. Look closely and you could see that he was holding them tight, the way people hold onto their dreams. Five years later that old man acquired both a name (Carl Fredrickson) and a pair of square spectacles. From a simple beginning in felt-tip and coloured crayon, he emerged as one of the highest earners in Hollywood: star of a $400m cinematic phenomenon called *Up*.

Up was 2009's smash hit from Pixar, a computer animation studio doing to 21st century animation what Disney did to 20th. Pixar makes cartoons that both children and adults adore. To critics, it can do no wrong. 'You have to go back to Disney in the Thirties and Forties, when they lifted audiences out of the Great Depression with Snow White, Bambi, Pinocchio and Dumbo, in quick succession, to get anything close,' wrote the respected film critic Tom Shone. 'This is living history, right under our noses. Your grandkids will ask about this.'

Pixar never sits still. When the firm takes risks, they get big results. The studio's 2008 film had been Wall-E, an odd love story about a garbage-eating robot. The film's hero communicated in bleeps and clicks. Its script contained barely a word of dialogue. On paper, it should never have worked. Instead,

line 38

it made $521m, and won an Oscar for Best Animation. So then we had *Up*. The film is part action adventure, part about the meaning of happiness, love and loss. Critics, needless to say, adored it. They laughed a lot at its subplots and raved about its supporting characters. They called it tender, thrilling, and very, very funny.

So, what is the secret of their success? Pixar Studios are in Oakland but spiritually, their home is more Silicon Valley. Round the office are pool, ping-pong and air hockey tables. Most of them are in use, throughout the working day. Grown men whizz down corridors on skateboards and scooters. Ask a guide why, and he'll shrug his shoulders and simply say: 'Because they're creative.' What they mean is that Pixar is a professional playground for happy,

inventive people. The firm's PR people are proud that the senior production staff on Up have been on the payroll for over a decade. They are the best in the world at what they do, and deserve everything that goes with it – from ping-pong to company yoga days.

'Most Hollywood studios are run by businessmen, says *Up* director, Peter Docter. 'The problem with that is that if you start out on any film with the goal of simply making money, the chances are that you're not going to make a great movie.' Pixar approaches film-making from the opposite direction. They take talented people, allow them to enjoy themselves, and let that childish freedom rub off on films. As a result it encourages brave ideas that might, in a normal studio environment, end up on the cutting room floor. With *Up* people might have said, 'It won't appeal to kids, they hate old people.' Or, 'You can't have an action adventure film that stars a 78-year-old man.' But from the top, Pixar is different,' added Docter.

In *Up*, the creative process was more complicated than usual. The film was one of the first major new products to be widely released in 3D in 2009. Around 100 UK cinemas are now kitted out with suitable projecting equipment. For film studios, 3D is a good investment. Tickets to 3D cinemas are expensive and their films are almost impossible to pirate. But Pixar used the technology to add to *Up's* narrative, creating a 'depth script' that varied the levels of contrast in the 3D according to the storyline. 'Carl, our main character, goes on an emotional journey,' said Bob Whitehill, the man responsible. 'When he's a boy, his life is very rich and full, so 3D in that section is pretty deep. When he loses his wife, his life is claustrophobic, so we reduce the depth, and make everything very shallow. Then when he lifts off to go on the adventure, things deepen again.'

'In the future,' Whitehill says, 'every Pixar film will be made in three dimensions.' That pioneering way of thinking – and the effect it has had on other major studios, who are putting a lot of money into their own 3D titles ensures that right now, the location where Silicon Valley meets Hollywood is an exciting place to be.

5 Read the article again carefully. For questions 1–8, choose the answer (**A, B, C** or **D**) which you think fits best according to the text.

Help

- Read the article first for an overall understanding.
- Then underline important words in the questions or stems.
- The questions are in the same order as the information in the text. Find the part of the text where the question is focused. Read it again with the question in mind.
- Eliminate those options which are clearly wrong. Decide on the best answer. If you are not sure, choose one. Marks are not deducted for incorrect answers.

1 What do we learn about the main character in the first paragraph?
   A He was not a very pleasant person.
   B He had a lot of money.
   C He was easy to design.
   D He changed a little over the years.

2 What does the writer say about Pixar and Disney?
   A They have both had a big impact on audiences but at different times.
   B They have both had financial problems.
   C They both have a tradition of producing films very quickly.
   D They are both technically ahead of any other company.

3 The film Wall-E is mentioned to show
   A that a good script is necessary for a successful film.
   B that films about robots will always be successful.
   C that Pixar does not always choose safe options.
   D that Pixar has a lot of money to invest in the business.

4 What does 'it' in line 38 refer to?
   A the hero
   B the dialogue
   C the film
   D Pixar

5 What is good about the working environment at Pixar?
   A It was designed by the people who work there themselves.
   B It suits the type of people who work there.
   C It encourages workers to take breaks from their work.
   D It is available for employees' families to enjoy too.

6 What does Pete Docter think about film making?
   A The need for financial success can restrict creativity.
   B Filmmakers should sometimes listen more to children's ideas.
   C Statistics about films do not always tell the truth.
   D More money should be given to encourage new talent.

7 Why is 3D important to the film 'Up!'?
   A People are interested in new technology and will see the film for this reason.
   B It shows that Pixar is ahead of their competitors in this field.
   C The visual techniques help the development of the story.
   D Many cinemas today need 3D films to pay for their investment in equipment.

8 In the last paragraph the writer suggests that in the future Pixar might
   A go in a new direction.
   B move location.
   C develop new technology.
   D have more competition.

6 🗨 'This is living history, right under our noses.' Can we say this about anything today?

Language focus: Present simple and continuous

1 Look at these examples from the listening and reading practice in this unit. <u>Underline</u> the examples of the present simple. (Circle) the examples of the present continuous.

1 *Pixar never sits still.*

2 *The major studios are putting a lot of money into their own 3D titles.*

3 *Pixar makes cartoons that both children and adults adore.*

4 *There's something in the newspapers about all the eating disorders young kids are suffering from today.*

5 *People are always moaning about something!*

6 *And it's getting worse!*

7 *Carl, our main character, goes on an emotional journey.*

2 <u>Underline</u> the correct word in *italics*. Then match each use a–g to sentences 1–7 in exercise 1. It is possible to match two sentences with one use.

a The present *simple/continuous* is used with *always* to talk about a repeated event that annoys us.

b The present *simple/continuous* is used to talk about something that is always true, a fact.

c The present *simple/continuous* is used to talk about something that is in progress now.

d The present *simple/continuous* is used to talk about a situation that is in the process of changing.

e The present *simple/continuous* is used to talk about a temporary situation.

f The present *simple/continuous* is used to talk about regular action, often with a frequency adverb.

g The present *simple/continuous* to is used to describe events in a story.

3 Explain the difference in the use of tenses in these pairs of sentences.

1 a He always plays music in his room in the evening.

b He's always playing music in his room in the evening.

2 a I can't talk at the moment because I'm driving.

b I'm driving to work these days because the railway station is closed for repairs.

3 a Dave gets to Level 4 on this computer game every time!

b Computer games are getting more and more difficult.

www Read more about present simple and continuous in the Grammar Reference.

4 <u>Underline</u> the correct option in *italics*.

1 They *sell/are selling* some really cheap handbags at the market in town. I think they might have been stolen from that robbery at the airport.

2 It's not a permanent job. I *only work/'m only working* there to get some experience.

3 I'm sorry. I *don't understand/am not understanding* what *you say/you're saying*.

4 We *don't usually take/aren't usually taking* photos when we're on holiday.

5 The number of polar bears in the Arctic *goes/is going* down.

6 It's a real pain! Adverts *always pop up/are always popping up* on my screen when I'm in the middle of working.

FCE Listening Part 1: Multiple choice

 1.13–1.28 You will hear people talking in eight different situations. For questions 1–8, choose the best answer (**A, B or C**).

Help	• You will hear eight short extracts. These are either monologues or conversations. • Before each extract is played, you will hear the question and three options. <u>Underline</u> the important words in the questions as you listen to them being read out. • You will hear distractors. Always listen carefully both times to the whole extract before you decide which option to choose.

1 You hear a man talking on a radio phone-in about a quiz programme he saw on TV. Why is he phoning?

   A He thinks the topic is not good for the quiz.

   B He doesn't enjoy this quiz show.

   C He disagrees with a few answers.

2 You overhear two friends talking about a film they've just seen. What sort of film was it?

   A a horror film

   B an action film

   C a comedy film

3 You hear someone leaving a voicemail message. What does he want to do?

   A change an arrangement

   B ask for some advice

   C make a complaint

4 You hear two mothers talking about their children's birthday parties. What did the magician do at both parties?

   A card tricks

   B an animal trick

   C an egg trick

5 You hear part of a TV review programme. What is the reviewer's opinion of the first episode of the new series?

   A It made a good impression.

   B It was disappointing.

   C It showed promise.

6 You hear Dave phoning his friend Greta. Why is he phoning her?

   A to invite her to a live concert

   B to make travel arrangements

   C to check whether she's going to see the new film

7 You hear a newscaster talking about an art exhibition at a local gallery. Why won't one painting be in the exhibition?

   A It might be a fake.

   B It has been stolen.

   C It wasn't allowed out of the USA.

8 You hear a writer talking about her work. What does she feel about writing?

   A It is lonely.

   B It is unpredictable.

   C It is tiring.

FCE Speaking Part 3: Collaborative task

1 Would you like to work in the film industry? Why/Why not?

2 Here are some jobs in the film industry. Talk to each other about the good and bad points of doing these different jobs and then decide which two jobs would be the most difficult for someone with little training.

Before you do the exercise, read the information in the Help box on page 128.

> • What are the good and bad points of doing these different jobs?
> • Which two jobs would be most difficult to do with little training?

scriptwriter

make-up artist

director

stuntman

cameraman

animator

37

Useful language

Make suggestions:

Let's start with

Shall we move on to …

We ought to think about …

Ask for your partner's opinion/ reaction:

What do you think about … ?

Don't you think … ?

How about you?

Agree/disagree with your partner:

I completely agree.

That's true.

You've got a point.

FCE Speaking Part 4: Further discussion

1 In the Part 4 speaking test the examiner will ask you some questions related to the topic you talked about in Part 3.

Work in pairs. Take turns to answer the questions. Add a comment to your partner's answer.

Help

- In Part 4 the examiner will ask you and your partner questions in turns. Sometimes if one student has spoken less than the other during the rest of the speaking test he or she may be asked more Part 4 questions.
- The examiner may ask you and your partner the same question.
- If you have an opinion about a question which your partner has been asked or want to comment on his/ her opinion, you can.
- When you reply to a Part 4 question try to say more than one sentence. Give your opinion and reason if you can.

1 Do you think that films in 3D will become more and more popular in the future? Why/Why not?

2 Many people prefer seeing films at the cinema to watching them on DVD. Why do you think this is?

3 How important do you think it is to have age limits for watching some films? Why?

4 Some people say it's better for film makers to show us more of the real world than invent new ones. How far do you agree?

5 Do you think films that cost a lot of money to make are usually better films than those that cost less? Why/Why not?

6 What do you think are the disadvantages of being a famous film star?

FCE Writing Part 2: Reviews

1 Work in pairs. Discuss these questions.

1 Have you seen a new TV drama programme recently? What did you like/not like about it?

2 Do you usually read reviews for films or TV programmes? Why/Why not?

3 What was the last review you read? Was it good/bad? Did you agree with it?

4 What do you expect to read about in a short film or TV drama review?

2 a Read these comments from reviews. Then write down an example of a film or drama they could be describing. *e.g. 1 Seven Years in Tibet.*

1 The leading **role** is played by Brad Pitt and he gives an excellent **performance**.

2 The **direction** is very imaginative.

3 The **special effects** are stunning.

4 The **stunts** are electrifying.

5 The **storyline** is simple but moving.

6 If you liked the previous film then this **sequel** will be disappointing.

7 It's a light hearted **look** at society today.

8 The **pace** is frenetic.

9 The **plot** is quite complex and confusing.

10 The final **scene** is really gripping.

b Compare your examples with those of your partner.

3 Read this short review of a TV drama series at the top of page 39. Then find information about 1–5 below.

1 the plot   2 the actors   3 the setting   4 the special effects   5 the writer's opinion

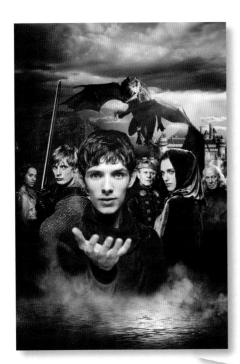

Merlin

Do you like TV series that are exciting and dramatic, set in a historical period but with a very modern interpretation? Then 'Merlin' is definitely for you. It's a wonderful new series which is based on the legends of King Arthur but written to appeal to a 21ˢᵗ century audience.

The series tells the story of Merlin the wizard and King Arthur when they were both young. Each week they have a new adventure, often fighting magical monsters. The plots are especially clever and bring in characters from the old legends in new situations.

Playing the roles of the young friends are newcomers Bradley James and Colin Morgan, whose acting is superb. The series is also visually stunning. It was filmed on location in a spectacular French castle and the Welsh forests, and there is also excellent use of special effects to create the monsters.

I was really impressed by the first few episodes of this series. It's well acted, cleverly written and directed, and magically addictive! I guarantee that if you watch one episode, you'll watch the rest

4 Match each sentence beginning **1–5** to an ending **a–e**. The completed sentences all contain phrases from the review.

1	It is based	**a**	location in Egypt.
2	It is set	**b**	by the special effects.
3	It appeals	**c**	on a true story.
4	I was impressed	**d**	to a younger audience.
5	It was filmed on	**e**	in the USA in the last century.

5 Sentences **1–4** describe the purpose of each paragraph in the review. Put the paragraphs into the correct order.
1 The writer sums up his opinion and says whether he thinks other people will enjoy it.
2 We are told the name of the series and generally what it's about.
3 We learn about some aspects of the series that the writer particularly liked.
4 We learn some details about the characters and the plot.

6 You recently saw an episode of a TV series. A local weekly newspaper wants to publish a review in its next edition and has asked you to write it. In your review tell readers what the episode was about and say what you liked or didn't like about it. Mention whether you would recommend watching the series.

Write your answer in 120–180 words in an appropriate style.

Help
- Underline key words in the question to ensure you include all the points in your answer.
- Plan your review well and divide it into clear paragraphs. See exercise 5 above.
- Write in a style which is appropriate to the target reader: e.g. informal for readers of a school magazine, neutral or formal for readers of a newspaper
- You could begin your review with a question to attract your readers' attention, e.g. *Do you like TV series that are exciting and dramatic?*
- Use conjunctions such as *but, because* and *so* to link ideas.
- Relative pronouns can also be used.
  Playing the roles of young friends are newcomers Bradley James and Colin Morgan, <u>whose</u> acting is superb.
- See page 144 for more information on writing reviews.

Review

Language focus

Complete each gap in these short dialogues with a modal verb and the correct form of the verb in brackets.

1 A: Do you think Rex invited Helen to the party?

  B: He .... her because she was telling everyone about it this morning! (invite)

2 A: Jack .... at work because his car's still outside his house. (be)

  B: He .... in bed! I know he was out late last night and his curtains are still closed. (be)

3 A: You .... much time on this work Rose. It's terrible. (spend)

  B: You're right. I did it really quickly.

4 A: I'm going to check my messages. I'm meeting Ted later and he .... while I was in class. (phone)

  B: I don't think so. He's been in a lecture for the last two hours.

5 A: You .... Spanish really well. You lived in Spain for five years didn't you? (speak)

  B: Yes, but I've forgotten it all now.

Vocabulary

<u>Underline</u> the correct word in *italics*.

1 I often can't *say/make/tell* the difference between a genuine designer shirt and a fake.

2 The man on the phone *made/gave/took* out that he was from the government. But I realised straight away that he wasn't.

3 The student was sent out of the room for *faking/imitating/cheating* in the exam.

4 Don't *give/take/have* offence but I think you're a bit old for that concert!

5 She's had *bending/crooked/curved* teeth since she was a child.

6 The old lady was taken *out/over/in* by the competition scam and she lost a lot of money.

7 I would never take the *danger/risk/worry* of driving a car without full insurance.

8 The adverts promise that this cream will give you a *straight/slim/clear* complexion.

Use of English Part 2: Open cloze

For questions 1–12, read the text below and think of the word which best fits each gap. Use only one word in each gap. There is an example at the beginning (0).

Where's the magic?

The fascination with magic usually (**0**) __BEGINS__ early. I remember (**1**) .... amazed by a magician for the first time at a friend's birthday party when I was six. I just (**2**) .... not understand how he (**3**) .... to find a coin behind my right ear! I was even (**4**) .... surprised when a rabbit appeared on the table in front of me. It (**5**) .... certainly not been there before!

As an adult I continue to be amazed even though I know it's all an illusion. Rabbits (**6**) .... not simply appear from nowhere and magicians (**7**) .... been fooling us for centuries. It's a shame really. The magic is slowly disappearing from our lives. People are (**8**) .... telling me to grow up but I still get taken in by street magicians! I'm the person standing there shouting confidently, 'It (**9**) .... be under that cup!' And of course I'm always wrong and it (**10**) .... is! Scientists tell us that it's all misdirection and the magician (**11**) .... us look in the wrong place, but I like (**12**) .... think that there's still a bit of real magic left in the world for children like the six-year-old me to find.

Use of English Part 1: Multiple-choice cloze

For questions 1–12, read the text below and decide which answer (A, B, C or D) best fits each gap. There is an example at the beginning (0).

A new look?

Most of us take it for (0) .... that as we get older our bodies will show the signs of ageing. (1) .... complexions become wrinkled and (2) .... hair starts to thin. However, many people today do not accept that this is inevitable and look for ways to halt or delay the different signs. Some get excited (3) .... expensive skin creams or injections that (4) .... wrinkles to disappear and lips to look fuller. Others (5) .... for expensive surgery to change their (6) .... But with the increase in people looking for surgical answers comes an increase in those ready to (7) .... advantage of this need. When looking for a reputable surgeon you need to be on your (8) .... Hundreds of people have been conned (9) .... of a lot of money or had operations that (10) .... badly wrong. We've all seen the documentaries and read the articles over the last few years. So don't (11) .... for unrealistic promises but make sure you (12) .... out the organisation you plan to use. There is a lot of choice out there, so if you're really determined to go ahead then do some research and find the best person to do the job.

0	**A** account	**B** <u>granted</u>	**C** normal	**D** seen
1	**A** Plain	**B** Flat	**C** Smooth	**D** Soft
2	**A** thick	**B** long	**C** heavy	**D** broad
3	**A** for	**B** on	**C** about	**D** of
4	**A** cause	**B** let	**C** do	**D** make
5	**A** choose	**B** take	**C** select	**D** go
6	**A** attitude	**B** looking	**C** appearance	**D** form
7	**A** have	**B** make	**C** get	**D** take
8	**A** safety	**B** guard	**C** protection	**D** care
9	**A** from	**B** off	**C** up	**D** out
10	**A** fell	**B** went	**C** made	**D** resulted
11	**A** fall	**B** go	**C** take	**D** look
12	**A** look	**B** check	**C** search	**D** find

Writing practice: Informal email

1 You have heard about a computer or phone scam. Write an email to your friend to warn him or her about it. Include the following points:

- What the scam is
- How you know about it
- What to do if he encounters it

Write **120–150** words.

2 You have recently seen a film that you really enjoyed. Write an email to your friend to tell him or her about it. Include the following points:

- When and where you saw the film
- General information about the film
- The good points
- A recommendation

Write **120–150** words.

Speaking: Holidays

1 💬 Which of the following types of holiday have you been on? Tell your partner, giving details.

> package   coach   adventure
> camping   skiing   working   sailing

Would you like to go on any of those you haven't yet experienced? Why/Why not?

2 💬 Discuss these questions with your partner.

Where do you usually **spend** your **summer holiday**?

Do you prefer **going on holiday** with your family or your friends? Why?

Do you enjoy, or think you would enjoy, going to **seaside holiday resorts**? Which one(s)?

If you could afford your very own **holiday home**, where would you buy it? Why?

What did you do on the last **public holiday**? Did you **go away**?

FCE Reading Part 3: Multiple matching

1 Apart from clothes and other essential items, what things do you usually take with you when you go on holiday? Give details.

Example:

I always take three or four books in case it rains and we can't go anywhere. They're nearly always crime novels because ...

2 You are going to read a magazine article about parents of young children and what they take on holiday with them. For questions 1–15, choose from the parents (A–E). The parents may be chosen more than once. When more than one answer is required, these may be given in any order.

Which parents

do not allow their children to do certain activities when travelling.	1
are generally pleased at their children's growing desire for independence.	2
have children who grow tired of each other's company on holiday.	3
have avoided one problem but created another.	4
accept that they are sometimes overcautious.	5
think well in advance about what to take for their children.	6
have experience of their children being unwell as the result of an activity.	7
keep something secret from their children until it is needed.	8
have displayed examples of their children's handiwork for others to look at.	9
are amused by the results of their children's activities.	10
keep their children busy at specific times so that they can both relax.	11
have no objections to the repetitive nature of a particular activity.	12
have not needed to make use of something they always take on holiday.	13
take things on holiday for their children which are deliberately inexpensive.	14 15

A Robbie and Trudi Jones

When we go away we always take a first aid kit, with all the usual children's medicines and plasters and so on. Amazingly, we've never once had to get it out on holiday, but I bet that if we didn't take it, the kids would fall ill and we'd regret not having it with us. It's the same with their clothes. We always pack something for every type of weather and they end up wearing the same three or four t-shirts all fortnight because, despite our fears to the contrary, it doesn't rain or snow or blow a gale. I guess for some things we're guilty of worrying a little too much about what might go wrong. Maybe we should relax a bit more. After all, that's what holidays are all about.

B Tanya and Steve Simpson

We usually spend our summer holiday camping in the south of France, so the main challenge for us is keeping the children entertained during the long journey down. Reading is not an option because it makes them feel sick, as we've learnt to

our cost in the past! And we don't believe in letting them watch videos or play with game consoles when we go away, especially not when there are so many more interesting things to see out of the window. So we always take loads of CDs of music and stories with us. The children have their favourites of course, and we often have to listen to the same ones again and again, but it's a small price to pay and we don't mind it. In fact, we rather enjoy the stories, so it's really not a problem.

C Dale and Paula Lambert

My wife and I are interested in photography and we own expensive camera equipment. Our young daughters have now reached an age where they increasingly want to do things for themselves, which we both think is great, of course. But for a while they kept asking us to let them take their own photos with our cameras. We did sometimes, but to prevent costly accidents we now buy them each a low-cost disposable camera before we go on holiday. We don't have to worry about them being dropped or broken and the girls have stopped asking to use our cameras. The only thing now is that when we're in the car, they keep wanting us to stop to take photos every five minutes, which can be very irritating. Having said

that, we always enjoy looking at their photos when we get back home. My wife and I have a private laugh when we see the images of headless people or little girls' fingers, but our daughters are proud of their efforts and that's the main thing.

D Helen and Tom Wright

When we are on holiday, we always have what we call 'hush moments', usually after lunch or whenever our three young children get overexcited. They have to stop rushing around and do something quietly. We have a special bag reserved for their things and we start packing it as much as a fortnight or so before we leave. It's important to get that right because if they're occupied it means we can get a bit of peace and quiet and maybe even sleep or read. Books are at the top of the list, followed by felt-tip pens and crayons. They'll happily sit

together drawing and colouring in for over an hour before they get tired of it. And they sometimes create souvenirs: we still have pictures of mountains and castles on our kitchen wall that they did in Spain last year. Everyone who sees them comments on them.

E Gerry and Hannah Naylor

Our two boys generally get on quite well, but after a few days on holiday, they get fed up with being together all the time and tempers are often lost. So we always make a point just before we go of buying a few new toys and games to take with us. They give us a chance to calm things down at moments of high tension and help restore the peace between them. We don't tell the boys we've bought these things, so it comes as a pleasant surprise for them when we suddenly produce them. That's part of the trick, of course. The other thing is that because these disputes are quite frequent when we're away, we only buy fairly cheap things - otherwise we couldn't afford to have a holiday!

3 Where did you use to go on holiday as a young child?

How did you spend your time there?

What types of things did you take with you?

Language focus: Gerunds and infinitives

1 a Sentences 1–8 below are taken from the reading on page 43. Without referring to the text, complete each gap using one of the following forms of the verb in brackets:

a) the gerund: e.g. *finding*

b) the infinitive with *to*: e.g. *to find*

c) the infinitive without *to*: e.g. *find*

e.g. *We're guilty of* ..worrying... *(worry) a little too much about what might* ..go.. *(go) wrong.* (A)

1 If we didn't take it ... we'd regret .... (not have) it with us. (A)

2 .... (read) is not an option. (B)

3 We don't believe in .... (let) them .... (watch) videos. (B)

4 .... (prevent) costly accidents we now buy them each a low-cost disposable camera. (C)

5 We always enjoy .... (look) at their photos when we get back home. (C)

6 It's important .... (get) that right. (D)

7 They give us a chance .... (calm) things down at moments of high tension and help .... (restore) the peace. (E)

8 ... otherwise we couldn't .... (afford) .... (have) a holiday. (E)

b Check your answers in the relevant sections of the reading text as indicated by the letter in the brackets.

2 Match each of the answers in exercise 1 to one of the explanations below.

e.g. **0** *worrying*: b a gerund after a preposition

go: h an infinitive without *to* after a modal verb

A gerund is used:

a as the subject, object or complement of a clause or sentence.
The main challenge for us is **keeping** *the children entertained.*

b after prepositions.
They get fed up **with being** *together.*

c after certain verbs.
Paul **suggested staying** *in a campsite.*

An infinitive with *to* is used:

d to say why you do something
We went to York **to see** *the cathedral.*

e after certain adjectives
It's **lovely to see** *you again.*

f after certain nouns
I admire her **ability to keep** *calm.*

g after certain verbs
They **want to do** *things for themselves.*

An infinitive without *to* is used:

h after modal verbs
It means we **can get** *a bit of peace and quiet.*

i after *help, let, make, would rather, had better*
I **'d rather go** *on holiday with my friends.*

www Read more about gerunds and infinitives in the Grammar Reference.

3 Two of the sentences **1–10** below are grammatically correct. The others each contain one mistake. Find the mistakes and correct them. There is an example at the beginning **(0)**.

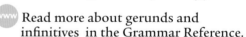

Top ten tips: staying safe in the sun

to follow
0 Failure ~~following~~ the advice below can result in serious damage to your skin.

1 Always use a high-factor sun cream for protect your skin.

2 Apply sun cream to your skin at least 30 minutes before go to the beach or pool.

3 80% of ultraviolet radiation can pass through clouds, so you still need put on sun cream on cloudy days.

4 Avoid to go out in the sun between 12 noon and 3pm.

5 Never sunbathe for more than 30 minutes at a time and do not let your skin to burn.

6 Remember to take water with you when travelling – and don't forget drinking it!

7 You should avoid alcohol, tea, coffee and fizzy drinks as they dehydrate you.

8 Choose light-coloured, loose-fitting clothing and get used to wear a hat.

9 It is essential to wear sunglasses that block ultraviolet rays.

10 Spend time on sunbeds can be just as dangerous as overexposure to the sun, and should be avoided.

4 Which of the above advice do you normally follow? Do you disagree with any of it?

Vocabulary: Travel

1 For sentences **1–8**, complete the gaps with two of the answers **A–D**.

Example:

When we used to take the caravan to Wales, my dad would ....drive........ and my mum used to .....navigate... Now she doesn't need to, because we've got a satnav.

    A navigate   **B** ride   **C** pilot   **D** drive

1 Charlie watched as Lucy's plane .... along the runway, ... and disappeared into the cloudless sky.

    A landed   **B** took off   **C** taxied   **D** touched down

2 I can .... to London on Friday – I'm going there for the day. And when you come back on Sunday, phone me from the train and I'll .... at the station.

    A see you off   **B** drop you off   **C** pick you up   **D** give you a lift

3 I'm going to have a .... when I'm on holiday, but I also want to .... myself.

    A relax   **B** enjoy   **C** unwind   **D** rest

4 Tim's just called from the airport; his flight's been .... by three hours so he hasn't .... the plane yet.

    A delayed   **B** booked   **C** boarded   **D** cancelled

5 I spent the holiday weekend in Dublin. My brother .... me up for two nights and I .... at Jane's house on Sunday.

    A lived   **B** put   **C** accommodated   **D** stayed

6 We .... for a few days at Easter to Scotland. We started off in Aberdeen and then .... to Inverness.

    A went on   **B** went out   **C** went away   **D** went back

7 To get to Camden Town, take the Piccadilly line from Heathrow airport, ... trains at Leicester Square and .... on the Northern Line.

    A catch   **B** get   **C** change   **D** miss

8 Cerys and Jim have just got back from their .... to California. When they were there, they went on a .... of all the movie stars' homes in Beverly Hills.

    A travel   **B** journey   **C** tour   **D** trip

2 a Write five gapped sentences, each testing one of the unused options in exercise 1.

Example:

Amelia Earhart was the first woman to .... a plane across the Atlantic Ocean.
                 (pilot)

b Give your sentences to your partner, who will try to complete the gaps.

FCE Speaking Part 3: Collaborative task

🗨 Work in pairs. Look at the pictures on these two pages. They show ways of getting around on a safari holiday. First talk to each other about the advantages and disadvantages of using the different forms of travel for watching animals. Then decide which two would be best for getting around on a safari.

> **Help**
>
> - When talking about the advantages and disadvantages of each form of travel, consider the following areas.
>
>   possible effect on animals   user's ability to see animals   personal safety   speed   comfort   other
> - Use modal verbs to speculate about these areas.
>
>   e.g. *The noise of the engine might scare the animals.*
> - Use language of comparisons when deciding on the best three forms of travel
>
>   e.g. *You wouldn't be able to see as many animals from an elephant because it's slower than a horse.*
> - Read again the Help box on page 128.

FCE Use of English Part 2: Open cloze

1 In Part 2 of the Use of English paper there is a text with 12 gaps to be filled. Here are some examples of the types of words which are tested in Part 2. Most are grammatical, though some are part of vocabulary items, such as phrasal verbs or set phrases.

Complete each gap with one word.

1 **Phrasal verbs:** I'm much fitter now that I've given .... smoking.

2 **Prepositions:** Rosie had spent all her pocket money .... sweets.

3 **Pronouns:** I can't drink coffee because .... gives me a headache.

4 **Relative pronouns:** We only employ people .... have some experience.

5 **Conjunctions:** I wore my coat .... it was cold when I got up this morning.

6 **Auxiliary verbs:** This is the worst snow we .... had for a long time.

7 **Negatives:** The hotel staff were rude and .... at all helpful.

8 **Articles:** It was .... first time Lionel had been to Paris.

9 **Determiners:** Then add the herbs and a .... salt to the mixture.

10 **Set phrases:** We would like to wish Harry .... the best in his new job.

2 Read the text below, ignoring the gaps, and answer these questions.

What was the 'mistake' mentioned in the title? What caused it?

What did the victim of the error have to do?

An expensive mistake

A holidaymaker **(0)** W̲H̲O̲ booked a three-week holiday ended **(1)** .... 1,300 miles away from her chosen destination after her travel agent mixed up her flights. Samantha Lazzaris booked a trip **(2)** .... a lifetime to Costa Rica, in Central America, but found herself in the US territory of Puerto Rico. Miss Lazzaris did not realise she was in Puerto Rico **(3)** .... she got into a taxi and the driver told her she was in the wrong country. "I asked the taxi driver to take me to the hotel I **(4)** .... pre-booked. He looked **(5)** .... amazement at me, then he laughed and said, 'This is not Costa Rica. It's Puerto Rico'. I was in shock. I looked around **(6)** .... airport, saw posters of Puerto Rico everywhere, and thought: What am I going to do?"

(7) .... a result of the mix-up, Miss Lazzaris had to spend £800 on three extra flights to get **(8)** .... her intended destination, losing four days of her holiday. **(9)** .... seems the travel agent had used the booking code for San Juan, capital of Puerto Rico, **(10)** .... of the code for San Jose, capital of Costa Rica. The airport codes are similar to each **(11)** .... : SJO for San Jose and SJU for the airport in San Juan. A spokesman for the travel agent promised it **(12)** .... fully investigate the complaint as soon as possible.

3 Read the text again and think of the word which best fits each gap. Use only **one** word in each gap. There is an example at the beginning **(0).**

Help

- Read the whole sentence carefully before you decide which word to put in a gap. Adverbs such as *very, quite, rather, fairly* seem to fit into the following gap.

  We enjoyed the holiday, but sometimes it was .... *windy by the seaside ...*

  However, when you read to the end of the sentence, you see that the answer is so.

  We enjoyed the holiday, but sometimes it was <u>*so*</u> *windy by the seaside that we could hardly walk.*

4 Match the answers in exercise 3 to the categories in exercise 1.

Example:

0 *who* – relative pronoun

5 Have you or anyone you know been the victim of a mistake on holiday? What happened?

FCE Listening Part 2: Sentence completion

1 You are going to hear part of a radio programme about 'food miles'.

What do you think 'food miles' are?

2 1.29 Listen to the recording and for questions **1–10**, complete the sentences.

> **Help**
> - You may hear distractors, information which could fit the gap but does not answer the question.
>   *For questions 2, 7 and 9 in this particular task, you will hear more than one mention of a percentage, a month and a figure in millions. Listen carefully to ensure you choose the right one for each.*
> - Read the Help box on page 11 in unit 1.

Food miles

Mark Mitchell says that food miles measure how far food travels from 'field to [**1**]'.

The UK imports [**2**] per cent of its fruit.

Some consumers are worried that food transported by air is contributing to rising [**3**].

Some UK supermarkets put a sticker with a picture of [**4**] on food imported by air.

'Locavores' are people who buy [**5**] fruit and vegetables if they can.

Critics of the concept of food miles say it is too [**6**] and does not help shoppers.

From the month of [**7**] it is more environmentally-friendly to import apples from New Zealand to the UK.

As well as food miles, we need to consider the time of year food travels and the [**8**] used.

There are [**9**] million Africans working in the business of supplying fruit and vegetables to the UK.

Kenyan farming methods do not include the use of [**10**] or chemical fertilizers for growing green beans.

3 Consumers are used to having a wide choice and eating fruit and vegetables when they are out of season. Do you think this is a good thing? Why/Why not?

Word formation: Prefixes

1 Write the correct negative form of the adjectives in brackets to complete these extracts from the recording.

  a Some experts now say that the whole idea of food miles is too simplistic and therefore .... (helpful) to environmentally conscious consumers.

  b 'Environmentally .... (friendly),' say some. 'Not at all,' say others.

  c The concept of food miles, then, is not wrong; it is simply .... (complete)

2 Make each adjective negative using an appropriate prefix from the box.

| un-   in-   dis-   im-   ir-   il- |

  1 honest   **2** lucky   **3** legal   **4** practical   **5** correct   **6** rational

3 Now do the exercise on page 128.

FCE Speaking Part 2: Talking about photos

1 ◯ Look at photographs 1 and 2. They show places where people live.

Student A: Compare the photographs and say what you think it would be like to live and work in places like these.

Student B: When your partner has finished, answer the following question.

Where would you prefer to live?

Help

Always try to use a good range of vocabulary and structures in the FCE Speaking paper.

Structures: The language of comparisons and modal verbs of speculation and deduction will be useful in Part 2.

Vocabulary: Use your dictionary to help you match the words below to photographs 1–4 on these pages. You may use some words more than once and others not at all.

exciting   inhospitable   overcrowded   appealing   bleak

bustling   dreary   unhurried   dull   vibrant

pleasant   stressful   monotonous   relaxed   depressing

What would it be like to live and work in places like these?

2 Now change roles. Look at the photographs on page 49 and follow the instructions above.

FCE Reading Part 2: Gapped text

1 ◯ You are going to read an extract from an autobiography in which West Indian author and actress Floella Benjamin writes about her childhood experiences in the late 1950s and early 1960s. Read the base text only (the main text with the gaps) and answer the following questions.

How was the writer personally affected by the wave of emigration to Britain in the 1960s? How did she feel about what happened?

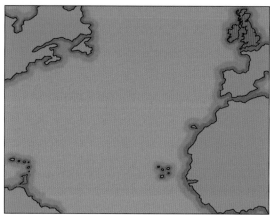

Coming to England

There was always talk of someone who had left the island, who had gone to England to be met with open arms. Fantastic stories of how life was wonderful and much money could be made, of how the islanders were wanted and needed to help Britain build herself up again in the years after the war, and how people could better themselves overnight. The streets were said to be paved with gold.

Life was far from unbearable in Trinidad but many people were tempted by these stories and couldn't resist the opportunity. ☐ 1 ☐ As children we didn't take much notice of all this talk. It was almost like the stories Dardie* had made up for us.

☐ 2 ☐ While in bed one night, Sandra and I overheard Dardie telling Marmie* that he wanted to go and make a new life in England. He was frustrated by not being able to play jazz, the music he had heard so much about but got so little opportunity to play because the music in Trinidad was calypso, Latin and steel pan. A friend who had settled in England had written and told him he would not only get a chance to play jazz but also to make lots of money.

The discussion went on into the night and over the next weeks newspapers advertising jobs and boat journeys to Britain were left around the

house. Some nights, in bed, I could hear Marmie crying, saying she would never leave us. **3** I started to have nightmares of being left alone, falling with no one to catch me.

I told not a soul of my dreams and anxieties – if I did, then perhaps they would come true and I didn't want them to. **4** But the talk of going to England never stopped.

Then finally it was decided that all eight of us couldn't go at once, so Dardie would go first and send for us later. I was so relieved that Marmie wasn't going to leave us too.

I was sad to see Dardie go. **5** Life hadn't changed much as Marmie was still with us, things were almost back to normal, no more constant talk of going to England.

But then the unthinkable happened. Marmie started asking family and friends if they would look after us, because she was going to join Dardie in England without us. **6** She had said she would never leave us.

I wished night after night that it wouldn't happen. I thought my wish had come true when none of my family would take us – they all had too many children. Grandparents usually took care of the children when parents left for a new world. **7**

Unexpectedly, two of our godparents said they would take us. We couldn't stay together though. Lester and Ellington would stay south in San Fernando, Sandra and I would go north to Tunapuna. The lucky two were Cynthia and Junior, the two youngest, who would go with Marmie to England. This was the day when a veil of unhappiness came down on my life.

Dardie and Marmie: the words the author uses for her father and mother

2 Seven sentences have been removed from the extract. Choose from the sentences **A–H** the one which fits each gap **(1–7)**. There is one extra sentence which you do not need to use.

Remember

- First predict the type of information that could go in each gap.

- Then read the missing sentences and decide where each one should go. Underline any words which help you make your choices.

- When you have finished, read through the completed text to ensure that it makes sense. Check that the extra sentence does not fit into any of the gaps.

A I cried a little when he left, but was soon back to my old self.

B Marmie was pleased at the news, but also slightly nervous about what the future might hold.

C I felt so reassured by those words; they were my only comfort during those restless nights.

D They were not only unskilled workers; artists, writers, musicians also made the decision to leave their tropical island home.

E I was devastated: she was going to break her promise.

F So I kept silent, pretended I didn't know what was going on.

G But that was not to be the case with us – we had none.

H But all of a sudden the stories got very close to home.

3 🗨 Discuss the following questions.

What difficulties do you think people faced when emigrating from tropical islands in the West Indies to Britain in the early 1960s?

Would you like to live and work in a different country? Why/Why not?

Vocabulary: Verb collocations

1 In the following extracts from the reading text and missing sentences on page 49, complete the gaps with the correct form of a word from the box. You will need to use two of the verbs more than once.

break	come	get	keep	make	take

1 Artists, writers, musicians also .... **the decision to** leave their tropical island home.

2 As children we didn't .... **much notice of** all this talk.

3 It was almost like the **stories** Dardie had .... **up** for us.

4 A friend .... told him he would not only .... **a chance to** play jazz but also to .... lots of **money**.

5 So I .... **silent**, pretended I didn't know what was going on.

6 I was devastated: she was going to .... her **promise**.

7 I thought my wish had .... **true** when none of my family would take us.

8 Grandparents usually .... **care of** the children when parents left for a new world.

Check your answers in the text.

2 Express the meaning of the collocations in exercise 1 in your own words where possible.

Example:

1 *make the decision to* = decided to   2 *take much notice of* = pay much attention to
Now do the exercises on page 129.

FCE Writing Part 1: Letter

1 Read the following Part 1 task and answer these questions:

- Is Ian Webster's letter written in a formal or informal style?
- What features of the language tell you this? Give examples.
- What style would you use for your reply to Ian Webster? Why?

You are helping to organise a visit to a college in an English-speaking country for a group of students. Read the letter from Ian Webster, the College Director, and the notes you have made. Then write a letter to Mr Webster using all your notes.

We are delighted you have chosen to come to our college to study English in August.

Accommodation is usually with English-speaking families. I hope you are happy with this arrangement.

Yes, because...

The second Monday of your visit is a public holiday. Some of our teachers will be available to give classes, although you might like to have the day free to do as you wish. Could you tell me which option you would prefer?

Say which and why

All students take a level test when they arrive, but it would help me to know in advance what the general level of your students is.

Tell Mr Webster

If you require any further information, please do not hesitate to ask.

Yours sincerely

Ian Webster

Ask him about ..

2 Work in pairs. Discuss how you could develop the notes when you reply to Ian Webster.

e.g. *Yes, because ...* → *It will mean that we can practise more English and also ...*

3 Read the example answer opposite. Does Ana mention any of the ideas you discussed in 2?

Dear Mr Webster,

Thank you for your recent letter. First of all, I would like to say we are very pleased to be staying with familys, becuase this will give us more chance to learn about the food and custums of your country and practise our English. In answer to your question about our level, we are all takeing the First Certificate examination in June and are confidente of passing.

With regard to the public holiday, we all agree that we would preffer to have more free time. As the holiday comes imediately after a weekend, we will probably take the oportunity to organise a trip to another part of the country. Finally, we would be intrested to know whether you offer a programe of evening activities, since we are keen to socialise with other students after lessons.

I look forward to hearing from you.

Yours sincerely,

Ana Crespo

4 a Ana does not begin answering the four points in the notes immediately. What does she do first? How does she end her letter?

b Which words or expressions does Ana use to introduce each of the four points mentioned in the notes.

e.g. Yes, because ... → *First of all ...*

c Which words does Ana use to avoid repeating 'because' in the second paragraph?

d Ana's reply has ten spelling mistakes. Find the mistakes and correct them. There are five in each of the two main paragraphs.

5 Answer the following Part 1 task.

You are helping to organise a visit for a group of British teenagers who are coming to your area. Read the letter from Mrs Cummings, the leader of the group, and the notes you have made. Then write a letter to Mrs Cummings using **all** your notes.

Say which and why   Tell Mrs Cummings

We are not sure whether to travel by coach or train from the airport to our hotel. Which do you think is better?

We understand that our visit coincides with the Festival of Arts and Culture. Could you possibly tell me something about it?

Many of our students have expressed a wish to see a sporting event during their stay. Is there anything that you would recommend?

We are very much looking forward to our visit. If there is anything else you would like to know, please do not hesitate to ask.

Yours sincerely,

Amanda Cummings

Ask Mrs Cummings about ...   Suggest ...

Write your letter in **120–150** words. You must use grammatically correct sentences with accurate spelling and punctuation in a style appropriate for the situation.

Remember

- Plan how you will answer and develop each of the four notes.

- Organise your ideas into logical paragraphs.

- Write in a formal style.

- Begin and end your letter in a suitable way.

- Use appropriate words and expressions to introduce the points in the notes.

e.g.
First of all / Secondly / Finally

With regard to ...
As far as ... is concerned

In answer to your question about ...

- Check your spelling.

For questions **1–10**, read the text below. Use the word given in capitals at the end of some of the lines to form a word that fits in the gap in the same line. There is an example at the beginning **(0)**.

Remember

- Read the whole text through first.
- Decide what part of speech (noun, adjective, adverb or verb) is required.
- Check whether you need a negative or a plural form.
- Read the whole sentence before deciding on your answer.
- Check your spelling.

Brighton

It is no **(0)** ..EXAGGERATION.. to say that Brighton is one of the most   **EXAGGERATE**
delightful, exciting and **(1)** .... seaside cities in Britain. Its   **ORDINARY**
temperate climate, **(2)** .... regency architecture, cosmopolitan   **ATTRACT**
atmosphere and vibrant nightlife give this resort its unique character
and charm and make it one of the country's prime holiday destinations.
Situated on the coast **(3)** .... south of London, this one-time   **DIRECT**
fishing village offers its eight million annual **(4)** .... a variety   **VISIT**
of **(5)** .... , with its theatres and concert halls, pubs and clubs,   **ENTERTAIN**
amusement parks and arcades, and a wide **(6)** .... of restaurants   **CHOOSE**
and cafés. Brighton is also an excellent place for shopping, and a trip to
the city would be **(7)** .... without a stroll around the narrow,   **COMPLETE**
historic streets known as 'The Lanes', where the numerous independent
shops tempt you with antiques, clothes, gifts, and items of **(8)** ....   **JEWEL**
Also not to be missed is the Royal Pavilion, King George IV's former
seaside **(9)** .... with its Indian domes and minarets, and lavish   **RESIDENT**
Chinese interiors. And if you are too tired for a walk along the seafront
or out to sea on the pier, then have a ride on the Volk's Electric Railway,
which will **(10)** .... you to sit back and admire some fine regency   **ABLE**
buildings as you travel along the beach to the impressive Brighton Marina.

Vocabulary

<u>Underline</u> the correct alternative in italics.

1 Could you keep *a look/an eye/a care/a search* on my bag for me? I'm just going to the toilet.
2 It came *with/like/to/as* no surprise to hear that Bob had resigned – he wasn't happy in his job.
3 In this week's programme, we take a *near/strong/close/large* look at the issue of food miles.
4 I can't understand what you've written here – it doesn't make *understanding/logic/reason/sense*.
5 The Cold War *came/reached/got/arrived* to an end in the late 1980s and early 1990s.
6 I don't often get *an occasion/an ability/a chance/an option* to play tennis these days.
7 I haven't been able to *come/get/speak/make* in touch with Lina. I've tried phoning, emailing and texting her, but without any luck.
8 Make *check/safe/sure/confident* you lock the door when you leave the house.

Language focus

Complete each gap with the correct form of the verb in brackets.

Amsterdam

There is no city I enjoy **(1)** .... (visit) more than Amsterdam. If you ever get the chance **(2)** .... (go), don't hesitate **(3)** .... (do) so!

There are some great parks and fascinating museums, and even if you don't normally like **(4)** .... (look) at paintings, I'd still recommend you **(5)** .... (go) to the Van Gogh museum. It's well worth **(6)** .... (see) and you'd be sorry **(7)** .... (miss) it. If you want to avoid **(8)** .... (have) to wait for hours in a long queue, don't forget **(9)** .... (buy) your tickets on the internet before **(10)** .... (leave) home.

(11) .... (travel) within the city is easy. If you'd rather **(12)** .... (not walk), the best way **(13)** .... (get) around is by bike. Everywhere is flat so it's easy **(14)** .... (cycle). But I couldn't **(15)** .... (imagine) anyone **(16)** .... (go) to Amsterdam without **(17)** .... (have) a ride on a canal boat. They're clean, dry and comfortable and they enable you **(18)** .... (get) the best views of the beautiful buildings which line the canals.

If you feel like **(19)** .... (get) out of the city, then why not take the train and bus to Keukenhof **(20)** .... (see) the tulips? Go in April and May, when the flowers are in full bloom. It's an experience you won't forget!

Phrasal verbs revision

For 1–4, complete each gap with the correct form of one of the four verbs. The resulting phrasal verb should have the same meaning as the definition in brackets.

1 give   end   set   come

Sue (thought of) .... **up with** the idea for her new business when she was working in a bank. She (stopped doing) .... **up** her job there and (started) .... **up** her own company. Unfortunately, things didn't go according to plan and she (finished by) .... **up** having to ask for her old job back.

2 touch   see   take   drop

Alan told Emily he didn't have time to park the car and go into the airport to (say goodbye) .... her **off**, so he just (took to a place without getting out of the car) .... her **off** outside and drove away. When the plane (left the ground) .... **off**, Emily began to cry quietly and when it (landed) .... **down** two hours later, her eyes were still red.

3 fall   talk   make (x 2)   take

My brother Tom's always (inventing) .... **up** stories and telling lies. Yesterday he (pretended) .... out he was ill and nearly managed to (persuade) .... my mum **into** keeping him off school for the day. She was completely (fooled) .... **in**! My dad didn't (believe) .... **for** it, though – he made Tom get out of bed and drove him to school himself.

4 break   grow   let   look (x 2)

When I (think about a time in the past) .... **back**, it's not difficult to understand why I felt so (disappointed) .... **down** by my father. All the time I was (going from childhood to adulthood) .... **up** I (admired and respected) .... **up to** him, he was my role model. Then, when I was 21, he was imprisoned for (entering by force) .... **into** a shop.

FCE Writing Part 2

Write an answer to **one** of these questions in **120–180** words in an appropriate style.

1 You have seen this notice in an international magazine.

> **Competition**
>
> Write an article about your favourite town or city, explaining to our readers why you like it so much.
>
> The best article will be published in next month's magazine.

2 You have seen this announcement on an international travel website.

> **Reviews wanted!**
>
> Write us a review of a campsite you have been to anywhere in the world. Describe both the good and the bad features of the campsite and say why you did or did not enjoy staying there.

Help

- For information on these writing types, look again at the following units.

  Articles: Unit 2 page 27. See also the two texts on Brighton and Amsterdam above.

  Reviews: Unit 3 page 38

UNIT 5 Fitting in

FCE Speaking Part 2: Talking about photos

1 Look at photographs 1 and 2. They show young people together.

Student A: Compare the photographs and say why you think one of the people in each photograph is unhappy.

Student B: When your partner has finished, answer the following question.

Which person do you think will be unhappy longer?

> Why do you think one of the people in each photograph is unhappy?

Useful language

- Use modal verbs to speculate about what happened to make the person unhappy.

They **might/could/may have had** *an argument.*

- Avoid repetition of *unhappy* by using alternatives.

She is **sad/miserable/fed up/upset/ in a bad mood/feeling down.**

She is **feeling sorry for herself.**

Help

The question for student B is always different to the question in the main task. Your answer should not be too long. It is not another one-minute talk. On the other hand, it should not just be a one word answer. Try to give one or two sentences.

2 Now change roles and look at photographs 3 & 4. They show groups of people in different places.

Student A: Compare the photographs and say why one of the people in each photograph is not doing the same as the other people.

Student B: When your partner has finished, answer the following question.

Do you prefer to be on your own or with a group of people?

> Why is one of the people in each photograph not doing the same as the other people?

3 🗨 What advice would you give to the young people who made the following statements?

'I don't enjoy going to parties because I never know what to say to people.'

'I'm a bit nervous because I'm changing to a different school and I won't know anyone there.'

'I'm going abroad to study and I'll be staying with a family. I'm worried because I don't speak their language very well.'

'I live with my parents in the city, but we're moving soon to a house in the countryside. How will I make friends?'

FCE Listening Part 3: Multiple matching

1 🎧 1.30–1.34 You will hear five different people talking about experiences they have had settling in to a new situation. For questions **1–5**, choose from the list (**A–F**) what each speaker says. Use the letters only once. There is one extra letter which you do not need to use.

A All the time I was there I didn't make any friends.

B I regretted my decision to ignore people's advice.

C Some people laughed at the way I spoke.

D It was a long time before I felt accepted by the others.

E A recent experience has made me consider leaving.

F I wasn't looking forward to the new situation.

Speaker 1 ☐ **1**

Speaker 2 ☐ **2**

Speaker 3 ☐ **3**

Speaker 4 ☐ **4**

Speaker 5 ☐ **5**

2 🗨 Have you been in any situations similar to those of the speakers? Tell your partner about them and say how you felt.

Vocabulary: Phrasal verbs

1 Work in pairs. Look at the listening script on page 154 and use the context to help you guess the meanings of the phrasal verbs in bold.

e.g. *I felt I was being* **left out** – in this context it probably means she felt ignored, not included in the group

2 Check your ideas in the Phrasal verbs list on pages 158–159.

3 Record the phrasal verbs in your notebook. Include:

- the definition
- original example sentence with enough context to illustrate the meaning

e.g. *leave someone/something out* = to not include someone or something

I felt I was being left out ... . They would all go out for a drink after work, but they'd never ask me if I wanted to go.

4 Write four sentences, each including one of the phrasal verbs you recorded in exercise 3. Leave a gap where the phrasal verbs should be. Your sentences should contain enough information to illustrate the meanings of the phrasal verbs.

e.g. *We've invited Emily to the party, so we have to ask her brother to come, too – it wouldn't be fair to .... him ....*

5 🗨 Show your sentences from exercise 4 to another student, who will tell you what your phrasal verbs are.

Language focus: Time linkers with past tenses

1 Complete each gap in these extracts from the listening with a word from the box. The word should be the same as the one used by the speaker. The first one has been done for you.

> after ~~at~~ at before by eventually
> for for for soon until when
> whenever while

Speaker 1

1 I often laugh about it now, but ....*at*.... the time it was quite hurtful.

2 They'd all been working together .... years.

3 .... someone had a birthday, they would all go out for a drink after work.

4 It wasn't .... I'd been in the job .... about nine months that I began to feel like I was one of the crowd.

Speaker 2

5 .... my dad got promotion, we had to move to a different part of the country.

6 It wasn't long .... I'd settled in, though.

7 .... the end of the first week I'd got in with a group of lads from my class.

Speaker 3

8 .... first it used to get me down.

Speaker 4

9 I stuck with it .... a while, but I left .... , not long .... my mum and dad had bought the uniform.

Speaker 5

10 Almost as .... as I'd moved in, I made a really good group of friends.

11 .... I was sleeping upstairs, someone broke into my cottage.

Check your answers in the listening script on page 154.

2 Identify the tenses or forms of the verbs in exercise 1.

e.g. **1** *I often laugh* – present simple;
it was – past simple

www **Read more about time linkers in the Grammar Reference.**

3 In each sentence there is one mistake in the use of time linkers or tenses. Correct the mistakes.

1 Not long time after I started at this school I made lots of new friends.

2 It wasn't until I have been studying English for about three years that I began to feel comfortable speaking it.

3 I watched a little bit of television before of leaving the house this morning.

4 I wasn't paying very much attention whenever I was reading the Grammar reference just now.

5 As soon as I was getting up this morning I had a shower.

6 I spoke to one of my friends during over half an hour on my mobile yesterday.

7 Last night I lay awake for more than an hour after that I went to bed.

8 I wasn't sure what to do last Saturday evening: at first I thought about going to the cinema, but at last I decided to stay at home and play on the computer.

4 💬 Work in pairs. Discuss how true the sentences in exercise 3 are for you.

FCE Writing Part 2: Story

1 Read the following Part 2 question and the two example answers. Which do you think would receive a higher mark? Give reasons for your opinion.

Your English teacher has asked you to write a story for the college magazine.

The story must begin with the following words:

I will never forget my first day in ...

Write your **story** in **120–180** words.

a It was my first day at my primary school. I was seven years old. I didn't know anyone. I was very sad. I was alone - nobody talked to me. My teacher was old and she shouted a lot.

I will never forget my first day in the class. A boy sat next to me. He cried a lot. I wanted to cry. But I didn't. I forgot to say the reason I didn't know anyone: we moved and all my friends went to a different school. That's the reason. It's amazing - I can remember the colour of the chairs, yellow, and the door, red. Also, I will never forget the thing we ate at school on my first day. We ate soup - maybe vegetable soup – and chicken. I remember because I like chicken. It's my favourite meal and I was a bit happier on that first day. Later I made some friends and things were better.

b I will never forget my first day in Ireland on a school exchange trip. I'd been looking forward to going for a long time. My exchange partner, Liam, had stayed at my house a few months before and we'd got on really well with each other.

When I arrived at the airport, though, things didn't go according to plan. Liam and his parents weren't there to pick me up because they'd been involved in a car accident that morning. It wasn't serious but I ended up spending the rest of the day with Liam's uncle, while they were sorting everything out.

At first I thought it was going to be terrible. The uncle was very shy and during the car journey to his house we hardly spoke a word. It wasn't until we got there that I found out he had his own farm, so I spent the afternoon riding in his tractor, feeding the animals and even milking the cows. I had a wonderful time and when Liam eventually came to collect me I didn't want to leave!

Help

- Choose the setting for your story. Here are some examples for your first day:

  a new school   a job
  a college or university
  a team or organization
  a foreign country   a new house

- Plan your story, organizing your ideas into logical paragraphs. Consider:

  1 The background to the events
  2 How the events develop
  3 The outcome

- Write the story, including a variety of past tenses, a range of vocabulary and appropriate linking words.

- Check your answer for spelling and grammar mistakes.

2 The ideas and events in a story should be organized into logical paragraphs.

What is the purpose of each of the three paragraphs in answer B above

3 A good story contains the following features

- a variety of tenses: e.g. past simple, past continuous, past perfect

- a wide range of vocabulary: e.g. collocations, phrasal verbs

- suitable linking words: e.g. *when, though, because*

Find examples of each of these features in example answer b above.

4 Write your own answer to the question in exercise 1 in **120–180** words. Remember, this is a story, so it does not have to be true.

FCE Reading Part 1: Multiple choice

1 💬 Imagine a member of a small tribe on an island in the Pacific Ocean came to visit your country for the first time. What aspects of your society and its way of life would he or she find strangest and/or most difficult to adapt to?

2 Read the text quite quickly. Were any of your ideas from exercise 1 mentioned?

Outsiders looking in

Guy Adams takes a look at an extraordinary social experiment.

It's a bright morning in St James's Park and a stream of tourists approaches Buckingham Palace. In the middle of the crowd walk five very short, very unusual-looking men. They
5 carry camcorders, gesticulate wildly, and talk in a language no one can understand. In the heart of picture-postcard London, this group of people stands out like a sore thumb.

Further investigation reveals that a film crew is
10 following the party, at a discreet distance. For not so long ago, a British TV company invited a small tribe called the Kastam, from the tiny South Pacific island of Tanna, to send a delegation to England, a country none of its
15 people had ever visited before. They spent a month living here, learning the customs, and making a film about the way the strange and alien inhabitants of a modern western democracy live. The five men walking up the
20 Mall are this delegation.

The three-part documentary called *Meet the Natives* marks a scientific first: for generations, western anthropologists have travelled to faraway lands to live among native tribes and
25 document their way of life. But, until now, anthropology has always been a one-way street; alien cultures have never 'gone native'over here. The project was an experiment in what one might call reverse
30 anthropology.

The five men, whose names are Yapa, Joel, JJ, Posen and Albi, come from a small hillside village on Tanna, which is the southern tip of the archipelago that makes up the island nation
35 of Vanuatu. At home, they live in mud huts, and spend their time growing crops, looking after their animals and sitting contentedly in the shade of the banyan tree. The hurly-burly of central London couldn't be more different.
40 For men who grew up in a place where the only form of currency is animals, and innovations like electricity, television and the internal combustion engine never caught on, the land of skyscrapers and capitalism isn't just
45 another country. It might as well be another planet.

In a strange way, however, Yapa, Joel, JJ, Posen and Albi were ideally equipped to study our frenetic society: as the ultimate outsiders, their
50 opinion of everything from household gadgets to domestic relations and workplace convention promised to be unique. Over the three episodes of *Meet the Natives* the group lives amongst the three great English tribes: the
55 middle-class, upper-class and working-class. They spend a week on a Norfolk farm, a week on a Manchester housing estate, and a week at Chillingham Castle in Northumberland. 'We had four weeks to give them a sense of the
60 enormous diversity of England, and decided this was the best way to show them a snapshot of what was here,' says Will Anderson, the series producer.

Most surprising is what Yapa, Joel, JJ, Posen
65 and Albi find either enjoyable, or shocking. In Manchester they were amazed by the phenomenon of homelessness (in Tanna, your family provides a home, whatever happens), but felt relatively at home in a nightclub, since
70 ritual dancing is an important part of their culture. They learnt to love fish and chips, but were left cold by the hustle and bustle of city living. They are astonished at the amount of time Britons spend cleaning and washing up,
75 which is regarded as a waste of time and effort.

British culture, meanwhile, can also learn a thing or two from watching *Meet the Natives*. The visitors from a village in the hills of Tanna are also able to educate us in some of the
80 things we may have got wrong. They are, for example, amazed at the fact we spend most of our lives working; they are also staggered by the apparent breakdown of family life in sections of our society. In one of the most
85 instructive episodes of the documentary, viewers see them on London Bridge during rush hour, attempting to film pedestrians and engage commuters in a conversation, with

predictably unsuccessful results. This they
90 thought was 'crazy': a rejection of the most
important things in life, which they believe to
be 'love, happiness, peace and respect'.

'One of the problems of our modern world is
that for too long we've regarded these cultures
95 as a sort of exotic creature, thinking how
primitive they are,' says anthropologist Kirk
Huffman, who acted as a consultant to the
project. 'But I've spent 18 years living with
them, and there's a lot we can learn. They are
100 much more open-minded, and interested in the
big questions. In the West, we are obsessed by
little things. Our culture is all about how: to
travel faster, to live longer, and make more
money. Smart cultures are more about why.
105 They are more reflective. That's what they can
teach us.'

3 Choose the answer (**A**, **B**, **C** or **D**) which you think fits best according to the text.

1 What do we learn about the visitors
from Tanna in the first paragraph?

A They are not at all like the other
tourists.

B They are very excited to be visiting
London.

C They would prefer to keep away from
other tourists.

D They have problems communicating
with each other.

2 What does the writer say in the third
paragraph about *Meet the Natives*?

A It questions the methods used by
western anthropologists.

B It introduces a new area of
anthropology.

C It aims to compare life under two
political systems.

D It forms part of a series of films on
different western cultures.

3 In line 45, the writer says 'It might as
well be another planet' to highlight

A the enormous distance that separates
England from Tanna.

B the great lack of open spaces in
London compared to Tanna.

C the high cost of living in London
compared with that on Tanna.

D the huge differences between life in
England and life on Tanna.

4 What does the writer say about the five
visitors from Tanna in paragraph 5?

A They have no class system in Tanna.

B They were surprised at the size of
England.

C They were the right people for the
project.

D They were reluctant to express their
opinions.

5 The writer is surprised by

A the Kastam's mistrust of homeless
people.

B the Kastam's style of dancing.

C how easily the Kastam find
somewhere to live.

D how comfortable the Kastam felt in a
nightclub.

6 The writer suggests we can learn from
the Kastam because

A they work harder than we do.

B some of their moral values are better
than ours.

C they have more experience than us in
some areas of life.

D they have more highly developed
communication skills than us.

7 What does 'they' in line 89 refer to?

A the five visitors from Tanna

B the pedestrians and commuters

C the television viewers

D the television cameramen

8 What does Kirk Huffman say in the last
paragraph about people like the
Kastam?

A They are unwilling to adopt a more
western lifestyle.

B They have been undervalued by
western cultures.

C They pay a great deal of attention to
their appearance.

D They think more than we do before
taking action.

Help

- In most cases in
FCE reading texts
you should be able
to guess the
meaning of words
you are unfamiliar
with.

In paragraph 4 use
the context to help
you decide on the
meaning of
hurly-burly and
caught on.

4 Discuss the following in small groups. Give reasons for your opinions.

- In the penultimate paragraph the writer mentions some aspects of modern society that
'we may have got wrong'. Do you agree with this view? What, if anything, would you add to
the list of *things* he mentions in that paragraph?

- Kirk Huffman says that people in the West *'are obsessed by little things'*. How true is that for
people in your country? And you?

Word formation: Nouns

1 Write the appropriate noun form of the words in brackets to complete these extracts from the reading text on page 58 and 59. Check your answers in the text.

People

1 A stream of ..tourists.. (tour) approaches Buckingham Palace.

2 ... a film about the way the strange and alien .... (inhabit) of a modern western democracy live.

3 The .... (visit) from Tanna are also able to educate us in some of the things we may have got wrong.

4 .... (view) see them attempting to engage .... (commute) in a conversation.

Other nouns

5 Further .... (investigate) reveals that a film crew is following the party, at a discreet .... (distant).

6 a place where .... (innovate) like .... (electric) and television never caught on.

7 In Manchester they were amazed by the phenomenon of .... (homeless).

8 They were left cold by the hustle and bustle of city .... (live).

2 a Record the singular form of the answers from exercise 1 in your notebook. Place the words in columns with these suffixes as the titles for the columns.

-ist   -ant   -er   -or   -ion

-ance   -ity   -ness   -ing

-ist	-ant	-er
tourist	inhabitant	viewer

b Add the noun forms of each pair of words below to the correct column in your notebook. Use the same noun suffix for both words in each pair. Make any necessary spelling changes.

-ist
tourist
cyclist
scientist

able/generous	appear/perform
assist/participate	build/meet
compete/spectate	~~cycle/science~~
employ/win	predict/reduce
tired/weak	

3 In each extract below there is one spelling mistake. Correct the mistakes.

a Over 900,000 signatures opposing the proposal to reduce unemployment payments were handed over to a goverment politician yesterday.

b With the growth of violence among youths in this neihgbourhood, many here are concerned for their own safety.

c The magician could not hide his disappointment and embarrassment at his failure to make himself disappear and he clearly began to lose confidance in himself.

d During his childhood and adolescence he won many junior championships, so his anouncement that he was turning professional surprised no one.

e Margaret had difficulty getting used to retirement and missed the friendships she had formed as a librarian. Her presence was missed as well; the new arrival, Margaret's replacement, did not have the same personal warmth and unlimited patients.

4 Underline all the nouns in exercise 3 then write down the word from which each noun is formed.

Sentence a: *signatures* – sign
proposal – propose *unemployment* – employ
payments – pay *government* – govern
politician – politics

5 Record the singular form of the nouns from exercise 3 in your notebook. Place the nouns in columns with these suffixes as the titles for the columns.

-ure   -al   -ment   -ian

-th   -ence   -hood   -y   -ship

-ure	-al	-ment
signature	proposal	unemployment

Now do exercises 1–3 on page 130.

Vocabulary: Personality

1 For **1–8**, <u>underline</u> the adjective in each group which is very different in meaning to the other three. In each case say in what way it is different. Use a dictionary to help you.

Example:

cheerful   <u>*fussy*</u>   *enthusiastic*   *lively*

A fussy person is someone who worries too much about small details. The other three are all positive adjectives describing happy, keen or energetic people.

1 friendly   outgoing   reserved   sociable
2 patient   grumpy   moody   bad-tempered
3 considerable   responsible   sensible   reliable
4 tough   brave   adventurous   sensitive
5 easy-going   relaxed   nervous   even-tempered
6 confident   tolerant   decisive   self-assured
7 kind   caring   thoughtful   lazy
8 rude   practical   impolite   bad-mannered

2 Which of the adjectives in exercises 1 would you use to describe the following people? Tell your partner, explaining your choices and giving examples.

yourself   a parent or relative   a friend
a character in a TV programme or a film

FCE Speaking Part 3: Collaborative task

🗩 Work in pairs. Here are some people whose jobs are in isolated places. Talk to each other about the personal qualities people need to do these jobs and then decide which job would be the most difficult to do.

> • What personal qualities do people need to do these jobs?
>
> • Which job would be the most difficult to do?

Now do the FCE Speaking Part 4 on page 131.

Useful language

• Use different structures to talk about the qualities needed.

You need/have to be patient.

It's important/essential to have a cheerful nature.

You should never lose your temper with others.

You can't afford to be fussy.

• Decide which adjectives you could use to talk about the jobs in the photographs.

Think about those qualities you need (e.g. *patient*) and those which would not be helpful (e.g. *fussy*).

• Give reasons for your opinions.

that's because …

the (main) reason for this is …

in order (not) to …

FCE Listening Part 1: Multiple choice

1 🎧 **1.35–1.50** You will hear people talking in eight different situations. For questions 1–8, choose the best answer (A, B or C).

1 You hear a teenager talking to a friend about becoming a firefighter.

What has prevented her from making an application?

A her age

B her eyesight

C her height

2 You hear a wildlife cameraman talking on the radio about his work.

What aspect of his work does he particularly enjoy?

A the solitude

B the danger

C the unpredictability

3 You hear a woman talking about a walking holiday she is going on soon with some friends.

Why are they going without a guide?

A They will have more freedom to do what they want.

B They cannot find a guide for the place they are going to.

C They have had a bad experience with a guide in the past.

4 You hear a commercial fisherman being interviewed on the radio.

How does he feel about life at sea?

A He often misses his family.

B He dislikes the lack of privacy.

C He doesn't get on with the crew.

5 You hear a British woman talking about travelling to Mongolia.

What advice does she give to tourists who visit Mongolia?

A They should be tolerant of discomfort.

B They should avoid some of the local food.

C They should take gifts for the nomads.

6 You hear an elderly man talking about retirement.

How does he say he sometimes feels now that he has retired?

A isolated

B bad-tempered

C anxious

7 You overhear a woman talking about her husband.

What is her husband's job?

A an army officer

B a prison officer

C a police officer

8 You hear an extract from a radio play.

What is the man's relationship with the teenage girl?

A He is her father.

B He is her employer.

C He is one of her teachers.

Language focus: The future

Each of the highlighted sentences in the listening script on pages 155–156 refers to the future. Write each sentence below the corresponding explanation 1–10.

e.g. **1** *Will* is used to make predictions and talk about expectations.

I don't think it'll be a problem.

2 *Will* is used for events the speaker knows or believes are certain to happen.

....

3 The present simple is used after some time linkers.

....

4 *May/might/could* express uncertainty.

....

5 *Should* expresses probability.

....

6 *Be likely to* also expresses probability.

....

7 *Going to* expresses intentions or plans.

....

8 The present continuous is used for confirmed arrangements.

....

9 The future continuous is used for actions in progress at a certain time in the future and fixed plans.

....

10 The future perfect continuous is used for actions which continue up to, and possibly beyond a certain time in the future.

....

🌐 **Read more about expressing the future in the Grammar Reference.**

Remember!

• In each extract you will hear words which relate to each option, A, B and C.

• Listen carefully both times to the whole extract before you choose the correct option.

2 Circle the correct alternative in *italics*.

1 I'm probably *about/going/thinking* to spend a fortnight camping in France next year.

2 Charlotte's not feeling too well, but she *should/hope/can* be better in a few days.

3 I may *well/be/try* get in touch with Lucy this weekend.

4 Tom and I *will play/be playing/are playing* tennis tomorrow afternoon. We've booked the court.

5 I'm going straight home as soon as this class *will finish/has finished/is finishing*.

6 My dad is *certainly/possibly/likely* to get angry if I don't get home before midnight tonight.

7 I'll *learn/be learning/have been learning* English for three years by the end of this year.

8 I *hope/expect/want* that Steve goes to the party on Saturday.

3 Choose five of the sentences in exercise 2 and write new ones by changing the underlined sections. Your new sentences should be true. You may also change the time expressions at the end of the sentences if necessary.

Example:

1 *I'm probably going to play tennis with my cousin on Sunday morning.*

4 Work in pairs. Compare and discuss your sentences from exercise 3.

FCE Writing Part 2: Letter of application

1 Read the following Part 2 task. Which of the jobs would you apply for? Why?

You have seen this advertisement in a local English language magazine.

FREE LANGUAGE LESSONS!

EU Languages is opening a new school in this area. Work part-time for us this summer and we will give you free language lessons – and the possibility of a longer contract. We have the following vacancies:

- Receptionists
- Bar staff
- Social events organisers
- Library assistants

Write, in English please, to the director, Mrs Jameson, saying which job interests you and why you would be suitable.

Write your **letter of application**.

2 Read the letter of application opposite. Do you think the writer would be suitable for the job? Give reasons for your answer.

3 **What is the purpose of each paragraph in Elena's letter in exercise 2?**

Example:

Paragraph 1: to say which job she is applying for

4 Underline words and phrases in Elena's letter which might be useful when you write a letter of application.

5 Write a letter of application for one of the other jobs available in the new EU Languages school, saying why you would be suitable. Write **120–180** words.

Dear Mrs Jameson

I have seen your advertisement in the latest issue of 'English Weekly' and I am writing to apply for the job as a library assistant in your new school.

I am 18 years old and about to start a university degree course in German, one of the languages your schools normally offer. I will also soon be taking the Cambridge FCE examination. As a result of my studies I have a good knowledge of English and German graded readers, and am a keen reader of novels in both languages.

I also spent the last year working three hours a week in my school library, sometimes taking charge when the librarian was absent. Using my computer skills I helped her to maintain the library database and catalogue new books.

In addition to my knowledge, experience and enthusiasm for books I have a patient and friendly nature, which I think is important for library work, and I feel I would be well suited to a job in your school.

I look forward to hearing from you.

Yours sincerely

Elena Campos

Help

- Plan your letter and organise your ideas into paragraphs. Include relevant personal information, knowledge, experience and personal qualities.
- Begin and end your letter appropriately.
- Write your letter in a consistently formal style.
- See page 148 for more information on writing letters of application.

FCE Use of English Part 4: Transformations

For questions 1–8, complete the second sentence so that it has a similar meaning to the first sentence, using the word given. **Do not change the word given.** You must use between **two** and **five** words, including the word given.

1 John ate a big meal shortly before he went swimming.

   LONG

   John went swimming

   .... eaten a big meal.

2 I had to discover who the murderer was before I could put my book down.

   UNTIL

   I could not put my book down

   .... out who the murderer was.

3 You will be met by one of our tour guides immediately on your arrival at the airport.

   SOON

   One of our tour guides will meet you

   .... at the airport.

4 United probably won't beat City on Saturday.

   UNLIKELY

   United is ....

   against City on Saturday.

5 The government lost the election because it had completely failed to reduce unemployment.

   ITS

   The government lost the election because of ....

   reduce unemployment.

6 Alan was so disappointed by his exam marks.

   SUCH

   Alan's exam marks ....

   to him.

7 The hotel will send you confirmation of your reservation after you have paid the deposit.

   FOLLOWING

   The hotel will send you confirmation of your reservation ....

   the deposit.

8 Paul's interest in music began when he was a child in Liverpool.

   DURING

   Paul's interest in music began

   .... in Liverpool.

Vocabulary

1 **Complete the compound adjectives so that they have a similar meaning to the word in brackets. The first letter has been given to you.**

   1 He's such a bad-m..................... (rude) child – he never says 'please' or 'thank you'.

   2 They're like chalk and cheese: Lina is very shy, whereas her sister is extremely self-a..................... (confident).

   3 Helen never gets angry or upset – she's so even-t..................... (calm).

   4 Paul is very open-m..................... (tolerant) and wouldn't criticize anyone for their religious beliefs.

   5 Our last teacher was very strict – the new one is so much more easy-g..................... (relaxed).

   6 Don't go near Mike on a Monday morning – he's always bad-t..................... (easily annoyed) then.

2 **Write the opposite of each of the following adjectives. In each group of three, one adjective requires a different prefix or suffix to the other two. The first one has been done for you.**

   1 enthusiastic adventurous decisive

   unenthusiastic unadventurous indecisive

   2 sociable responsible reliable

   3 friendly patient polite

   4 thoughtful tolerant sensitive

   5 kind caring practical

Phrasal verbs revision

1 Match each sentence beginning 1–8 with an appropriate ending **a–h**.

1 We had to move because we couldn't **put**
2 Jo and I used to be friends but we don't **get**
3 Darren was arrested not long after he **got**
4 I'll be waiting at the station. I'm so **looking**
5 Charlene wore her ring to school to **show** it
6 I can't concentrate very well now. I'll **carry**
7 Jim's formed a rock band. He hasn't **come**
8 I think the person I most admire and **look**

a **in with** a group of boys from the other side of town.
b **on with** each other very well now.
c **on with** this work after I've had a cup of coffee.
d **up with** the noise from the neighbours any more.
e **up with** a name for it yet, though. Any ideas?
f **up to** is my grandfather. He's a role model to me.
g **off to** everyone. I pretended I wasn't interested.
h **forward to** seeing you again after all this time.

2 Study the sentences for two minutes. Then cover up the endings **a–h** and look at the beginnings 1–8. How many of the endings can you remember?

Language focus

Complete each gap with an appropriate form of the verb in brackets. There may be more than one possible answer.

a

I **(1)** .... (go) into town with my mum to get some shoes this afternoon. I hope it **(2)** .... (not take) too long – Colleen **(3)** .... (come) round at seven and I want to do a few things before she **(4)** .... (get) here.

b

Claire: Where **(5)** .... (we/go) on Saturday? Any ideas what we can do?

Paul: Sorry Claire but I **(6)** .... (stay) at home and work on Saturday. My exams **(7)** .... (start) on Monday so I **(8)** .... (revise) all weekend.

Claire: Alright then. I **(9)** .... (phone) Tony later and see if he wants to do anything.

Paul: Don't call him between eight and ten – he **(10)** .... (watch) the football then.

c

I'm just about **(11)** .... (start) packing for our holiday. We're planning on **(12)** .... (set off) at about five on Sunday morning. There isn't likely **(13)** .... (be) much traffic around at that time so we **(14)** .... (probably/get) to the coast by midday. I **(15)** .... (give) you a ring when we **(16)** .... (get) to the hotel, if you like.

FCE Writing Part 2

Write an answer to one of these questions in **120–180** words in an appropriate style.

1 You have decided to enter a short story competition in an international magazine. The competition rules say that the story must **begin** with the following words.

When I walked out of my house, I saw an unusual-looking man running towards me.

Write your **story**.

2 You see this notice on your school noticeboard.

MY FAVOURITE RELATIVE

Write us an article about a favourite relative of yours. Include a brief description of the relative and say why he or she is so special to you.

We will include the most interesting articles in the school magazine.

Write your **article**.

Useful language

- The article requires you to describe the relative; you could also include a brief description of the 'unusual-looking man' in the story. See page 31 in Unit 3 for some vocabulary to describe appearance.

- See page 61 in this unit for some vocabulary to describe the personality of your relative in the article.

UNIT 6 A matter of opinion

Vocabulary 1: Expressing your opinion

1 💬 These photographs show people expressing their opinions in different ways. With a partner, discuss how they are doing this.

2 Read the instant messaging conversation below, ignoring the gaps, and answer these questions.

Which picture does the conversation relate to?

What concerns does Beth have about this method of expressing an opinion?

Dave says:

What did you think of the protest march last Saturday through central London? I thought it **went (0)** .....OFF..... really **well**. It was very peaceful. I really admire people who **take (1)** .... in this way, actually doing something that gets noticed rather than just **(2)** .... **about** things all the time. It's a great way to **get your point (3)** .... and make yourself heard. Some people have never **been on any (4)** .... or marches in their life, which I think is a great shame.

Beth says:

Yeah, maybe. I suppose if you **feel (5)** .... **about** something, you need to show it in some way. But, you know, I think sometimes **things go too (6)** .... on these marches. The one last weekend was peaceful but they can **cause** a lot of **(7)** .... Shops have to close, traffic is diverted, and sometimes people get quite violent. And really, I**'m in two (8)** .... **about** whether they can ever achieve anything. Do politicians actually listen or do they just think 'Oh no, not another protest!'

---

3 a Complete each gap with one of the words in the box. There is an example at the beginning **(0)**.

| action   demonstrations   disruption   minds |

| across   ~~off~~   far   strongly   complaining |

b 💬 Do you agree or disagree with Dave and Beth's opinions? Why?

Do you feel strongly about anything which is in the news at the moment?

FCE Reading Part 3: Multiple matching

1 💬 Have you done, or would you ever do any of a–g below. Why/Why not?

  a go on a protest march   **e** go on a TV debate show
  b sign a petition   **f** take part in a sit-in
  c post a comment on a website   **g** take part in a flashmob protest
  d go on strike

2 Texts **A–D** are extracts from people's blogs about different protests. Read the texts quickly to see which of the activities in exercise 1 are mentioned.

3 Now read the texts again. For questions **1–15**, choose from the people **(A–D)**. The people may be chosen more than once.

Which person mentions

not having a clear understanding of why the protest happened [1]

accidentally becoming part of a group? [2]

not achieving the desired result? [3]

people's concern about a global problem? [4]

not having strong opinions about the protest he/she was involved in? [5]

an event that relied on technology for its organisation? [6]

the possible effect of an event on people's travelling plans? [7]

a rather frightening situation? [8]

an event that became more ordered as it continued? [9]

a way forward that was acceptable to both sides in the dispute? [10]

not being able to participate as fully as he/she had wanted? [11]

bad weather at the time of an event? [12]

attending an event with family members? [13]

the unintended release of secret information? [14]

being prompted by nostalgia? [15]

A   Mike

When I was at university I experienced a flashmob protest and it's something I shall never forget! What amazed me was the speed at which everything happened. One moment I was sitting quietly reading a book on the steps outside the main Arts building. Then I got a text message on my mobile saying that a really unpopular politician was about to arrive at the main entrance – which was at the Arts building - and everyone should get there as fast as possible. The result was that students started running from all directions and within seconds I was surrounded by hundreds and hundreds of people. I couldn't tell you where they all came from! It was incredible that one message could bring people together so quickly. Obviously the university had been trying to keep this particular visit quiet but the news had leaked out and we had an instant protest! I must admit it was quite scary. Everyone was pushing and shouting and I'm surprised no one got hurt in the crush. The politician was astonished at the unexpected reception he had when he came out. I think we got our point across.

B   Dave

The organisers had taken a long time to plan the day and we all knew exactly where we were going and when the speeches would happen and so on. So there was a sense of calm among the crowds. And the whole thing went off really well, in spite of the rain. OK, normal transport services were obviously disrupted, which might have caused problems for some people, but there were no fights with the police, not even a little scuffle! A lot of people, including myself, were there with their whole family and it was a great feeling to be marching alongside other people from all over the country who felt the same way as I did. We wanted to show the government how strongly people felt about the need to do something more about climate change and get results. When you're in the middle of something like that – and that march was enormous, there were half a million people there – it makes you realise how strongly people feel about the problem. I'm really glad I made the effort to go.

C   Sara

I was only a teenager at the time but I remember being really angry. My brothers and I had often played in the woods as kids and when they announced that they were going to cut all the trees down to make way for a new stretch of motorway it upset a lot of people with good memories of the place, including me. I suppose, looking back, it was quite idealistic but the local people really believed that they could stop the road being built. For weeks people camped in the woods so that they couldn't cut down the trees. Some people even built tree houses and stayed in them! Luckily the weather held up. I don't think they'd have been there long if it had been raining all the time. I thought this was all fantastic. I used to go down every day after school to take soup and coffee to the people there and I really wanted to stay in one of the tree houses. But my mum said she drew the line at that and wouldn't let me! For a teenager like me then, it was a very exciting time. Unfortunately the road was eventually built but maybe the protest made them think twice about where to build the next one.

D   Rose

I don't think I ever knew exactly why the sit-in started but it was definitely the most memorable event of my second year at college! I think it was something to do with cutting some lecturers' jobs, but anyway, it was something that a lot of people felt really strongly about. The news of the sit-in spread very quickly and soon the building was completely full of students with sleeping bags, sandwiches, hot flasks of coffee and so on. At first things weren't that well organised but in a really short time they set up food centres and started talking to the authorities, trying to sort out a compromise. I was quite immature at the time and I know that I got involved just to be part of the event and because a good friend of mine was there too, not because of my views! I sat in for two days and nights and I'll never forget the atmosphere. There was such a communal spirit - with everyone standing together against the authorities! The occupation lasted just over a week until the students got an agreement to have a series of formal discussions about their complaints.

---

4 ◯ Which do you think is more effective, an online protest or a protest march? Why?

Language focus: Reported speech

Reported statements

1 In extract C of the reading text on page 67 Sara says her mother would not let her stay in a tree house. Look at her mother's words and the way Sara reports them. What change does Sara make to the verb?

Sara's mother: *'I draw the line at that.'*

Sara: *My mum said she drew the line at that.*

2 a Look at these other examples of direct statements and how they were reported. <u>Underline</u> the verbs in each pair of sentences and describe the changes made to the tenses or verbs.

e.g. **1** The past simple 'went off' in direct speech changes to 'had gone off' in reported speech.

   1 *'The protest march <u>went off</u> well yesterday.'*

    She said that the protest march <u>had gone off</u> well the previous day.

   2 *'We must take action to reduce pollution.'*

    She said that they had to take action to reduce pollution.

   3 *'They'll agree to talks soon.'*

    She said they would agree to talks soon.

   4 *'We're having a sit-in to get our point across.'*

    They said that they were having a sit-in to get their point across.

   5 *'We can stop the council building a new motorway here.'*

    He said that they could stop the council building a new motorway there.

   6 *'News of the politician's visit has leaked out.'*

    He told me that news of the politician's visit had leaked out.

b What other words and expressions change when using reported speech? Give examples from 1–6 in exercise 2a.

e.g. **1** *Yesterday* in direct speech changes to *the previous day* in reported speech.

 Read more about reported statements in the Grammar Reference.

3 Write down four things people in your class have said during this lesson. Use direct speech. Exchange your list with a partner and use reported speech to tell another student what your partner has written.

Reporting verbs

1 In reported speech we can use other verbs apart from *say* and *tell*. <u>Underline</u> the reporting verb which best describes what the people are doing in these statements.

   1 *'Don't forget to hand in your essay tomorrow,'* Ben said to me.
                 recommending/reminding

   2 *'Roy Green will win the election. I know it!'* said Maria.   **promising/predicting**

   3 *'Don't be late this evening or dad will be angry,'* said my brother.
                 warning/threatening

   4 *'No, I won't sign this petition,'* said the student.   **complaining/refusing**

   5 *'Come on! You're tired. Take a break,'* my friend said to me. So I did.
                 persuading/begging

   6 *'Sit down at once!'* the teacher said to the class.   **encouraging/ordering**

   7 *'I'll help you with the research,'* Mike said to me.   **explaining/offering**

   8 *'It's a good idea to compare prices before buying a computer,'* my dad said to my brother.   **advising/insisiting**

2 Report the statements in exercise 1 using the simple past of the verbs you have underlined, together with one of the following verb patterns.

   1 verb + infinitive
     *He **promised to arrive** early.*

   2 verb + object + infinitive
     *He **urged me to** stop smoking.*

   3 verb + that + clause
     *He **explained that it was not serious**.*

e.g. **1** Ben reminded me to hand in my essay the following day.

 Read more about reporting verbs in the Grammar Reference.

3 a Write a direct statement for each of the following. Imagine you are talking to your partner.

   1 a recommendation   **3** a threat
   2 a promise   **4** a complaint

e.g. *1 You should do your homework as soon as you get home.*

b Exchange your sentences with your partner. Then report your partner's sentences to another student.

e.g. *1 Ana recommended me to do my homework as soon as I get home.*

Vocabulary: Making decisions

1 Look at these comments that people have made about making decisions. <u>Underline</u> the correct word in *italics*. Use a dictionary if necessary.

1 I usually take a long time to make decisions because I try to **take everything into *consideration*/*understanding***.

2 Once I've decided something, I rarely **change my *mind*/*head***. I don't like ***going*/*looking* back on a decision** once I've made it.

3 I agree. It's not a good idea to **rush/ speed into a decision** because you need to ***stand*/*weigh* up the pros and the cons**.

4 My problem is that I can never **make/ take up my mind**! I usually put off making a decision until the last possible moment.

5 Whenever there's an opinion to be expressed, my sister always **sits on the *half*/ *fence*** – she just won't support either side in an argument.

6 I never **go for the easiest *option*/ *election***. I prefer a bit of a challenge. How about you?

7 In my case – I usually **let my heart *decide*/*rule* my head**, and that's not always a good thing! I should think more about decisions and not get too emotional.

2 💬 Work in pairs. Tell your partner if you are like any of the people who made comments 1–7? Give reasons and examples.

Example:

I'm a bit like Speaker 4. Last week I waited so long to decide whether to go to the concert or not, there were no tickets left!

FCE Speaking Part 3: Collaborative task

1 Here are some decisions people often have to make. Talk to each other about what people need to consider when making these decisions. Then decide which is the most difficult decision to make.

Remember

- Don't just describe the photos and what you can see in them. Answer the questions printed above the photos.
- Don't rush through the pictures. Spend some time talking about each one before you move on to the next.
- You do not have to agree with your partner about which is the most difficult decision.

- What do people need to consider when making these decisions?
- Which decision is the most difficult to make?

Useful language

- Avoid repeating the words *consider* and *difficult*. Here are some alternatives:

*You need to **think about/bear in mind/ take into account** a number of factors.*

*It's a **hard/ complicated/tricky/ tough** decision to make.*

*It **isn't a/an easy/ simple/straightforward** decision.*

*Deciding what to do **is no easy matter**.*

FCE Listening Part 4: Multiple choice

1 🗨 Look at the photographs of the same place at different times. Where is it and what usually happens here?

2 🎧 **1.51** You will hear part of an interview with a member of the UKYP, the United Kingdom Youth Parliament. For questions 1–7, choose the best answer (A, B or C)

1 What was different about the House of Commons on Friday 30th November?

A The people were all dressed very smartly.

B The place was unusually full.

C Young people joined the normal MPs.

2 Why had the event been opposed?

A The Youth Parliament had not asked for permission in the right way.

B The MPs thought the event would cause too much disruption to their routine.

C An event like this had never been held in the House of Commons before.

3 According to Vince the majority of UKYP members want to be members because

A they want to make a difference in the world.

B they think it is good training for a future in politics.

C they think the politicians need to be replaced.

4 In his time as a member of UKYP Vince

A has been the leader of an international youth council.

B has concentrated on local problems.

C has worked with people who had similar views to his.

5 How did the UKYP members break with tradition in the House of Commons?

A They wore brightly coloured clothes.

B They sometimes used rude language.

C They talked to the press before the debate.

6 What is Vince proud of in relation to the day in the House of Commons?

A The results of the discussions.

B The support they gave to abolishing tuition fees.

C The admiration shown in some newspaper reports.

7 When compared with the normal MPs, Vince believes that the UKYP

A showed their feelings about the topics more.

B were more serious about their views.

C spoke out more in favour of equality in all aspects of life.

3 🗨 Do you have a youth parliament in your country? Do you think it's a good thing? Why/Why not?

4 🗨 Work in pairs. The Youth Parliament had to choose one of the following to campaign for over the coming year. Rank the issues in order of importance and then decide which one you think they chose and why.

1 University fees. University education should be free for all students.

2 Public transport and young people. Young people should have free public transport.

3 Jobs for young people and the economy. The government should give more help to young people in finding work.

4 Lowering the voting age. People of 16 should be allowed to vote.

5 Youth crime and what to do about it. Young offenders should not be sent to prison.

5 🗨 Choose one of the statements in exercise 4 for a class discussion. Before you start, think of two points for and two points against the statement. In the discussion use expressions from the Useful language box.

Useful language

In my opinion students should pay their way like everybody else.

I feel very strongly that the government should help students who come from poor backgrounds.

Surely education is the only way out of poverty? **I firmly believe that** all education should be free!

Don't you think there are better things the government should spend its money on?

That's a good point but you've got to look at the bigger picture.

FCE Writing Part 2: Essay

1 Read the following Part 2 question. Do you agree or disagree with the statement? Think of two points you might make to support your view when answering the question.

After a class discussion on youth crime, your teacher has asked you to write an essay, giving your opinion on the following statement.

Young offenders should not be sent to prison.

Write your essay in **120–180** words.

2 Read the model answer below. Does the writer mention the same points as you?

> Young offenders should not be sent to prison.
>
> Youth crime is increasing today and more and more young people are ending up in prison, often for long periods. Is this the best way to punish these young people? Personally, I do not think it is.
>
> Firstly, we have to consider the type of crime. For more serious, violent crimes perhaps prison is the right punishment as society needs to be protected. However, many young people in prison are there for minor crimes such as theft. In my opinion there should be different punishments for them.
>
> Secondly, young people who are in prison often have to share a cell with older, more experienced criminals. This is not a good thing because they can learn more about crime. I firmly believe that we should try to help young people leave crime behind.
>
> To conclude, whilst I fully agree that people who do something wrong should be punished, I feel that a punishment such as working to help the local community would be much better for many young people than being locked up in prison.

3 Read the model answer again. Find examples of linking words and phrases that can be used for each of the functions 1–6 below. Write the words and phrases next to the functions.

1 introduce a contrast
2 indicate the sequence of different points
3 introduce a reason
4 introduce an example
5 indicate that you are coming to the end of the essay
6 introduce your opinion

4 a Work in pairs. Read the following Part 2 question. Then choose a topic for your essay. Discuss and note down points you could use in the essay.

After a class discussion on the issues in exercise 4 on page 70, your teacher has asked you to write an essay, giving your opinion on one of the statements **1–4**.

Write your **essay** in **120–180** words.

b Make a plan for the essay using this guide and the notes you have made. Then write the essay.

Paragraph 1: Introduction - write about the situation now and give your general opinion.

Paragraph 2: Talk about your first point.

Paragraph 3: Talk about your second point.

Paragraph 4: Conclusion - summarize your ideas and restate your opinion.

Help

- Use a variety of linking devices. Think about contrast, addition, reason and sequence as used in the model answer in exercise 2
- Give examples to make your points clear.
- Use a formal or semi-formal style.

Language focus: Reported questions

1 In the listening on page 70 you heard an interview with Vince Martin, a member of the UKYP. Read this extract from a newspaper report of the interview and write down the direct questions that the interviewer asked.

In his interview with Vince Martin yesterday, Mark Hutchings asked Vince how many members of the Youth Parliament had spoken in the debate and if the UKYP members were going to campaign for any of the matters that they had discussed. He also asked whether the Youth parliament would return to the House of Commons at a future date.

Example:

How many UKYP members spoke in the debate?

2 Answer these questions about reported questions.

1 How is the word order in reported questions different from direct questions?
2 Are the changes in verb tenses the same as for reported statements?
3 What happens to the auxiliary verbs *do*, *does*, *did*?
4 Which two words can we use after the verb *ask* when reporting questions that require a yes/no answer?

www Read more about reported questions in the Grammar Reference.

3 Report these other questions that the interviewer asked Vince. Start your answers *The interviewer asked Vince …*

1 Did you enjoy the experience?
2 Was anyone wearing a suit and tie?
3 How long has the Youth Parliament been trying to get to the House of Commons?
4 Are you going to stand for election again next year?
5 Do you think the MPs were impressed by the debates?

4 a Work in pairs. Think of some more questions you would like to ask Vince about the Youth Parliament and their day in the House of Commons.

b Exchange your questions with another pair of students. Imagine how Vince might answer the questions that you have been given. Then write a short report.

Example:

How did all the members travel to the House of Commons?

Most came by train or coach.

The interviewer asked Vince how all the members had travelled to the House of Commons and he told her that most had gone by train or coach. …

Speaking: The news

1 Work in pairs. These pictures show people getting the news in different ways. Compare the pictures and say what the advantages are of getting the news in these ways. Then answer the questions.

1 What other ways are there of getting the news?
2 Do you keep up to date with national and world news? Why/Why not?
3 Which way of getting the news do you (or your parents) prefer? Why?

FCE Use of English Part 1: Multiple-choice cloze

1 Read the text below, ignoring the gaps. Choose the best title for the article.
   a The importance of keeping informed.
   b The death of the newspaper?
   c A career in journalism.
   d Which newspaper is best?

2 For questions 1–12, read the text below and decide which answer (A, B, C or D) best fits each gap. There is an example at the beginning (0).

The future of the daily newspaper is in (0) .... With changes in people's reading habits and financial concerns, it seems that more and more of us are turning (1) .... from the traditional daily newspaper as a means of getting our information and going online or to TV news for the (2) .... and main stories instead. Does this mean that newspapers will (3) .... become a thing of the past?

Many experts believe that newspapers will survive in some form in the future (4) .... the convenience of the internet, their main rival. The main reason for thinking this is that a large percentage of the population is (5) .... 35 and has a strong newspaper reading habit. For many of these people, reading newspapers is not simply a way of getting the information about (6) .... events but part of a traditional routine. For them, catching up with the main stories electronically from news websites or TV news (7) .... will never be a real substitute for turning the pages of a paper on the train or at the table.

However, the main competition for newspapers (8) .... from their own online versions. Access to these is currently free of charge but for how much longer? Many newspaper corporations are (9) .... that the only way forward for all newspapers is to charge customers to read the online versions. Apparently, surveys (10) .... that as many as 48% of British and American consumers are prepared to pay for this service, although they are not prepared to pay very (11) ....! Would you be willing to pay for online access to news websites or should it continue to be free for everyone? Can you (12) .... a world without newspapers? Post your comment below.

0 A problems	B <u>danger</u>	C fear	D worry
1 A out	B over	C away	D forward
2 A titles	B signs	C descriptions	D headlines
3 A shortly	B next	C lately	D early
4 A although	B however	C despite	D but
5 A over	B more	C after	D further
6 A modern	B current	C late	D ultimate
7 A emissions	B sendings	C hearings	D broadcasts
8 A gets	B goes	C gives	D comes
9 A accepted	B insisted	C convinced	D chosen
10 A tell	B show	C allow	D describe
11 A lot	B much	C largely	D enough
12 A imagine	B predict	C believe	D fancy

3 With a partner, discuss the two questions at the end of the article.

FCE Reading Part 2: Gapped text

1 🗪 Look at the photographs, all of which appeared in a daily newspaper. Discuss these questions with a partner.

What do you think the story might be behind each one?

Which story would interest you the most? And the least?

2 a 🗪 Work in pairs. You are going to read about the life of a breakfast radio news presenter. What do you think he likes/doesn't like about his job? What sort of problems might he have?

b Read the article, ignoring the gaps, and check your ideas.

3 Read the article again. Seven sentences have been removed from the article. Choose from the sentences A–H the one which best fits each gap (1–7). There is one extra sentence which you do not need to use.

A day in the life of a radio news presenter

Without doubt, the worst part of my job is the unearthly hour that I have to get up at every day. This puts me in a foul mood for at least two hours as I am not, nor have I ever been, a morning person! In fact I cannot imagine what it must be like to be a 'morning person'. **1** [ ] Unfortunately for me, this only happens at the weekends these days.

'Why?' people ask me, 'Why do you have a job that means you have to get up at 3.45 in the morning?' The simple answer is that the job of presenting the weekday breakfast news programme on a radio station is what I have always wanted to do **2** [ ] But there are no two ways about it – I am still not a morning person!

Having hauled myself out of bed, I get a taxi to the radio station (I wouldn't trust myself driving at that hour), and when we arrive it is still dark with only a few brave birds daring to break the silence with their song. Singing is the last thing I feel like doing. **3** [ ]

In much better spirits now. I sit in on the news conference, which is where the editors make the big decisions on which news stories we are going to run with and in which order. They discuss events that have happened overnight and developments in any stories we ran yesterday. **4** [ ] You can feel the excitement in the air on mornings like these, particularly if it's an event with important national or international implications.

The discussions are fierce. Which stories do we report and in how much depth? Then the big question – which stories get priority? We may have five big stories but which do we lead with? Is it the celebrity who has been caught for dangerous driving or is it yet another political scandal? Is it the murder of a homeless person or the fact that Australia has just won an important cricket match?

People in the meeting pull in different directions. **5** [ ] Others think that local crimes need to be top of the list. The team thrashes out the possibilities and eventually I am nearly ready to go on air.

This is when the adrenalin really kicks in. It is a buzz presenting a show live but there is not much room for mistakes and things do not always go smoothly. My job is to appear to be in control and I have to be alert and able to think on my feet. **6** [ ] Then there are the times when I get linked with the wrong reporter. Last week for example, I was talking about a break-in at a country house hotel and got linked to a reporter on another story who was at a zoo. So, my question about 'Was anything valuable stolen' prompted the rather puzzled response 'Er … no … all the elephants are definitely still here!'

Of course, there are also those callers on the phone-in sections who see it as an opportunity to go way off topic and complain about everything from taxation to the quality of the burgers in the restaurant down the road! There's a lot of mental gymnastics that goes on and afterwards I always feel completely exhausted. **7** [ ]

Before leaving the studio there's another meeting to discuss items for tomorrow's show. We might have a special guest – like a politician or an actor and we talk about the questions I should or shouldn't ask. Eventually the heart stops pounding and I can relax. I'm out of the door, determined to enjoy the rest of the day before I need to go to bed at the obscenely early time of 8.30!

A There may even be a breaking news story happening at the time.

B Of course, I realize there's a contradiction here, and I shouldn't be moaning about getting up early, particularly when my job is the envy of hundreds of other would-be presenters in Australia.

C What I love to do most in the whole world is to snuggle up in bed until lunchtime.

D When you're talking on the radio, you have to imagine that you're talking to one person face to face.

E Sometimes sound links with reporters in the field can go wrong and I'm left talking to complete silence.

F Some want to win the popular vote – celebrity stories attract listeners, the more sensational the better.

G However, that's all part of the job and the unpredictability is one of the reasons I love it so much.

H A couple of strong coffees later, however, I feel better able to face the day and my grumpiness begins to lift.

4 Work in pairs. Look at list of news headlines below. Imagine you are going to plan a news bulletin and decide the following points. Give reasons.

- What would be the lead story?

- What order would you present the other items in?

1 Celebrity arrested for dangerous driving

2 Government reduces money for hospitals

3 *Airport strike*

4 **Murder of homeless man**

5 Politician fails to pay his taxes

6 **Outbreak of dangerous spiders**

7 *Dog saves its master from freezing river*

8 Small country wins big sports trophy

FCE Writing Part 1: Email

Answer the following Part 1 task.

Your English friend Jack, has sent you an email asking you for help in improving his knowledge of your language. Read Jack's email and the notes you have made. Then write an email to Jack using **all** your notes. Write **120–150** words.

Email

From: Jack Barnes

Sent: 18th April

Subject: Advice please!

I really need your advice! Before I come to visit you next summer I must improve my language as I don't want to speak English all the time. I've been having some private lessons and last week my teacher told me to read magazines and books to improve my vocabulary. Do you read a lot in English? I prefer reading newspapers to reading books so I was wondering if you could suggest some newspapers that I could read online?

Are there any interesting news stories in your country at the moment? Here in the UK the government's trying to increase university fees for students. Everyone's really angry! There's been a big online campaign against it and even an online petition! Have you ever signed one of these?

Write soon!

Best wishes

Jack

…es – tell …m what

Good idea – make suggestions

Yes – outline a story

…es – say …hen and …hy

When you have finished writing, check your email by answering the questions in the Help box on page 131.

Language focus

Read this voicemail message from Paul to Helen.

Hi Helen! I've just got back from the Climate Change protest march. I was expecting to see you on the train but I couldn't find you. Did you go? It was amazing. I'm sitting here watching the march on TV. Are you watching it too? It looks really impressive! Well, it's been a long day so I'm going to bed early. I'll give you a ring soon. Bye!

The next day, Helen told her friend Andy, what Paul had said in his message. Complete her words using reported speech.

Hi Andy. Paul phoned last night and left a message. He told me he'd just got back from the Climate Change protest march and said that he ...

Vocabulary

1 Complete each gap with the correct verb. You will need to use one verb twice.

1 A lot of people .... **action** when they get angry about something the government has done.

2 I can't .... **up my mind** whether to go to Italy or Japan on holiday this year.

3 The group of protesters .... **disruption** to our travel when they blocked the entrances to the airport terminal.

4 You need to .... a lot of things **into consideration** before making a big decision about a future career.

5 Sometimes when my brother is discussing politics, he .... **too far** and offends people.

6 The protestors carried placards and banners to try to .... **their point about unemployment across**.

2 Underline the correct alternative in *italics*.

1 I'm in two *minds/heads* about whether to go to the party tonight or not.

2 Most parents would draw the *point/line* at letting children of five have a mobile phone.

3 I *balanced/weighed* up the pros and the cons before deciding which course to follow at university.

4 Do you feel *strongly/hardly* about the new motorway they are planning to build?

5 I saw the big *manifestation/demonstration* against taxes on the news last night.

6 The *lead/front* story in the newspaper this morning was about the accident in the centre of Paris.

Phrasal verbs revision

Complete each gap with the correct particle(s).

1 up   up with

a Come and visit us anytime. We can **put** you .... for a week if you like.

b The teacher couldn't **put** .... Jan's bad behaviour any longer and sent her home.

2 off   back on

a The organisers spent a long time preparing for the party and it **went** .... very well. Everyone had a good time.

b I'm so angry! My dad **went** .... his decision to let me use his car next weekend. It's not fair.

3 to   on

a Do you know if the paper is **taking** .... any more staff at the moment? I might apply if they are.

b We met Dan's new girlfriend last night. She's so friendly. I **took** .... her immediately.

4 after   for

a Can you help me? I'm **looking** .... a book about Australia.

b It isn't my dog! I'm just **looking** .... it while my sister's on holiday.

FCE Use of English Part 2: Open cloze

For questions **1–12**, read the text below and think of the word which best fits each gap. Use only one word in each gap. There is an example at the beginning **(0)**.

Judging the judges!

Everyone is **(0)** ..AN.. armchair critic these days. A quick look **(1)** .... any TV schedule shows that reality TV programmes dominate our screens and most of these ask the viewers to vote on which contestant or participant should **(2)** .... eliminated from the show and which should progress to the next level. But **(3)** .... do we make our choice? What do we base our opinions on? In general it's a personal reaction to **(4)** .... we see. We are not experts, but often we rely **(5)** .... guidance from the professional judges on the show.

So, what makes a good professional judge? Perhaps it's easier to point out what makes a bad one. We **(6)** .... all seen the judges on reality talent shows and **(7)** .... is probably fair to say that many of them often resort to generalities. They comment on the contestant's performance without giving detailed reasons **(8)** .... it was good or poor. How many times have we heard 'Well, that just wasn't as good **(9)** .... last week.' or 'Great. You deserve your place on this stage.' A good professional judge needs to be **(10)** .... to give constructive criticism and articulate his or her opinions about the strength or weakness of a performance. He needs to be an expert in his field, **(11)** .... it is music or cookery, and also **(12)** .... be afraid of telling the truth as he sees it. It is definitely not the judge's job to be popular.

Writing FCE Part 2

Write an answer to one of these questions in **120–180** words in an appropriate style.

1 You recently saw this notice in a TV guide.

> **What do you think?**
>
> There are a lot of reality shows on TV at the moment and we'd like to know what you think about them. Write a review of one of the shows and say what you like or don't like about it. We'll publish the best reviews in next week's edition.

Write your **review**.

2 You have seen this advertisement for summer jobs.

> **Are you an animal lover?**
>
> We're looking for people aged 14–19 to support some of our animal rescue centres in the evenings and at weekends. Would you be suitable and willing to give some time to help?
>
> Activities include
>
> • fund raising
>
> • looking after the animals
>
> • dealing with enquiries
>
> Write to Mr. Franks, saying which activities you could help with and why you would be suitable.

Write your **letter of application**.

Speaking

1 Look at the items shown in the photographs and answer the following questions about each one. Give reasons.

What aspects of the modern world threaten their survival?

Do you think it is important for us to try to keep them in the future? Why/Why not?

What, if anything, can be done to help them survive?

2 How easy or difficult is it for people of your grandparents' generation to survive in today's fast-moving world?

Do you think life in the future will be better or worse than it is now? Why?

3 a Rank the following from **1–8** where **1** is the one you would find it most difficult to survive without and **8** is the one you would miss the least if you didn't have it.

washing machine	television
mobile phone	central heating
fridge	mp4 player
computer	dishwasher

b Work in pairs. Compare your lists, giving reasons for your decisions.

Books

Letters

Small shops

Tropical rainforests

Cinemas

Whales

Board games

Vocabulary: Surviving

1 Complete each gap with a word from the box.

get	get	live	make	stay

1 I don't need a powerful computer; I can .... **by with** just a small laptop.

2 My grandparents receive a very small pension and **find it hard to** .... **ends** meet.

3 I never work during the summer holidays; I can .... **on the money** my parents give me.

4 If I was lost in the mountains or a forest, I'd know what plants, berries and other food I could eat in order to .... **alive**.

5 I need at least three cups of coffee to help me .... **through the day**.

2 Match the highlighted phrasal verbs and expressions which you completed in exercise 1 to a definition **a–e**.

a continue to live when you are in a dangerous situation

b have enough of something (e.g. equipment, knowledge) to be able to do what you need to do

c have enough money to pay for the things you need

d manage to deal with the situations you encounter during the day

e have trouble paying for the things you need in order to live

3 Look again at the sentences in exercise 1 and say how true each one is for you. Develop your answers.

FCE Listening Part 1: Multiple choice

🎧 **2.1–2.16 You will hear people talking in eight different situations. For questions 1–8, choose the best answer (A, B or C).**

1 You hear a man talking about a documentary he saw on television.

What aspect of the documentary's location surprised him?

A the beauty of the scenery

B the variety of the wildlife

C the severity of the climate

2 You hear a shop owner being interviewed on the radio.

What does she say is the main threat to her business?

A the current economic situation

B the competition from large stores

C the import of cheap foreign goods

3 You hear a teacher being interviewed on the radio.

Why is his school celebrating Tiger Day?

A to make children aware of the tiger's situation

B to collect money to help with tiger conservation

C to protest against keeping tigers in zoos

4 You hear a woman talking about books and eBook readers.

Why does she prefer books to eBook readers?

A They will last longer than eBook readers.

B They are easier to keep clean than eBook readers.

C They are more pleasant to hold than eBook readers.

5 You overhear this man speaking on his mobile phone.

Who is he talking to?

A his boss

B his brother

C his neighbour

6 You overhear a student speaking about her financial situation.

What is she complaining about?

A She gets no help from her parents.

B She is having trouble finding a job.

C She has to repay money she borrows.

7 You hear a man speaking on the radio.

What is his occupation?

A a professor

B an author

C a reporter

8 You hear a woman talking to a friend about her first week as a teacher.

What has she found most tiring about it?

A planning her lessons

B the length of her teaching day

C maintaining discipline

Language focus: Countable and uncountable nouns

1 A **countable** noun has a plural form and can be used after *a/an* when it is singular.

e.g. *book   letter   shop   match*

An **uncountable** noun has no plural form and is not used after *a/an*.

e.g. *furniture   health   progress*

In sentences 1–10, which are taken from the listening on page 79, some of the nouns have been <u>underlined</u>. Write **C** in the square brackets if the noun is countable, and **U** if it is uncountable.

e.g. ***Many*** *small businesses* [**C**] *are having to close.*

1 **A large number of** <u>hypermarkets</u> [ ] seem to be popping up everywhere.

2 There are **very few** <u>tigers</u> [ ] left in the wild.

3 My son downloaded **some** <u>eBooks</u> [ ] on it for me.

4 **Several** <u>schools</u> [ ] in the area are hoping to raise **a large amount of** <u>money</u>. [ ]

5 There wasn't **much** <u>damage</u> [ ] at all in our <u>street</u>. [ ]

6 **A lot of** <u>trees</u> [ ] were blown down.

7 I think the <u>house</u> [ ] next door lost **a couple of** <u>roof tiles</u>. [ ]

8 Clearly I had to have **some** <u>knowledge</u> [ ] of the subject and I did **a great deal of** <u>research</u>. [ ]

9 A <u>journalist</u> [ ] on a Welsh language newspaper gave me **a lot of** <u>help</u> [ ] and advice. [ ]

10 I did think I might have **a few** <u>problems</u> [ ] with bad <u>behaviour</u>. [ ]

2 Copy the table below into your notebook. Put the words and phrases in **bold** in exercise 1 into the correct columns.

Before [U] nouns	Before plural [C] nouns	Before [U] and plural [C] nouns
	many	

3 a Look again at sentences 2 and 10 in exercise 1 and complete the gaps in these definitions with *few* and *a few*.

1 We use .... with plural countable nouns to mean not many or not as many as you would like or expect.

2 We use .... with plural countable nouns to mean some or a small number of.

b Which words would be used instead of *few* and *a few* before **uncountable** nouns?

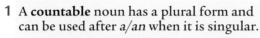 Read more about countable and uncountable nouns in the Grammar Reference.

4 In 1–6 there are **two** mistakes in each sentence. Correct the mistakes.

1 Kelly's not in a very good health and she's having trouble finding a work.

2 The news on the telly are depressing, it's a terrible weather outside and I've got an awful cold – I feel so miserable!

3 There was graffiti on the walls, and they did a lot of damages to the furnitures.

4 We went on a travel to Italy last year and two of our three luggages went missing.

5 We've just received this piece of traffic informations: the police are advising drivers to leave their cars at home and use public transports.

5 For 1–5 <u>underline</u> the correct alternative in *italics*.

1 *Any/Several/Every* sections of the art gallery were destroyed in the fire, but a surprisingly large *number/deal/amount* of works survived.

2 There weren't *no/much/many* people on the flight out and there were *plenty/most/lot* of free seats on the plane home, too. I don't know how that airline survives.

3 *All/Each/Some* time I go to Greece, I manage to get by with a *few/little/lot* words of Greek, a *few/little/lot* English and a *few/little/lot* of gestures.

4 A small *number/deal/amount* of salt each day is fine, but too *more/most/much* salt in your diet increases your chances of developing high blood pressure.

5 At high altitudes there is not *little/enough/some* oxygen to support human life, and very *few/fewer/a few* climbers have reached the top of Everest without supplementary supplies.

6 Work in pairs. Choose one of the topics in the photographs on page 78. Take turns talking about the topic for two minutes, using as many of the words and phrases as possible from exercises 2 and 5 above. Note how many words and phrases your partner uses correctly.

FCE Use of English Part 2: Open cloze

1 Work with a partner. <u>Underline</u> what you think is the correct alternative in *italics* in the following sentences about Wales.

Welsh Factfile
1 The capital of Wales is *Swansea/Cardiff/Newport*.
2 The population of Wales is approximately *three/six/nine* million.
3 About *five/twenty/fifty* per cent of the population speak Welsh.
4 The highest mountain in Wales at just over *one/two/three* thousand metres is Mount Snowdon.
5 *Football/Cricket/Rugby* is regarded as Wales' national game.
6 The Welsh are noted for their *choral singing/ballroom dancing/classical music*.
7 Hollywood celebrities from Wales include *Tim Burton/Anthony Perkins/Catherine Zeta-Jones*.
8 The title 'Prince of Wales' is traditionally given to the British king or queen's *eldest/second/youngest* son.

2.17 Listen to an extract from a radio programme and check your answers.

2 For questions **1–12**, read the text below and think of the word which best fits each gap. Use only **one** word in each gap. There is an example at the beginning **(0)**.

The survival of Welsh

Welsh is **(0)** ..ONE.. of the oldest surviving languages **(1)** .... Europe with a history going back over fifteen centuries. In Wales itself it **(2)** .... now spoken by over half a million people, around twenty per cent of the population. Welsh is **(3)** .... much in evidence there as English: street signs are written in **(4)** .... of the languages, all official documents in English must also be available in Welsh, and **(5)** .... child in Wales learns Welsh in school up to the age of 16.

Interestingly, Welsh did not enjoy equal status with English in public life **(6)** .... fairly recently, with the passing of the Welsh Language Acts in 1967 and 1993. **(7)** .... two laws put an end to the dominance of English in the legal and administrative systems, **(8)** .... began in 1536, when Wales was united politically with its larger neighbour and English became the only official language.

Welsh was preserved thanks largely **(9)** .... the translation of the Bible into Welsh and the continued use of the language in churches. Its general use, however, declined in the twentieth century: with very **(10)** .... job opportunities in the post-war depression of the 1920s and 1930s, many young Welsh speakers left Wales in search of work elsewhere. In addition, relatively cheap housing in recent years **(11)** .... led to the arrival of large numbers of English people and an anglicization of rural areas.

(12) .... this decline has been reversed and Welsh is currently enjoying a revival, the language is still struggling for survival and the number of children being brought up with Welsh as their mother tongue is falling.

3 Do you think minority languages like Welsh can continue to survive in today's world? Why/Why not?

Are any minority languages spoken in your country? What is being done to help their survival?

FCE Reading Part 2: Gapped text

1 💬 Would you like to be a secondary school teacher? Why/Why not?

2 You are going to read an extract from a teacher's autobiography. Read the base text only and answer this question:

How would you have dealt with Daryl Jones if you had been the teacher?

My first ever lesson

This was a GCSE English class. I was supposed to have another teacher in the class with me but I was entirely on my own. I knew from observing a couple of other GCSE classes that everyone else in the English Department was reading *A Taste of Honey* by Shelagh Delaney and asking them to do a piece of coursework on it.

The play was a bleak drama written in the 1960s about a teenage girl living in the poverty-stricken North. **1** However, I hadn't any time to prepare to teach it or even to think about whether I should teach it or not. It was the only suitable book I had seen in the stock cupboard and I pulled it out without a second thought.

"Now then," I said. "Could we have quiet please? I need to see who is reading what role in this play. Could you put up your hand if you want to read?" **2** Then when I said they had a part, they refused to take it. After ten minutes of trying to allocate roles, no one had a part.

I remember feeling a sense of rising panic. What was I supposed to do? I was banking on reading the play for part of the lesson and then setting a written exercise, where they predicted what happened next, for the remainder of the lesson. **3** How could they make a prediction from nothing?

These kids were laughing at me. I felt very vulnerable with my long ponytail. Sweat was beginning to seep through my shirt. I wandered around the class, trying to encourage kids on a one-to-one basis to take on a role. **4**

I succeeded in getting the play started with these readers. However, their faltering voices were virtually drowned out by the other kids who were still chatting very loudly. In particular, there was one kid, the surly, sunken-eyed Daryl Jones, who was pushing and shouting at the boy sitting next to him. **5** I decided that I had to take him on if I was going to get anywhere.

I asked him to be quiet and to listen. He didn't respond – or rather he did by **shoving** his friend so hard he fell off his seat. Everyone burst out laughing. **6** For the first time in the lesson, everyone was quiet. All eyes turned to watch me as I **stalked** with a red and furious face towards Jones. He grinned at everyone and then let his head **flop** on to the desk with a soft thud. He appeared to shut his eyes.

7 I picked up his book which had fallen on the floor and put it beside his tousled black hair. His face was still buried in the desk. "You have to follow this," I said in an angry but calmish voice, as I pointed at a page of *A Taste of Honey*. Jones didn't reply. "Did you hear me?" I said.

Jones groaned in a pseudo-sleepy voice, "What, what you say?" The class tittered. They were still watching with avid attention. "I said you need to follow this." "Oh, sir," said Jones, lifting his head slightly to show his hooded eyes. "I'm just trying to have a kip* here." There was an intake of breath and then an explosion of laughter from the class. I had been humiliated.

kip = a short sleep

3 Seven sentences have been removed from the extract. Choose from the sentences **A–H on page 83** the one which fits each gap (1–7). There is one extra sentence which you do not need to use.

A But they hadn't read anything.

B I didn't know what to say to him because he wasn't being noisy any more.

C I approached him as his friend picked himself off the floor.

D As I had predicted, however, this measure did not meet with much success.

E This worked a bit better because I managed to get a few of them to agree to read out aloud.

F I liked the text although I was aware that it was very dated in its references.

G He was by far the worst-behaved and noisiest kid in the class.

H Everyone started shouting out that they wanted a role.

4 ◯ Why do you think some children behave like Daryl Jones?

Should teachers have the power to punish children more severely? Why/Why not?

Vocabulary: Prepositions

1 Complete each gap in these sentences from the reading text on page 82 with a preposition.

a I was entirely .... my own.

b I hadn't any time to think .... whether I should teach it or not.

c These kids were laughing .... me.

d I succeeded .... getting the play started with these readers.

e He grinned .... everyone.

f I pointed .... a page of *A Taste of Honey*.

Check your answers in the reading text.

2 a Complete each gap with a preposition which can be used after all four verbs. The first one has been done for you.

about	at	for	~~in~~	on	to

1 invest believe participate result *in* something

2 belong listen object respond .... something/somebody

3 pay apologize save up apply .... something

4 depend concentrate insist agree .... something

5 worry dream complain forget .... something/somebody

6 smile look shout stare .... somebody

Remember

b Complete each gap with a preposition which can be used before all four nouns.

at	by	in	on	out of

1 .... purpose fire average offer

2 .... home risk work fault

3 .... heart bus accident chance

4 .... date breath order sight

5 .... theory practice danger charge

3 Complete each gap with a noun or the appropriate form of a verb from exercise 2.

1 The fire chief **in** .... of the operation said that the whole area was **on** .... , putting over two hundred homes **at** .... and the lives of residents **in** ....

2 I broke a chair at school **by** .... I kept telling them I hadn't done it **on** .... but they still made me .... **for** a new one.

3 The hand dryer in the toilet is always **out of** .... I keep .... **about** it to the caretaker but he just .... politely **at** me and shrugs his shoulders.

4 Over 150 countries .... **in** last month's conference, which .... **in** a decision to reduce carbon emissions by 15–20%. Representatives could not, however, ... **on** an exact figure.

4 Now do the exercise on page 131.

FCE Listening Part 2: Sentence completion

1 Work in pairs. Tell your partner about the last time you visited a museum.

Did you enjoy it? Why/Why not?

2 2.18 You will hear part of a radio programme about a new exhibition at a museum. For questions 1–10, complete the sentences.

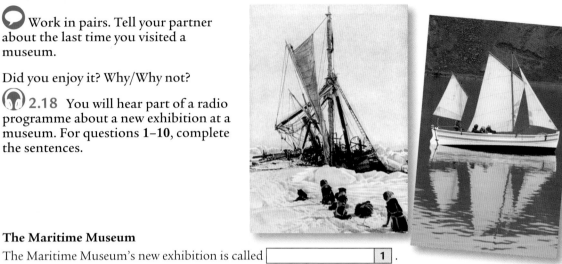

The Maritime Museum

The Maritime Museum's new exhibition is called [_____ 1] .

On display is the boat in which Ernest Shackleton and [_____ 2] members of his crew sailed to South Georgia in search of help.

Shackleton's ship, *Endurance*, became trapped in Antarctic ice in the month of [_____ 3] 1915.

In 1972, the Robertson family's yacht sank after an attack by [_____ 4] .

Initially, all the Robertsons had to eat were biscuits, sweets, fruit and a [_____ 5]

The Robertsons were rescued by a [_____ 6] fishing boat.

One part of the exhibition focuses on the skills and personal qualities needed to sail [_____ 7] .

The Maritime Museum has a large number of [_____ 8] exhibits.

John's son was particularly interested in the display of [_____ 9] .

Entry to the exhibition is free for [_____ 10] .

3 Tell the class about any other 'tales of endurance and survival against the odds' that you know.

Language focus:
Obligation, prohibition, advice and necessity

1 a Complete each gap in these sentences from the listening with one of the items from the box. Use the same words that the speakers used.

have to   had to   don't have to   mustn't   must   ought   need   should

1 If you enjoy tales of endurance and survival against the odds, then you really .... go along and see it.

2 They .... leave the rest of the crew behind on a small island in order to go and look for help.

3 The Maritime Museum is not one of those museums where you .... touch anything.

4 You'd love it - you .... to pay a visit.

5 And how much will I .... pay to get in?

6 Children under six .... pay ...

7 Students .... to show their student card, of course ...

8 ... and senior citizens .... take some proof of their age, just in case they're asked to provide it.

b Check your answers in the listening script on page 156.

2 Complete the table with the sentences from the box below. For each sentence on the left there are two sentences in the box which express a similar idea. The first one has been done for you.

Advice (present)

She should go out. ......*She'd better go out.*...... ....

Lack of necessity (present)

She doesn't need to go out. ....

Prohibition (present)

She mustn't go out. ....

Prohibition (past)

She couldn't go out. ....

Obligation (past)

She had to go out. ....

They made her go out.	~~She'd better go out.~~	There's no need for her to go out.
She isn't allowed to go out.	She needn't go out.	She wasn't allowed to go out.
They won't let her go out.	She ought to go out.	They wouldn't let her go out.
She was made to go out.		

Read more about obligation, prohibition, advice and necessity in the Grammar Reference.

3 There is a mistake in each sentence **1–8**. Correct the mistakes. You may need to delete a word or change one or more words. There is an example at the beginning **(0)**.

0 I think you should ~~to~~ stop now – you've been in front of that screen for too long.

1 You can touch and stroke them if you want to but you don't be allowed to feed them.

2 We would better clear this up before she gets back or she'll be really angry.

3 He made me to stay in during the break just because I was talking.

4 We mustn't wear a tie if we don't want to, but I think our customers prefer it if we do.

5 I needn't having spent so much time worrying – it was really easy.

6 Steve lent me his pair the last time I went birdwatching, but I dropped them and did must buy him some new ones.

7 It broke down on the way to work on Monday, so now I must walk or get the bus everywhere while it's being repaired.

8 We've got plenty here in the flat for you to use, whether in the bathroom or on the beach, so there's no need to you for bring your own.

4 a Work in pairs. Discuss the possible context for each of the sentences in exercise 3. Consider:

• who might be talking

• who they might be talking to

• what or who they might be talking about.

Example:

0 *This might be a parent telling their child to stop playing on the computer or watching television.*

b Work in pairs. Write a six-line dialogue. The first or last line of the dialogue must be one of the sentences in exercise 3.

c Read your dialogue to another pair of students, but do not read out the sentence from exercise 3. Can the other students guess which sentence you chose?

Word formation: Adverbs

1 Read the spelling rules and complete the gaps with the correct adverb form. The first one has been done for you.

a Many adverbs are formed by adding *ly* to the corresponding adjective.

slow slowly........

patient .... *careful* ....

If the adjective ends in *ll*, add only *y* to form the adverb.

full .... *dull* ....

b For adjectives ending in a consonant + *le*, omit the *e* and add *y*.

reasonable .... *gentle* ....

Omit the final *e* and add *ly* in these two cases:

true .... *whole* ....

In all other cases, the final *e* is kept.

immediate .... *brave* ....

c For adjectives ending in *y*, change the *y* to *i* and add *ly*.

happy .... *noisy* ....

d It is usually necessary to add *ally* to adjectives ending in *ic*.

automatic .... *scientific* ....

A common exception to this is:

public ....

2 a Complete each gap in these sentences from the listening on page 156 with the adverb form of the words in brackets. The first one has been done for you.

Adverbs can be used:

a with verbs.

1 ... you ....really...... (real) **must go along** and see it

2 And did everyone **get back** .... (safe)?

3 They were .... (eventual) **picked up** 300 miles west of Costa Rica.

4 Some sections .... (specific) **cater** for kids.

b with adjectives.

5 This year's exhibition ... promises to be just as successful as last year's .... (enormous) **popular** *Surf's Up* event.

6 I would be .... (extreme) **foolish** even to think of doing it!

7 It all sounds .... (absolute) **fascinating**, John.

c on their own at the beginning of a clause or sentence.

8 .... (incredible), Shackleton and all those who'd sailed on the *Endurance* lived to tell the tale.

9 And .... (remark), so did all five members of the Robertson family and a friend ...

10 .... (surprise), though, what my 12-year-old boy found most interesting was the display of navigation equipment.

b Check your answers in the listening script on page 00.

3 In each extract below, two of the adverbs have been spelt incorrectly. Correct the mistakes.

1 The President has publicly thanked the surgeons who successfuly removed the bullet from his back after last month's failed assassination attempt. "I am truly grateful to Dr Korben and his team for saving my life," said Mr Tobang, who is recovering slowly but steadily in hospital. He added that he felt "extremly lucky" to have survived.

2 The Iberian lynx is a criticly endangered species of cat native to the Iberian Peninsula in Southern Europe. There are estimated to be only two hundred or so lynx surviving in the wild. Fortunately, though, its numbers are slowly recovering; the lynx's habitat is now fully protected and it can no longer be legally hunted. Initialy, its decline was due to diseases like myxomatosis, which seriously affected the rabbit population, the lynx's most important prey. More recently, however, urban development, road deaths, poisoning and hunting have been to blame.

3 Personally, I don't think cinemas can survive much longer. We rarely go these days - it's so incredibely expensive with two children, so we normally wait for films to come out on DVD. When we do go, there's hardly anyone else there, so there's absolutely no atmosphere at all and we almost wish we'd stayed at home. Not surprisingally, the one near us closed last week.

FCE Writing Part 2: Reports

1 In Part 2 of the Writing paper one of the options might be to write a report, for which you will be expected to give factual information and make suggestions or recommendations.

Read the following Part 2 task. Which places would you recommend in your town and why?

A group of foreign students is going to be staying in your town for a fortnight this summer. The group leader has asked you to write a report suggesting ways in which the students might spend their free time in your town without having to spend much money. Give advice on cheap places to go for entertainment and say why you think they would be suitable for the students.

2 Read the answer below and write these paragraph headings on the appropriate lines.

The sea is free	Going dancing	Indoor water fun
Introduction	Conclusion	

Compton: surviving on a low budget and having fun

1 _____

The aim of this report is to suggest things to do in Compton which do not involve spending a great deal of money.

2 _____

Compton is noted for its large number of discotheques, including many which are specifically aimed at under-16s, so are ideally suited to your younger group members. Most town centre discotheques are not cheap so I would advise students to go to those on the seafront, where admission is inexpensive and drinks are affordably priced.

3 _____

There is of course no charge for entry to the beach, a must for all your students, who will love its fine sand and clean water. There are also plenty of amusements here which appeal to every age group, such as crazy golf, trampolines and even bungee jumping, and prices are reasonable.

4 _____

I would also recommend a visit to the indoor Aqua Park, which has two wave pools and several water slides. It is highly popular with young people and there are generous student discounts.

5 _____

It is clear that your students will be able to enjoy themselves in Compton without having to spend a fortune.

3 Who is the report written for and has the writer used a formal or informal style?

4 Find examples in the model of:

a words and phrases showing the amount or number of people/things.
e.g. **a great deal of** money

b words and phrases for describing price.
e.g. town centre discotheques are **not cheap**

c phrases for making recommendations.
e.g. **I would advise students to** go to those on the seafront

5 Apart from price, what other reasons does the writer give for recommending the different places to the students?

6 Read the Help box on page 132 before you do the following task.

A group of foreign students is going to be staying in your area for a fortnight this summer. You have been asked to write a report for the group leader about eating out both cheaply and healthily. Give advice on the best places for the students to eat healthy food in your area without having to spend a lot of money, and say why you would recommend them.

Write your **report** in **120–180** words.

Review

For questions **1–8**, complete the second sentence so that it has a similar meaning to the first sentence, using the word given. **Do not change the word given.** You must use between **two** and **five** words, including the word given.

1 In my opinion, they ought not to build the new airport so close to the town.

   SHOULD

   I don't think .... the new airport so close to the town.

2 Sarah wasn't allowed to go to the rock festival.

   LET

   Sarah's parents .... to the rock festival.

3 You ought to leave now or you'll miss the bus.

   BETTER

   You .... now or you'll miss the bus.

4 Ryan had to tidy his room before his mother gave him his pocket money.

   MADE

   Ryan's mother .... his room before she gave him his pocket money.

5 You don't need to phone John about the party because I emailed him yesterday.

   YOU

   There's .... phone John about the party because I emailed him yesterday.

6 Why can't we wear make-up to school?

   ALLOWED

   Why .... wear make-up to school?

7 Thank you for the flowers but it wasn't necessary to buy them for me.

   HAVE

   Thank you for the flowers, but you .... them for me.

8 Candidates are not allowed to remove question papers from the examination room.

   MUST

   Question papers .... by candidates from the examination room.

Vocabulary

Complete each gap with the correct preposition.

1 John insisted .... paying .... the drinks.

2 My dad apologized .... shouting .... me.

3 We're saving up .... a new car, so I've been putting in some extra hours .... work.

4 When I complained to the neighbours .... the noise, they just laughed .... me.

5 The panda is .... danger of extinction and is on the World Conservation Union's Red List, which identifies all animals, birds and plants which are .... risk.

6 I've been staring .... this poem for ages – I'll never be able to learn it .... heart!

7 .... theory we should win this match, but what happens .... practice is another matter entirely.

8 Listen .... the recording again and concentrate .... finding the answers you missed the first time.

Language focus

Complete each gap with one word.

1 If .... student in the school gave us one euro, think how .... money we'd raise!

2 I'm really stressed: I've got so .... things to do, but very .... time to do them.

3 A rather disappointing exam: you made quite a .... mistakes in Part 1 and you had very .... correct answers in Part 2.

4 I've got .... of paper: I can give you a .... of sheets. Will two be enough?

5 We've received a large .... of emails from customers congratulating us on the speed of our service and there haven't been .... complaints – none at all.

6 I've got .... good news; you'll be pleased to hear there's .... homework tonight.

FCE Use of English Part: Word formation

For questions 1–10, read the text below. Use the word given in capitals at the end of some of the lines to form a word that fits in the gap **in the same line**. There is an example (0).

Book Review

Perhaps the best non-fiction book I have read **(0)** RECENTLY is *Touching the Void* by Joe Simpson. It is a **(1)** .... remarkable tale of courage and **(2)** .... in extreme conditions, and is **(3)** .... well written.

	RECENT
	TRUE
	SURVIVE
	EXCEPTION

The author describes in chilling detail what happened in 1985 on a mountaineering expedition in the Peruvian Andes after he and his friend Simon Yates had **(4)** .... climbed the previously unconquered West Face of Siula Grande. During their descent from the summit, the weather changed **(5)** .... and, blinded by snowstorms, Simpson fell badly and broke his leg. **(6)** .... to walk, he had to be lowered by Yates down the mountain using their rope.

SUCCEED

DRAMA

ABLE

Disaster struck again when Simpson was left hanging **(7)** .... over a precipice and could not communicate his situation to his climbing partner. Yates made the only **(8)** .... available to him and cut the rope, sending Simpson plunging into a deep crevasse. **(9)** .... , Simpson managed to crawl his way out of it and then back to camp, where he met up again with Yates.

DANGER

DECIDE

AMAZE

I have no **(10)** .... in recommending this book to anyone who likes real-life adventure stories. Even though you know the author will survive, it holds your attention from start to finish.

HESITATE

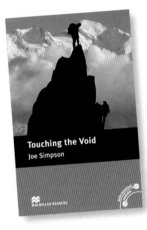

Touching the Void
Joe Simpson

Help

- For information on writing reviews see page 38 in Unit 3 and page 144 in the Writing Bank. You can structure your review like the one on this page.

- For information on writing stories see page 56 in Unit 5 and page 145 in the Writing Bank.

- Include some adverbs in your review or story.

FCE Writing Part 2

Write an answer to one of the following Part 2 tasks in **120–180** words in an appropriate style.

1 You see this announcement in your school English-language magazine. Write a **review**.

> ### Reviews needed!
> Have you read any good non-fiction books or seen any interesting films based on true-life events recently? If so, write us a review for the school magazine telling us what it is about, why you enjoyed it and who you would recommended it to.

2 Your teacher has asked you to write a **story**. Your story must end with the words:
It had been a difficult experience, but I had survived.

UNIT 8 Strength of mind

Vocabulary: Memory

1 💬 Discuss the following questions with your partner.

1 How easy do you find it to **remember names and faces**?

2 Do you have **a good memory for facts and figures**?

2 a Study the pictures for one minute. Then cover them up and write down what you can remember from them.

b 💬 Compare what you have written with your partner. Tell each other about any techniques you used to remember the information.

3 <u>Underline</u> the correct word in *italics*. Which images are the people talking about?

1 I saw it last year when it first came out. The **story is** *forgetful/unforgettable*. You'll love it!

2 When we get tests Jan usually **memorizes/reminds** **long lists** of equations and rules but that doesn't work for me.

3 I envy people who have a **photographic/photographed memory**. Passing exams is no problem for them!

4 I can remember songs from twenty years ago! If you repeat something often enough it goes into your **long/past term memory**.

5 Looking at these **brings/takes** **back memories of** a wonderful holiday. We had such a good time that summer.

6 I sometimes break long numbers down into three or four small groups, or 'chunks' of numbers, and that makes them more **memorable/remembered**.

7 Can you **write down** *of/from* **memory** ten people's phone numbers?

4 💬 Tell your partner about 1–5 below.

1 A memorable event during your last holiday.

2 An unforgettable film you've seen.

3 Someone you know who is quite forgetful.

4 Some things you regularly memorize.

5 A song which brings back memories of something or someone.

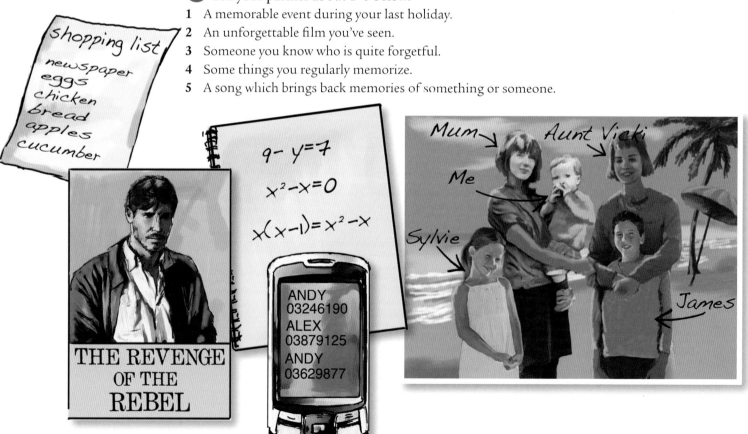

FCE Listening Part 4: Multiple choice

1 You will hear part of a radio interview about memory. Look at the picture. What do you think the connection is with memory?

2  **2.19** Listen to the interview. For questions 1–7, choose the best answers, (A, B or C).

1 What is the interviewer's memory like?
   A It's usually extremely good.
   B It used to be better.
   C It's improving with practice.

2 How did Roberta remember the appointment?
   A She kept it in her head because it was interesting.
   B She kept a record of it.
   C She needed to be reminded

3 Roberta says that one way to remember something is
   A to create an unusual mental image of it.
   B to make an amusing sentence about it.
   C to relax and think about something else.

4 According to Roberta, actors often learn their lines
   A immediately after rehearsals.
   B by repeating them.
   C extremely quickly.

5 When he was younger, the presenter says
   A he did well because of his photographic memory.
   B he always wanted a photographic memory.
   C he was irritated by someone else's photographic memory.

6 What did the chimps have to do?
   A type their name on the computer.
   B do mathematical problems.
   C remember missing numbers.

7 What does Roberta think might be true?
   A Only chimps have a photographic memory.
   B A photographic memory is more common in young people.
   C A photographic memory stays with you for life.

3 Work in pairs. Look at this list of things you have to buy. Make a memorable picture in your head involving all the items. Describe it to your partner. Are your pictures very different?

shopping list
eggs
fish
tomatoes
stamps
books
shampoo
a cucumber

4 Discuss these questions with your partner.

1 Do you think having a good memory is the same as being intelligent?

2 What's a good way to improve your memory?

3 Do you think some animals are as intelligent as human beings?

Vocabulary: Expressions with mind

1 Sentences 1–7 all contain an expression with *mind*. Match each sentence to a follow up sentence (a–g).

1 Finishing that work is **a real weight off my mind**.

2 **I've set my mind on** studying in Paris.

3 **I don't mind** walking to school.

4 I tried to **take my mind off** the exam last night.

5 I meant to phone Ronnie last night but **it completely slipped my mind**.

6 One thing I have to **bear in mind** when writing my answer is the target reader.

7 When the examiner asked me a question **my mind went blank**.

a I won't even consider going anywhere else.

b There was a long pause and then she asked me another question.

c It only takes twenty minutes and it's good exercise for me.

d I'd been worrying for days about getting it done on time.

e I'll text him later on.

f I watched a really good film and relaxed, which is what I needed.

g This determines whether I need to use a formal or an informal style.

2 Match the highlighted phrases in *italics* in exercise 1 to their meanings a–g below.

a I forgot it   b remember and consider   c a relief   d I'm determined to
e I couldn't remember anything   f it's not a problem for me   g stop thinking about

3 Write three sentences which are true for you, using the expressions in *italics* in exercise 1. Compare your sentences with your partner's.

Example:
I've set my mind on buying a Ferrari when I'm older!

FCE Speaking Part 2: Talking about photos

1 Look at the photographs 1 and 2. They show people who are remembering different things.

Student A: Compare the photographs and say what sort of things you think the people are remembering.

Student B: When your partner has finished, answer the following question.

How do you think the people are feeling?

2 In Part 2 of the Speaking paper you are sometimes asked to say how the people might be feeling.

Work in pairs. Take turns to find photographs with people in them in previous units in this book. Ask each other the question:

How do you think he/she is feeling?

When answering, use the useful language in the box.

3 Now change roles. Turn to page 132 and follow the instructions.

4 a With a partner, take turns to explain which of the alternatives in each of these pairs you would prefer and why.

be a pilot/businessman or woman   go on a beach holiday/activity holiday
go skiing/work out in a gym   have a meal in a restaurant/picnic in a forest

b Write three more pairs of alternatives for your partner to talk about.

Useful language

When talking about how people may be feeling:

• use adjectives like: *happy/depressed/angry/tired/bored/exhausted enthusiastic/worried/fed-up*

• use words like: *a bit/quite/really/very/extremely* with the adjectives.

• use patterns like:
They look *really happy.*
I think they must be quite tired. **They look as if** *they're concentrating hard.*

Language focus:
The passive

1 These are comments made by people in the photographs on page 92 and 132. Decide which of the four photographs the speaker is from.

a *I don't remember this one being taken!*

b *End of year exams are always held in the sports hall.*

c *The ruins were discovered 200 years ago.*

d *I have often been asked how I learned the names of all the roads in this enormous city!*

e *We had to stay in our seats until all the papers had been handed in.*

f *These should definitely be stored somewhere safe – we don't want to lose them.*

g *The results will be posted to us on 16th May.*

h *Some people want to be taken all round London. That's good money!*

i *We are being supervised by Miss Langton.*

2 Underline the passive forms in the comments in exercise 1. Then write the words you have underlined in the list below. The first one has been done for you.

Present simple: ....

Present continuous: ....

Present perfect: ....

Past simple: ....

Past perfect: ....

Future simple: ....

Gerund: ..... *being taken* ....

Infinitive with *to*: ....

Infinitive without *to*: ....

3 Complete these sentences about the passive.

To form the passive, we use the correct tense of the verb .... and the .... participle. To talk about the agent (the person or thing doing the action) in a passive construction we use the preposition ....

4 Reasons 1–4 below explain why the agent is often not mentioned in sentences containing the passive. Match each reason to a sentence a–d.

1 to avoid the use of 'you' in official notices

2 it is obvious who or what the agent is

3 the agent is unknown or unimportant

4 the agent is 'people in general'

a Three men have been arrested in connection with the theft of the painting.

b Dogs must be kept under control at all times in this park.

c Photographic memory is also known as eidetic memory, from the Greek *eidos* meaning 'form' or 'shape'.

d The vase was probably made in Italy in the sixteenth or seventeenth century. The gold rings were made in Roman times.

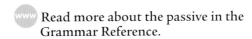 Read more about the passive in the Grammar Reference.

5 Rewrite sentences 1–6 using the passive. Begin with the word(s) in brackets and omit the agent if it is not needed.

1 Dominic O'Brien wrote *How to Develop a Perfect Memory* in 1993.   (How to Develop a Perfect Memory)

2 People will still remember this artist's work in two hundred years from now. (This artist's work)

3 The teacher was giving us a vocabulary test when the fire alarm went off. (We)

4 My neighbour has asked me not to play my music too loud. (I)

5 They regularly hold memory competitions all round the world. (Memory competitions)

6 You must switch off mobile phones before entering the classroom. (Mobile phones)

6 Rewrite the following notice using the passive and omitting the agents where appropriate.

Notice for Teachers

We have found an expensive laptop in the sports hall. A cleaner discovered it early this morning and someone must have left it there after yesterday's exam. At the moment we are keeping it in the head teacher's office. We shall put a notice about the laptop on the main school noticeboard asking the owner to go to the head teacher, and teachers should tell students in all classes about it. Teachers should also remind students that we do not permit laptops in exam rooms. When we know the name of the owner we shall confiscate the laptop for a period of one month.

FCE Writing Part 1: Letter

1 ⟲ Read the following Part 1 task. With a partner, discuss the points you have to write about and note down what you would include in the letter to Frank.

Your friend Frank is acting in a college play. Read the extract from Frank's letter, the flier he has sent you and your notes. Then write a letter to Frank using **all** your notes. Write **120–150** words.

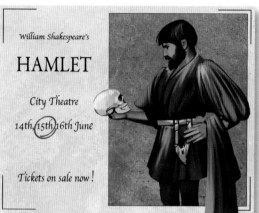

You're not going to believe this but I've agreed to take on a part in the end of year school play and I've been spending ages trying to learn the lines. You know me – I've got a terrible memory, so I'm finding it really hard. Any tips on how to go about it? I know you do some acting yourself. Have you done any recently?

And if you like Shakespeare then why not come along and have a laugh! I'm enclosing a flier for the show. Let me know if you can make it.

By the way – how did the exams go?

Do write soon!

Frank

Yes – give advice

No – say why

Tell him whe

Not well – say why

2 a Read this model answer and check if any of the ideas you wrote down for exercise 1 are included.

Dear Frank,

It was really nice to hear from you and catch up on your news. The play sounds great – I'd love to come and see you! Wednesday 15th looks the best day for me. By the way, which part are you playing? You didn't say.

I can understand the problems you must be having with the lines. I usually find the best way is just to keep repeating them over and over again, even when I'm out walking or on the train!

I haven't done any acting for a long time now because college is too busy. I've got to re-sit my exams – the ones you asked about. I did terribly! As soon as I looked at the paper my mind just went completely blank. I hope that doesn't happen when you're on stage!

Good luck and see you on the 15th.

Best wishes

Lara

b Is Lara's letter written in an appropriate style. Give examples to justify your answer.

3 <u>Underline</u> the linking words and phrases in the model answer.

e.g. *It was really nice to hear from you <u>and</u> catch up on your news.*

4 Write an answer to the following Part 1 task.

Your friend, Tony, has to give an acceptance speech at a dinner. Read Tony's letter, the invitation and your notes on page 95. Then write a letter to Tony using **all** your notes. Write **120–150** words.

PRIZE GIVING DINNER

SEPTEMBER 25TH

8PM AT
THE REGAL HOTEL

Remember!

- Begin by referring to the letter you have received.
- Address and develop all the points in the notes.
- Use an informal style throughout the letter.
- Include a variety of linking words.
- Make a suitable closing comment.

I've got some news. You know that short film I made for the college competition? Well – I won!   *Congratulate him*

The only problem is I have to make a speech at the ceremony when I accept the prize. My memory is terrible and there's no way I'm going to remember a whole speech! Do you think it's OK to use notes, or any suggestions on how I can remember it? You're really good at that sort of thing. Didn't you get a prize last year for a painting?   *Suggest ...*   *Yes – give details*

Also – there's a special dinner for the prize giving and I wondered if you'd like to come. I'm enclosing an invitation with date and times. It would be great if you could be there.   *No – because ...*

Let me know as soon as you can,

Best wishes

Tony

Vocabulary: Arts and culture

1 a For each of the words below, write down the first example you think of.

> a novel   a poem   a play
> a painting   a ballet   an opera

Example:

a novel Pride and Prejudice

b 💬 Compare your answers in small groups. Explain why you think you chose these examples.

Example:

I probably chose this novel because it brings back memories of my holiday last year, when I read it.

2 For each group of words, <u>underline</u> the one that doesn't fit. Give reasons for your choices. The first one has been done for you.

1 biography   paperback   <u>soap opera</u> best-seller

   You watch a soap opera on television: the other three are things you read.

2 studio   gallery   concert hall performance

3 cast   choir   ballerina   orchestra

4 exhibition   abstract   graffiti portrait

5 novelist   musician   instrument choreographer

6 classical   jazz   lyrics   hip hop

7 playwright   composer   poet sculpture

8 comic   graphic novel   stage cartoon

3 💬 Work in pairs. Take turns to choose one of the words from exercise 2 and describe it to your partner, without saying the word. Your partner must guess which word you have chosen.

Example:

It's a person who dances classical ballet ...

4 a Complete each gap with a word from exercise 2.

1 I've never acted on .... before. I think I'd be too nervous!

2 When I buy a book I usually go for a .... because I know other people have enjoyed it.

3 Some people think that .... is vandalism but I don't. I think it brightens up dull areas.

4 I prefer to listen to music in small venues rather than in a great big ....

5 I can remember the .... to songs I listened to when I was really young.

b 💬 Are these sentences true for you? Explain why/why not.

FCE Reading Part 1: Multiple choice

1 🗨 Work in small groups.

If you enjoy playing video games, tell your group which ones you play and why you like playing them?

If you do not enjoy playing video games, tell your group why not.

2 🗨 Look at the man in the photo. Which of the following adjectives do you think might describe his personality?

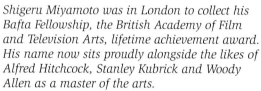

aggressive	attention-seeking	
modest	moody	placid
polite	rebellious	respectful
timid	vain	

3 The man in the photo is Shigeru Miyamoto, a Japanese designer of video games. Read the text about Shigeru Miyamoto quite quickly and check your ideas for exercise 2.

The brains behind the games

Shigeru Miyamoto was in London to collect his Bafta Fellowship, the British Academy of Film and Television Arts, lifetime achievement award. His name now sits proudly alongside the likes of Alfred Hitchcock, Stanley Kubrick and Woody Allen as a master of the arts.

Shigeru Miyamoto is the most successful artist of the last 50 years. He has single-handedly laid the foundations for the world's largest entertainment industry. Sales of his video games, from Super Mario Bros to Wii Sports, have topped an incredible 500 million, and show no signs of slowing down. Miyamoto, who joined Nintendo in 1977, has created eight of the top-10-selling video games of all time. His latest **smash**, Wii Fit, has sold 23 million copies, becoming the second biggest-selling game in history. It's made video games a daily part of life for a huge **demographic** of people who previously dismissed them as child's play.

Yet over and above his phenomenal sales success, what really sets Miyamoto apart from anyone else in any creative field is his marrying of genius with astonishing modesty. He cuts an unimposing, diminutive figure, sitting obediently in his chair. A Beatles T-shirt and moptop haircut are the only signs of cultural rebellion, smoothed at the edges by a quiet **reverence** and politeness. It's immediately apparent that unlike many of the Bafta Fellows to whose club he now rightly belongs, impassioned **tantrums** and theatrical outbursts are not his style.

line 36 Neither, as it turns out, are the glitz and glamour to which some may suggest he is entitled. "I'm not envious of the attention of movie stars. I enjoy not being recognised," he says. "It allows me to get on with my life. All I want is to be recognised through my work. It's funny – in America and the UK, they say I'm famous in Japan. In Japan, they say I'm famous in America and the UK." Miyamoto's placid temperament and genial timidity form a perfect fit with the universally loveable nature of his work. Miyamoto has never produced a title that wasn't suitable for families to play together, even in the days when video games were the unique **preserve** of teens in darkened bedrooms.

So what does he make of the more violent end of video games? His respectful nature, it seems, stretches even to peers who incorporate aggression into their gaming narrative. "When it comes to the question of how each designer creates their games, I don't think we should intervene in how they express themselves," he says. "However, our marketing people must be very careful as to how they promote which types of products to which audiences, especially children."

All of today's hottest developers cite Miyamoto as an inspiration. But growing up in the mountainous Kyoto, and with no video game industry in existence, how was Miyamoto himself inspired? Was his childhood a happy one? The great man silently shuts both eyes and compresses them tightly with his index fingers, simultaneously pulling in his legs. Miyamoto is visualising his youth. Ten seconds later, he blinks, catches my eye, and a smile reaches his lips.

"I have often taken inspiration from my childhood memories," he reveals. "It was a happy time for me, even though I had less around me in terms of material **prosperity** than others, certainly far less than children today. Wealthy families tended to have a lot of stuff, while all the others of us had a **scarcity** when it came to toys. But because of that, I used to make toys for myself with my own hands. A lot of the encounters and experiences I had and my conversations with other children still influence the way I make games today."

The next evening, Miyamoto excitedly skips along the red carpet of the Park Lane Hilton Hotel before collecting his Bafta Fellowship. A huge smile doesn't leave his face all evening. It no doubt masks a desire to escape **the limelight** he's reluctant to embrace; to return home to his wife, two children and his true out-of-work passion, playing and appreciating bluegrass music.

4 Match the highlighted nouns in the text to their meanings in this context **a–h**.

a an activity only one type of person does

b a strong feeling of respect and admiration for someone or something

c the situation in which there is not very much of something

d something that is extremely successful

e public attention and interest

f sudden short periods of unreasonable childish anger

g a group of people that a company wants to sell its products to

h the state of being rich and successful

5 Read the article again. For questions **1–8**, choose the answer (**A, B, C or D**) which you think fits best according to the text.

1 What does the writer say in the first paragraph about the games Miyamoto has created?

A Sales figures have been exaggerated.

B It looks as if they will continue to sell well.

C They are more popular with children than adults.

D The majority of people do not take them seriously.

2 According to the writer, Miyamoto's personality

A can be irritating to those meeting him for the first time.

B has led the artist to feel isolated within his profession.

C is unusual for someone so talented working in the arts.

D has caused him to reject some of his fellow artists.

3 What does 'It' in line 36 refer to?

A Miyamoto's fame

B the attention of movie stars

C people's failure to recognise Miyamoto

D Miyamoto's enjoyment of his work

4 When talking about the artist's work in paragraph 3, the writer suggests that.

A Miyamoto's love of nature is incorporated into many of his games.

B Miyamoto's games are more suited to individuals than families.

C Miyamoto's early work was designed specifically for teenagers.

D Miyamoto's personality is reflected in the games he creates.

5 What does Miyamoto say about violence in video games?

A He believes it should be illegal to sell games with violence to children.

B He recognizes the right of designers to include violence if they wish.

C He criticizes companies which advertise games with violent content.

D He admires designers who can create stories that contain no violence.

6 When the writer asks the artist about his inspiration, Miyamoto

A pauses to reflect on the past.

B finds the question amusing.

C demonstrates his tiredness.

D is reluctant to answer.

7 What do we learn about Miyamoto's childhood?

A He did not like the commercially available toys.

B His family could not afford to buy him many toys.

C He did not form friendships easily with other children.

D He did not have many other children to play with.

8 The writer suggests that on the evening that Miyamoto receives his Bafta Fellowship the artist

A has secret thoughts of changing his career.

B dislikes the physical contact at the ceremony.

C questions whether he deserves the award.

D would be happier if he were somewhere else.

6 a Imagine you had to design a video game which reflected your personality and your interests. Decide what type of game you would design. Make brief notes of the **general idea** for your game.

b 🗨 Share your ideas with other students in the class. Explain in what ways the game reflects your personality and your interests.

Language focus: Passive of reporting verbs

1 Some reporting verbs can be used with passive constructions to introduce generalized opinions and facts.

It + passive + that clause
It is said that Miyamoto dislikes being in the limelight.
Subject + passive + infinitive
Miyamoto is said to dislike being in the limelight.

<u>Underline</u> the infinitives in sentences **1–3** below and then write each one on the appropriate line in **a–c**.

1 Alfred Hitchcock is known to have appeared in most of his films.

2 The human brain is thought to be getting bigger.

3 Memory is said to improve the more often we use it.

    a continuous infinitive ....
    b simple infinitive ....
    c perfect infinitive ....

2 Rewrite sentences **1–3** using *It + passive + that* clause.

It is known that Alfred Hitchcock ...

www Read more about the passive of reporting verbs in the Grammar Reference. Then do the exercises on page 132.

Vocabulary: The senses

1 🗨 Discuss these questions in pairs.

1 Which senses do the pictures show?

2 Do certain sounds, smells or tastes make you remember things from the past?

3 Name one sound, taste, smell, texture and view that you like and one that you don't like.

2 <u>Underline</u> the correct word in *italics*.

1 Several people stopped and *stared/ glanced* open-mouthed at the strange man with the bright green hair.

2 Quite by accident I *eavesdropped/ overheard* our teachers talking about a possible trip to the city museum.

3 Sweets that you *suck/swallow* aren't good for your teeth because they stay in the mouth for a long time.

4 My cat loves being *squeezed/stroked* the 'wrong way' from her tail to her head.

5 In some cultures it's quite rude to *smell/ sniff* when you have a cold.

6 Don't *whisper/yell* at me. It hurts my ears!

7 I *gazed/glimpsed* at the view in wonder for half an hour because it was so beautiful.

8 Katy *scratched/rubbed* her eyes because she was very tired after watching the late film.

3 Write gapped sentences for four words you did not use in Exercise 2. Give your sentences to your partner to complete.

Example:

As I drove past Greg's house I .... someone at the window. [Answer: glimpsed]

FCE Listening Part 3: Multiple matching

1 🎧 2.20–2.24 You will hear five different people speaking about experiences involving the senses. For questions **1–5**, choose from the list (**A–F**) what each speaker says. Use the letters only once. There is one extra letter which you do not need to use.

A I was expecting something more straightforward.
B I enjoyed the experience much more the second time.
C I was continually distracted.
D I wasn't very enthusiastic before the experience.
E I had to concentrate on one sense.
F I didn't have the same reaction as someone else did.

Speaker 1   [| **1**]
Speaker 2   [| **2**]
Speaker 3   [| **3**]
Speaker 4   [| **4**]
Speaker 5   [| **5**]

2 🗨 Rank the speakers' five experiences from the one you would enjoy doing the most (1) to the one you would enjoy the least (5). Then tell your partner, giving reasons for your choices. Use some of the language for expressing preferences in the Useful language box on page 132.

FCE Writing Part 2: Essay

1 🔘 **Read the following Part 2 task and discuss questions 1 and 2.**

Your teacher has asked you to write an essay with the title:

Do you believe that people really have a sixth sense?

Write your **essay** in **120–180** words.

1 What do people mean by 'sixth sense?'

2 Do you agree or disagree that people have a sixth sense? Give reasons for your views.

2 **Read the model answer below. Does the writer mention any of the points you discussed in exercise 1?**

Do you believe that people really have a sixth sense?

People have always been fascinated by the brain and its powers. Do we have a special power that lets us know what other people are thinking or enables us to look into the future? Is there really a 'sixth sense'?

To support the idea, people give the example of twins who often communicate without language. In addition to this, some people have predicted events that actually happened. On a personal level, I know that I have often phoned someone at exactly the same time that they phoned me.

However, many people attribute these examples to coincidence and insist that there is no real evidence. They believe that if we cannot see or measure something, it does not exist. They insist that the people who say they can do these things are lying to make money.

I agree that there is no real proof but in my opinion there are too many examples to ignore. I, personally, believe that there is a sixth sense and one day we shall all be able to use it.

---

3 **What is the purpose of each paragraph in the essay in exercise 2?**

Example:

Paragraph 1: the writer introduces the subject and defines what he/she understands by 'sixth sense.'

4 **In the model answer the writer presents different points of view and concludes with his/her own opinion. Underline words and phrases in the essay that introduce 1–5 below.**

1 ideas which support one point of view

2 ideas which support a contrasting point of view

3 an additional point

4 an example from personal experience

5 a personal opinion

5 **Here are some more useful words and phrases. Add them to the appropriate group in exercise 4.**

On one hand …
From personal experience …
On the other hand …
As well as this …   Moreover …
Some people feel that …

There is an argument that …
On balance, I think …
Having looked at both sides, I feel that …
Others argue that …   Whereas …
My personal view is that …
What is more, …
I know myself that …
One point of view is that …

6 a **Read the following Part 2 questions.**

Your teacher has asked you to write an essay with one of the following titles.

1 Most animals are intelligent.

2 All films should be made in 3D in the future.

3 A good memory is all you need to pass examinations.

4 Young people today are not interested in arts and culture.

5 Artists, actors and writers do not need training to be successful.

b **Write a list of points for and against the idea in the statement you chose to write about. Organize your points into paragraphs. Then write your answer in 120–180 words.**

Review

FCE Use of English Part 4: Transformations

For questions **1–8**, complete the second sentence so that it has a similar meaning to the first sentence, using the word given. **Do not change the word given.** You must use between **two** and **five** words, including the word given.

1 The English teacher gave us the results.

    GIVEN

    We .... the English teacher.

2 You should give me your homework by Friday afternoon.

    TO

    Your homework .... me by Friday afternoon.

3 Police are currently questioning a 30-year-old man in relation to the incident.

    IS

    A 30-year-old man .... in relation to the incident.

4 Leo has just taken the children to school.

    DROPPED

    The children .... at school by Leo.

5 People do not think the film will make a lot of money.

    EXPECTED

    The film .... a lot of money.

6 They know that the two Monet paintings are fakes..

    BE

    The two Monet paintings .... fakes.

7 They think young people's hearing is getting worse because of too much loud music.

    THOUGHT

    Young people's hearing .... worse because of too much loud music.

8 It is believed that the accident occurred after midnight.

    HAVE

    The accident .... place after midnight.

Vocabulary

<u>Underline</u> the correct word in *italics* in the following sentences.

1 When the examiner asked me a question my mind *got/went* blank.

2 My grandfather's long *term/time* memory is still very good.

3 Our visit to the Paris opera was *unmemorable/unforgettable* - I loved it.

4 The play has an excellent *cast/choir* and it deserves a good review.

5 I only *glanced/stared* at the letter quickly and didn't read it carefully.

6 I invited Marie round to dinner to take her mind *out/off* her problems at work.

7 The doctor said you need to *swallow/stroke* these tablets with water.

8 My cousin wants to be an actress; she loves being in the *lamplight/limelight*.

9 Dave's popstar brother is very *modest/vain* about his success, and rarely talks about himself.

10 Video games are no longer the *reserve/preserve* of teenage boys; they are now played by people of both sexes and of all ages.

Language focus

Rewrite these sentences using the passive. Omit the agent when appropriate. Begin the sentence with the words <u>underlined</u>.

1 Two members of the paparazzi photographed <u>the celebrity</u> as he was leaving his house this morning.

2 You should take <u>these tablets</u> with food.

3 They say that <u>memory</u> gets worse with age.

4 Television presenter Mervyn Bagg was interviewing <u>the writer</u> when the lights suddenly went out in the studio.

5 They will make <u>all films</u> in 3D in the future.

6 They had chosen <u>Pat</u> to join the orchestra so he was celebrating all night.

7 The decorators must finish <u>the decorating</u> before we go on holiday.

8 Most critics have given <u>the play</u> positive reviews.

FCE Use of English Part 1: Multiple-choice cloze

For questions 1–12, read the text below and decide which answer (A, B, C or D) best fits each gap. There is an example at the beginning (0).

Memory Man

For a man carrying the **(0)** .... of a nation on his – slightly hunched – shoulders, Ben Pridmore, would-be World Memory Champion and **(1)** .... holder of the British title, cuts a rather laid-back figure. Stepping over mountains of clothing in the living room of his miniscule Derby flat (he uses his wardrobe to **(2)** .... his cartoon video collection) 30-year-old Ben directs me towards the one chair not obscured by **(3)** .... of papers or soft toys and **(4)** .... that he is taking a break from 'training.' Each day when Ben returns home from his job **(5)** .... an accountant, he cooks dinner, watches The Simpsons and **(6)** .... to an hour and a half of memorising. With the competition fast approaching, he has been practising for **(7)** .... at the weekends. When he first **(8)** .... the World Memory Championships several years ago he had to commit to memory almost 2,000 numbers in an hour and remember the order of a **(9)** .... of 52 cards in 26.28 seconds! This week's championships **(10)** .... of ten memory disciplines, most involving recounting a series of numbers over different lengths of time, and a few word-based exercises. But what is most amazing about this man is that in spite of his ability he also **(11)** .... to being very forgetful! I often leave my briefcase and all my papers at work!' He also has problems **(12)** .... which is his left and right hand and recently left his 'lucky' hat on a train!

	A	B	C	D
0	decisions	goals	<u>hopes</u>	plans
1	momentary	current	today	immediate
2	store	support	save	maintain
3	pieces	piles	shelves	blocks
4	tells	narrates	accounts	announces
5	as	to	at	like
6	catches up	settles down	runs down	puts off
7	better	further	longer	greater
8	earned	gained	won	elected
9	pack	block	stock	chunk
10	hold	include	make	consist
11	accepts	admits	realizes	agrees
12	memorising	remembering	reminding	retrieving

FCE Writing Part 2: Report

Write an answer to the following question. Write **120–180** words in an appropriate style.

Your teacher has asked you for a report on cultural activities in your local area. Write about the range of cultural activities available and recommend the most interesting activities for visitors to the area.

Write your **report**.

UNIT 9 A slave to routine

1 How do you usually feel when you wake up on a weekday?

What is your normal morning routine at home before you go to school, college or work? Are things calm in your house in the morning or is everything done in a rush?

How do you normally get to school, college or work? How do you spend your time on the journey?

2 The following text is an extract from a novel. The main characters are Polly, an overworked single mother and immigration lawyer, and her two children Tania and Robbie. Read the extract quite quickly. Then answer these questions with your partner. Give reasons.

Do you recognize yourself or anyone you know in any of the characters?

Who do you think Iryna is?

'Wake up!' she calls, going into each child's room and switching on their lights. Now the hour-long struggle begins. Tania **slumbers** on, her skin covered with sweat as Polly kisses her, but Robbie stirs and **burrows** deeper into his duvet. Polly notices with annoyance that Iryna has not put out his school clothes for him.

'Time to get up, my angel.'
'I hate school,' says Robbie, **lashing out** as his mother pulls the duvet off him.
'I hate Mondays,' says Tania, in turn. 'And I hate you.'
'Tough,' says Polly. 'Get dressed, or you'll be going to school in pyjamas.'
Each weekday morning, she has to make sure the children are dressed, fed, clean, have done their homework and get to school on time before going to her office. It does not sound like much, but there are days when she feels like she can't stand another minute of it.

'Robbie, you *still* haven't got your shoes on! Put them on, or you're going to school in your socks.'
'Why do I have to go to school? Why can't I stay with you?' *line 72*
Polly sighs. She is trying to **cram** a full working day **into** eight hours, and she keeps her watch five minutes fast in order to get to any appointment, tricking herself into tiny panic attacks that are like the miniature muffled explosions in a combustion engine.

'Outside this country, and also in it, are millions and millions of people who would kill to have what you do here,' she says. 'They are clever, fantastically hard-working and they are all learning English. When you grow up, you're going to be competing with them for places at university, and for jobs.'
'Yeah, yeah,' says Tania rudely.
'You *have* to do this stuff,' said Polly. 'If you don't get good marks, you'll never go to university, and if you don't go to university you'll end up **flipping** burgers and –'

'You mean if I don't read, I could have all the burgers I could eat, every day?'
'Then you'd get fat, Robbie,' says Tania, with horror.
'Who gives? But why must I learn *French*? Or *any* language when everyone in the world wants to learn English?' says Robbie, who won't even drink orange juice if it has bits.

'Because otherwise you won't know what they're saying about you in secret,' says Tania.
Polly smiles, for this is a far better answer than she could have given. Then her heart jumps with the clock, for they have just forty-eight seconds left to get out of the door.

Where are their coats?
'How should I know?' Robbie answers, calmly.
'You *must* have them!' It's freezing, it's January, you can't go out today without a coat. Look, I'm wearing my heaviest one again.'

'I can't find my school tie,' Polly's son complains. 'Iryna's hidden it.'
'Iryna!' Polly calls up the stairs. The girl is supposed to be down by now. No answer, and Robbie will be punished if he **turns up** without a school tie. She races upstairs to **fish** one **out** of the laundry basket, already nauseous with stress.
'I hate you!' Tania screams. 'I'm going to miss the school bus, and it's *all your fault!*'
Outside, Polly takes off like a rocket. They have only three minutes as a margin of error, never enough.
'Oh, damn and blast!' she says, trying to text Iryna at a traffic light. 'I wonder where she is?'

The car **surges** forward. It is only a momentary release of frustration because a second later her undercarriage hits a speed cushion with a bang. Polly dreams long tedious dreams in which she does the school run, endlessly **grinding** up Highgate Hill to the bus stop for Tania's school. But now, at last, she is passing Highgate Cemetery and Karl Marx's tomb, racing past the ornate iron gates of Waterlow Park, out of Pond Square and then, just in time, she stops in front of the school bus.

'Love you,' Polly says, **drawing up**.
'Huh!' says Tania, slipping off to join the gaggle of other girls in uniform. Every day, when she goes back into the heart of London, Polly thinks how glad she is that her children will be out in the suburbs, where it is leafy and safe.

3 Match the highlighted verbs in the text to their meanings in this context **a–j** below.

Phrasal verbs

a pull something out of a bag or other container

b suddenly try to hit someone

c arrive

d arrive and stop (in a vehicle)

e do many things in a short period of time

Other verbs

f push yourself under something so as to feel warmer or more comfortable

g move quickly and powerfully

h move slowly and with difficulty

i turn something over quickly (so as to cook it on both sides)

j sleep

4 Read the text again. For questions **1–8**, choose the answer (**A, B, C or D**) which you think fits best according to the text.

1 In the first paragraph we learn that Polly

  A normally finds it easy to wake her children up.

  B is irritated by somebody's failure to do something.

  C loves one of her two children more than the other.

  D usually asks somebody else to take her children to school.

2 How does Polly react to her children's anger at having to get up?

  A She threatens to leave the house without them.

  B She shows no sympathy towards them.

  C She complains to them about her routine.

  D She refuses to help them get ready.

3 The writer mentions a combustion engine to give an idea of

  A the complex nature of Polly's work.

  B the speed with which Polly has to do things.

  C how Polly's work sometimes affects her.

  D how Polly feels if she thinks she will be late.

4 Why does Polly talk to her children about 'millions and millions of people' who are learning English?

  A to show them how easily many people learn English

  B to convince them of the need to learn a foreign language

  C to encourage them to take their schoolwork seriously

  D to make them aware of the unemployment problem

5 What does the writer suggest about Robbie in paragraph 5?

  A He is fussy about what he will and will not eat and drink.

  B He intends to work in a restaurant when he leaves school.

  C He is not very good at learning languages.

  D He does not get on very well with his sister.

6 Polly's 'heart jumps' in line 72 because she realizes

  A how much she loves her daughter.

  B how intelligent her daughter is.

  C how late it is.

  D how cold it is.

7 When Robbie cannot find his school tie,

  A he appears to be unconcerned.

  B he blames somebody else.

  C Polly gets him a clean one.

  D Polly criticizes him.

8 What do we learn about Polly in the last paragraph?

  A She is pleased her children do not go to a city centre school.

  B She is amused at the sight of Tania's friends in uniform.

  C She is sad that Tania does not return her love.

  D She is relieved that she does not live in a dangerous area.

5 💬 If you are not a parent: how well would you cope if you had to get one or more children ready for school each day?

If you are a parent already: how well do/did you cope with getting your child or children ready for school?

Language focus: Conditionals

1 Identify the verb forms in **bold** in the following conditional sentences. The first one has been done for you.

a *If Tania* **misses** *the bus, Polly* **has to** *take her to school in the car.*

misses – present simple
has to – present simple

b *Robbie* **will be punished** *if he* **turns up** *without a school tie.*

c *Everything* **would be** *much easier if Iryna* **were** *here.*

d *If Polly* **had known** *last night that Iryna wasn't in the house, she* **would have put out** *Robbie's clothes herself.*

e *If we* **had got up** *earlier, we* **might not be** *in such a hurry now.*

2 Match each explanation **1–5** below to sentences **a–e** in exercise 1.

1 an imaginary situation entirely in the past

2 an imaginary situation in the past and its possible result in the present

3 an imaginary situation in the present

4 a situation which is always or generally true; *if* means *whenever* or *every time*.

5 the predicted result of a possible future situation

3 Rewrite the following sentence from the reading text using *as long as* and *unless* instead of *if.*

If you don't get good marks, you'll never go to university.

a *You'll go to university* **as long as** ....

b *You'll never go to university* **unless** ....

4 Complete the following sentences from the reading text with **one** word. Both words in this context mean *if not.*

a *Get dressed,* .... *you'll be going to school in pyjamas.*

b *(You have to learn French) because* .... *you won't know what they're saying about you in secret, says Tania.*

🌐 Read more about conditionals in the Grammar Reference.

5 Each of the following sentences contains one mistake. Correct the mistakes.

1 We'd better hurry up: Carla will be angry if we'll be late.

2 I'll hate it if I had to work during the night, like nurses or firefighters.

3 If we'd known the bus was going to take so long, Anita and I would walk home last night.

4 You're going to fail these exams unless you don't study more.

5 A good pair of shoes will last for years, as far as you look after them properly.

6 If we'd taking the motorway, we'd probably be at home by now.

6 Complete each gap with an appropriate form of the verb in brackets. The first one has been done for you.

1 I ...*won't speak*..... (not/speak) to Mike again unless he ...*apologizes*........ (apologize) for what happened the other night.

2 If I .... (not/have) an exam tomorrow, I .... (go) to the match with you tonight, but I really must stay in and study.

3 Paul should slow down at work, otherwise he .... (make) himself ill.

4 I'm sweating. If I .... (know) it was going to be as warm as this, I .... (not/bring) this coat with me.

5 Julie's taking the jumper back to the shop. I'm sure they .... (change) it for her, as long as she .... (show) them the receipt.

6 Stop complaining! If you .... (have) a bigger breakfast this morning, you .... (not/be) so hungry now.

7 I .... (stay) away from Sue this morning if I .... (be) you – she's in a really bad mood.

7 Work in pairs. You are going to complete some conditional sentences and then read out the sentences to your partner.

Student A: Turn to page 133 for your sentence beginnings.

Student B: Turn to page 135 for your sentence beginnings.

Vocabulary: Time

1 a These extracts from the reading text on page 102 contain expressions with the word *time*. Complete each gap with one word. The meaning of each expression is given in brackets.

1 '*[It is]* **Time** _____ *get up, my angel.*' (= it is the moment that something should happen)

2 *... she has to make sure the children ...get to school* _____ **time**. (= at the correct time, not late)

3 *... just* _____ **time**, *she stops in front of the school bus.* (= early enough [to catch the bus])

b Complete each gap in these extracts from the reading text with one word.

1 *... there are days when she feels like* **she can't stand another** .... **of it**.

2 *...* **she keeps her watch five minutes** .... *in order to get to any appointment.*

3 *...* **they have just forty-eight seconds** .... *to get out of the door.*

Explain the meaning of the expressions in bold.

2 Complete each gap with a phrase from the box which has the same meaning as the word(s) in brackets.

at a time at all times at the time by the time from time to time time after time

a I walk to school .... (occasionally).

b I wear a watch .... (always).

c .... (again and again) I forget where I've put my keys.

d I can't multi-task: I can only ever do one thing .... (at a particular moment).

e I can remember when I learnt to tell the time: I was six .... (at that moment).

f .... (when or before) I get home from work I'm usually exhausted.

3 a Complete each gap with an appropriate verb from the box.

find   have   make   pass   set   spend   take   waste

1 It can _____ me quite **a long time to** get ready in the morning.

2 I try to _____ **the most of my time** by planning my day carefully.

3 I normally _____ a really **good time** on Friday night when I go out.

4 I can never seem to _____ **the time to** read these days; I'm always busy.

5 I try to _____ **aside time** each day for sport or other physical exercise.

6 I _____ quite a lot of **time** every day speaking to friends on my mobile.

7 I really don't like to _____ my **time** watching television; it's so boring.

8 In order to help me _____ **the time** on bus or train journeys I do sudokus.

b 💬 Discuss sentences **1–8** with your partner. How true is each one for you?

4 a Write your own sentences using **five** of the red sentence beginnings in exercise 3a. The sentences should be true for you.

b Work in pairs. Compare and discuss your sentences.

FCE Writing Part 2: Set books

1 Each year there are two set books for the First Certificate exam. If you have read one of them, you may decide to answer the relevant question in Part 2 of the Writing Paper. This will be either an article, an essay, a letter, a report or a review.

Read the following Part 2 question. If you have read *The Time Machine*, say what you might include in your answer. If not, choose another classic novel you have read, and say how you might answer the question if it were about that book.

You see this notice in your college magazine.

> **Oldies but Goldies – Articles wanted**
>
> Have you read a classic novel recently? If so, write us an article about it, saying why you think it is still popular today.

Write your **article** with reference to *The Time Machine* by H G Wells.

2 Read the following sample answer. What are the main reasons the writer gives for the continued popularity of *The Time Machine*?

'The Time Machine'

'The Time Machine' is as exciting today as it was when it was first published over a hundred years ago and still gets positive reviews. So what makes it such a popular classic?

Firstly, it has everything - science-fiction, adventure, horror and suspense. Will the Time Traveller manage to defend himself against the 'queer little ape-like' Morlocks with his box of matches, find his time machine and return from the year 802,701? We know the answer already, but Wells is a brilliant storyteller who keeps the reader interested until the end.

Secondly, the novel's central themes are timeless, as relevant today as they were in 1895. The hero sees the consequences of the growing gap between rich and poor, the 'Haves' and the 'Have-nots', who have evolved into the unintelligent Eloi, 'exquisite creatures' that inhabit the Upperworld, and the 'bleached, obscene' Morlocks who live underground. It is an extreme version of evolution.

This pessimistic, but moving vision of the future is very short. It takes no time to read, but you'll be thinking and talking about it for a long time afterwards.

3 Read the article again and answer the following questions.

- What typical features of articles has the writer included in this answer?

  e.g. It is written in a fairly informal style.

- What examples are there of the writer quoting from *The Time Machine*?

4 Write an answer to the question in exercise 1 or one of the questions on page 134.

FCE Listening Part 2: Sentence completion

1 🎧 2.25 You will hear an interview with a writer called Greg Chandler, whose latest book offers alternatives to the fast pace of modern life. For questions 1–10, complete the sentences.

The title of Greg Chandler's latest book is ' [_____ 1_] '

Greg says that the first thing we do when we wake up is [_____ 2_]

Greg agrees with the suggestion that we are obsessed with [_____ 3_]

Greg says we need to slow down and [_____ 4_]

Greg's first piece of advice to anyone who shares his beliefs is not to [_____ 5_]

Greg recommends not eating breakfast [_____ 6_]

Greg says it's a good idea to sit quietly before [_____ 7_]

The Slow Food movement campaigns for good, clean and [_____ 8_] food.

Slow Cities form part of a worldwide network of towns which share over [_____ 9_] common aims and principles.

Slow Cities attach importance to more [_____ 10_] ways of doing things.

2 💬 Do you do the things Greg recommends in questions 6 and 7 of the listening? Why/Why not?

Which things do you like to do quickly and which do you do more slowly? Why?

3 💬 Which of the following would you consider doing to help you slow down? Give reasons for your answers. If you do any of them already, would you say they improve your quality of life?

Read long novels rather than magazines

Have a siesta after lunch

Have baths rather than showers

Open your emails only once a day

Walk more

Listen to music without doing anything else

Always wait for the green man, or similar signal, when crossing the road

Word formation: Nouns 2

1 Complete each gap in these extracts from the listening with the correct noun form of the verb in brackets. Then check your answers in the listening script on pages 156–157.

a *... it's the clock that determines our* .... (behave) *...*

b *What's your main* .... (advise)?

c *... it's important to embrace the* .... (believe) *that your life would be better if you took things more slowly.*

d *Food for* .... (think) *there, indeed.*

e *There are more than one hundred and twenty towns in the* .... (net) *now ...*

2 For 1–5, complete sentence b so that it has a similar meaning to sentence a. You will need to complete the gap in b with the noun form of the underlined verb in a. The first one has been done for you.

1 a Sue spoke for three hours. b Sue gave a three-hour *speech* .
2 a Ian's selling his house. b Ian's house is for ....
3 a It's the first time we've lost this season. b It's our first .... of the season.
4 a It took us six hours to fly to Rio. b Our .... to Rio took six hours.
5 a We gave Eli a present. b We presented Eli with a ....
6 a Tim suddenly started laughing. b Tim burst into ....

3 Study all the sentences in exercise 2 for one minute. Then cover up the sentence b's. How many can you remember?

Turn to page 135 and do the Word formation task.

FCE Speaking Part 3: Collaborative task

🗨 Your local Community Centre, which offers a range of activities to those aged 16 and over, is planning to introduce a number of new activities aimed at helping people relieve stress. Some of the activities they are thinking about are shown below.

Talk to your partner about what type of people these activities might appeal to. Then decide which two would be most popular.

Help

When discussing who these activities might appeal to, you could mention:

• people's age, their work or studies, where they live, their family situation

• why they might be suffering from stress

• why a particular activity might be suitable to them.

Vocabulary: Sleep

1 Complete each gap with one of the verbs from the box.

> fallen   get   getting   had   hits
> lie   overslept   sleeping

1 Do you normally .... **a good night's sleep** or do you think you need to sleep more?

2 Do you often .... **awake** in bed at night or do you usually go to sleep **as soon as your head** .... **the pillow**?

3 What advice would you give to someone who has difficulty .... **to sleep** at night?

4 Do you like .... **in** on Saturday and Sunday mornings? Why/Why not? What is the longest **lie-in** you have ever .... ?

5 Have you or has anyone you know ever .... **asleep** in an unexpected place, such as in a cinema or at school?

6 Have you ever been late for something because you .... ?

2 🗨 Discuss each of the questions in exercise 1 with a partner. Give as much detail as possible in your answers.

yoga

countryside walking

laughter therapy

self-massage

running

conversation club

FCE Reading Part 2: Gapped text

1 🗨 You are going to read a newspaper article about a school which has introduced a ten-o'clock start time to the school day.

What benefits might such a change bring for pupils at the school?

Why might some parents and pupils disapprove of the change?

2 Read the base text only and check your ideas.

To sleep, perchance to get better grades

A Tyneside high school is giving pupils a longer lie-in, in the hope it improves their concentration in lessons.

It is what many teenagers tell their parents: 'I'd do better at school if you'd only let me sleep in every morning.' Now an 850-pupil comprehensive school has taken students at their word and put back the start of the day in the hope they turn up better prepared for learning.

A five-month experiment was launched at Monkseaton High School in Whitley Bay, North Tyneside, after half-term with the support of pupils, teachers and parents. [1]

Before approving the change, the headteacher, Dr Paul Kelley, took advice from sleep experts, in particular Russell Foster, who is a professor of circadian* neuroscience at Brasenose College, Oxford. In his research, Professor Foster has highlighted studies which suggest that teenagers need more sleep than the rest of the population. [2] What is more, continual interruption to their sleep patterns is likely to have an impact on their health and mental capacity.

Professor Foster's tests appear to confirm that students perform better in the afternoons. 'Sleep,' he said, 'provides all of us with our sense of wellbeing and the faculty that helps make us human: our extraordinary capacity for creativity and innovation. [3] Most school regimes force teenagers to function at a time of day that is sub-optimal, and many university students are exposed to considerable dangers from sleep deprivation.'

Initially, Dr Kelley wanted to make a more radical change to the school's timetable, pushing back the start time by two hours to 11am. [4] Lessons carry on for an extra 30 minutes in the afternoons, with the school staying open for study until 5pm. 'My view is that this is a very, very important issue because here is something that schools can do to improve the health and mental health of their pupils,' Dr Kelley said. Research shows that depression can set in if a human is constantly interrupted and woken from sleep.

The experiment has not won 100 per cent support from the school community and Dr Kelley pointed out that Monkseaton High still remained open from 8am until 5pm, so that parents who have childcare problems, or families in which both partners had jobs, could still leave their child at school before going to work. To further improve the standard of learning, the school has a £23m new building which, its pupils say, is designed like a football stadium. [5]

Emelye Hood, 13, is a fan of the changes: 'I get up about 8.30 am to 8.45 am and, with getting more sleep, it means I can concentrate more on my lessons.' Ryan Thompson, also 13, agreed. 'I get a lie-in and you don't have to rush your breakfast in the morning,'he said. '[6] But I don't mind that.'

Dr Kelley said several schools in Canada and the United States had put back their starting times. [7] He did not know of any in the UK doing what Monkseaton had done but felt it would "catch on" if the experiment was successful.

* circadian: relating to the changes in people's and animals' bodies during each period of 24 hours

3 **Seven sentences have been removed from the article. Choose from the sentences A–H the one which fits each gap (1–7). There is one extra sentence which you do not need to use.**

A As a result, they are likely to be at their peak performance in the afternoon rather than the morning.

B It means you don't get your lunch at school until 2pm.

C It is cruel to impose a cultural pattern on teenagers that makes them underachieve.

D The school, whose teachers approved of the proposed change, was faced with a number of problems.

E However, a compromise deal saw it changed to 10am.

F Instead of going into school every morning at 9am, pupils can indulge in a big breakfast before starting lessons at 10am.

G The classrooms are lighter and more spacious, which helps children to concentrate better in lessons.

H However, some had abandoned the idea because it was more difficult to fit in sporting fixtures with schools sticking to traditional timetables.

4 🗨 Would you prefer to begin school, college or work an hour later each day? What advantages and disadvantages would such a change have for you?

Language focus: Relative clauses

1 Read the following sentences **a–g** from the reading text and missing sentences on page 109. Then answer questions 1–5.

   a The headteacher ... took advice from sleep experts, in particular Russell Foster, **who** is a professor of circadian neuroscience at Brasenose College, Oxford.

   b In his research, Professor Foster has highlighted studies **which** suggest that teenagers need more sleep than the rest of the population.

   c ... here is something **that** schools can do to improve the health and mental health of their pupils.

   d ... so that parents **who** have childcare problems, or families in **which** both partners had jobs could still leave their child at school before going to work

   e The classrooms are lighter and more spacious, **which** helps children to concentrate better in lessons.

   f He did not know of any in the UK doing **what** Monkseaton had done ...

   g The school, **whose** teachers approved of the proposed change, was faced with a number of unexpected problems.

   1 Why are commas used before the relative pronoun in sentences **a**, **e** and **g**, but not the others?

   2 In which sentences can *who* or *which* be replaced by *that*? Why?

   3 In which sentence can the relative pronoun be omitted? Why?

   4 In which sentence does the relative pronoun refer to the whole of the main clause and not just a person or a thing?

   5 Which of the relative pronouns means 'the thing which'?

   www Read more about relative clauses in the Grammar Reference.

2 Complete each gap with *who, which, whose, where, when, why* or *what*, adding commas where necessary. The first one has been done for you.

   1 My father, ...*who*.... has always been a light sleeper, woke up when he heard a noise ...*which*... sounded like a gunshot.

   2 Last Saturday .... she stayed at my house Sally slept in the attic .... my parents have converted into a guestroom.

3 I got exactly .... I wanted for my birthday – a new watch. It was the only thing .... I really needed.

4 I don't see any reason .... my parents won't let me have a sleepover party for my birthday.

5 Our headteacher .... is retiring at the end of the year has been at this school for over twenty years.

6 An equinox is one of two days during the year on .... night and day are of equal length.

7 There's a prize for anyone .... can tell me the name of the group .... first hit record was 'Love me do'.

8 I slept until half past nine this morning .... is very unusual for me.

9 The only person .... I really get on with at work is leaving next week. She's got a job at The Grand Hotel .... her dad works as a doorman.

3 Look again at your answers in exercise 2. Decide which of the words you have written:

   a can be omitted.

   b can be replaced by *that*.

Example:

Sentence 1

   a *neither* **who** *nor* **which** *can be omitted.*

   b *only* **which** *can be replaced by* **that**.

4 Work in pairs. You are each going to write definitions for six words using relative clauses. The words you have to define all appear in units **1–8** of this coursebook.

Student A: Turn to page 133.

Student B: Turn to page 136.

FCE Writing Part 2: Informal letters

1 💬 Read the following Part 2 question and Helena's answer. Do you think the advice she gives Robin is good? Why/Why not?

This is part of a letter from your English-speaking friend, Robin.

> I've got my exams soon and I'm having real problems sleeping at night. You never seem to have any trouble – do you have any advice you could give me on what to do to help me sleep?
>
> Thanks,
>
> Robin

Write your **letter** to Robin. Do not write any postal addresses.

Letter to Robin

I'm your friend Helena. I hope you are well. Guess what! I'm going to Scotland in August. I'm going to study English in Edinburgh. I'm realy looking forward to it. I'm sure my English will improve. Your probably looking forward to your holiday in Ireland. I'm sure it will be beautifull at this time of year. (I went last year at Easter. I went to Cork. The weather wasn't good. It rained a lot.) You will have a nice brake after your exams. I'm sure you will do very well. You say you are finding it dificult to sleep. It must be terrible for you. I would be very nervious. Here are some tips.

1   Never drink coffee after 5 o'clock.

2   Do exercise every day.

3   Don't eat two late.

4   Read a book before you go to bed. Don't study late.

5   Have a warm bath.

6   Drink herbal infusions.

That is all. I hope my advise is useful. If it doesn't work, you should go to the doctor's.

2 💬 Read Helena's letter again and discuss the following questions. Give examples from the letter to justify your answers.

Content	Is all the information given in the letter relevant?
Organisation	Is the letter organised into logical paragraphs?
Cohesion	Is there an appropriate range of linking words and expressions?
Range	Is there a range of grammatical structures and vocabulary?
Accuracy	Is the English reasonably accurate?
Register	Is the style of the letter appropriate and consistent?
Format	Is the answer clearly set out as a letter?
Target reader	Would Robin have enough advice to help him sleep?

3 Helena's letter contains eight spelling mistakes. Find the mistakes and correct them.

4 Helena's answer would not be given a high mark at First Certificate. Write your own **letter** to Robin in **120–180 words**.

Help

- Aim to ensure that the answer to each question in exercise 2 is *Yes* for your letter.

- See page 147 for more information on writing Part 2 Informal letters, together with useful language for giving advice.

Review

1 For questions 1–12, read the text below and think of the word which best fits each gap. Use only one word in each gap. There is an example at the beginning **(0)**.

Write your answers **IN CAPITAL LETTERS**, just as you will have to do in the First Certificate examination.

Bedtime routines

Parents should create a clear bedtime routine and clear bedtimes for their children from **(0)** ....*AN*... early age. This means following a fixed pattern **(1)** .... evening at a similar time. Give your children supper, allow them **(2)** .... play, watch television or finish homework and then put them in the bath. Afterwards, it's straight into pyjamas and bed. Parents can read a story for a **(3)** .... minutes (or let older children read themselves), but after **(4)** .... , the lights should be switched off. Children should receive the minimum of fuss and attention **(5)** .... they get out of bed or wake up during the night, so as **(6)** .... to reinforce their behaviour.

Parents should also be working on tight strategies to manage waking behaviour, for example, being clear about **(7)** .... time children should be permitted to go into their parents' bedroom in the morning, and rewarding children **(8)** .... stay in bed and sleep longer. Children who **(9)** .... poor at going to bed need a regular and calming routine **(10)** .... encourages them to fall asleep in their cots or beds alone and with no reinforcement for staying awake (bottles, rocking, endless stories or falling asleep in **(11)** .... of the television are common, but ultimately unhelpful, strategies). Encouraging your child to sleep as much **(12)** .... is needed is just as important as ensuring that they eat properly and go to school.

Language focus

1 Rewrite the following sentences using third or mixed conditionals. The first one has been done for you.

1 I'm only tired because I went to bed late last night.
If I hadn't gone to bed last last night, I wouldn't be tired.

2 Rachel only got to the station on time because her dad gave her a lift.

3 I read an article about Slow Food. That's why I know so much about it.

4 Richard only played football last Saturday because the usual goalkeeper had flu.

5 I didn't realize it was Jackie's birthday so I didn't buy her a present.

6 You've got wet feet because you didn't wear the right kind of shoes.

2 In each of the following sentences **one** word is incorrect. Find the word and change it. The first one has been done for you.

1 James walks to school every day with his sister, ~~which~~ *who* is five years old.

2 The last bus leaves at half past nine, what seems quite early to me.

3 I lent my sleeping bag to my friend Tony, that was going camping with the scouts.

4 Jake took a sleeping pill it had been prescribed by his doctor.

5 The regulations state that any worker who's working day is longer than six hours is entitled to a break of at least 20 minutes.

6 He's a terrible manager: it's a clear example of someone being promoted to a position for that they're not qualified.

7 Do you have any idea of the reason for he decided to resign?

8 After school on Fridays we usually go to the café where is next to the bus station.

9 They met on December 14th, which it snowed all day.

Vocabulary

<u>Underline</u> the correct word in *italics* in the following sentences.

1 I *lied/lay/laid* awake thinking about work last night and didn't *get/fall/take* to sleep until after midnight.

2 You've got a busy day tomorrow, so you need to get a *right/good/well* night's sleep tonight.

3 I can have a *lie-down/lie-back/lie-in* tomorrow morning – I don't need to get up early.

4 Nika's bus *spent/took/lasted* a long time to arrive and she was late for school.

5 You could make the *fast/most/last* of your time at the doctor's and do some homework while we're waiting to see her.

6 The tour guide told us to carry our passports with us at *each/every/all* times.

7 Time *to/and/after* time I've told you not to go into my bedroom without asking!

8 Don't put so much food in your mouth. Eat the biscuits one *in/at/of* a time.

9 Your watch is ten minutes *fast/quick/long* – it's twenty past three not half past.

10 Parents should *set/pass/find* aside time each day to read to their children.

Phrasal verbs revision

1 Complete both gaps in each pair of sentences with the same particle. The first one has been done for you.

1 Is that story true or did you **make** it ....up......... .
I'm so unfit – I need to join a gym or **take** .....up....... a sport.

2 Our plane took off late but **touched** .... early!
My parents felt **let** .... when I told them I'd failed all my exams.

3 I'm used to my new job now, but it took me a long time to **settle** ....
I was a fool to believe he would keep his promise – I was completely **taken** ....

4 Sting worked as an English teacher before **going** .... to become lead singer with *The Police*.
They said that television would never **catch** .... but look how popular it became!

5 I managed to **talk** Tim .... lending me his car, but it wasn't easy to persuade him.
Someone **broke** .... our school and stole all the computers.

6 They tried to keep the wedding a secret but the news **leaked** .... and the paparazzi were everywhere.
I need a calculator to **work** .... the total cost.

7 **Talking** things .... together is the first step to solving problems.
I can't **get** .... the day without coffee – I must be addicted.

8 'I had meat the last time I ate here, so I think I'll **go** .... the fish.'
I don't trust you and I'm not going to **fall** .... your lies again!

2 Write down the meaning of each of the phrasal verbs in exercise 1.
e.g. **1** *make up* = invent   *take up* = start doing something new

Writing

Write an answer to one of the following in **120–180** words. Use an appropriate style.

1 Your teacher has asked you to write a story for the college magazine. The story must **begin** with the following words:
I had overslept, so I would have to hurry if I wanted to get there on time.
Write your **story**.

2 Your teacher has asked you to write an essay giving your opinions on the following statement:
The pace of life in the modern world is too fast.
Write your **essay**.

UNIT 10 Changes

Vocabulary and speaking: Age

Where possible, match the nouns, adjectives and phrases in the boxes to the people in the photographs on these two pages. It may be possible to match more than one item with some of the photographs.

adolescent	elderly	middle-aged	retired

preteen	toddler	youngster	newborn	teenager	senior citizen

in their twenties	past thirty	getting on

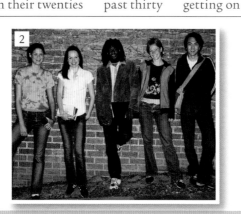

FCE Listening Part 3: Multiple matching

1 ⭕ Work in pairs. What do you think are the biggest sources of conflict between parents and teenagers these days?

2 🎧 2.26–2.30 You will hear five different people speaking about their relationships with their parents when they were teenagers. For questions 1–5, choose from the list (A–F) what each speaker says about their relationship. Use the letters only once. There is one extra letter which you do not need to use.

A I didn't think my parents' rules were unreasonable.

B I am still angry about a particular event.

C I made a decision that I now think was wrong.

D I thought my parents had little understanding of a teenager's life.

E I was allowed to go on holiday with friends when I was quite young.

F My parents each had a different approach to dealing with a particular problem.

Speaker 1		1
Speaker 2		2
Speaker 3		3
Speaker 4		4
Speaker 5		5

3 Are you like any of the speakers?

4 Underline the correct word in *italics* in the following sentences. The words in **bold** are from the listening.

1 I once **went** *through/by* **a stage** of not eating meat.

2 I've got far too many old clothes; I need to **get rid** *off/of* some.

3 My parents **approve** *of/for* most of my friends.

4 I often **stay** *to/out* **late** on Saturday and sometimes don't get home until two or three in the morning.

5 I don't always **stick** *to/for* **the rules**; rules are made to be broken.

5 ⭕ Work in pairs. Discuss how true the sentences in exercise 4 are for you. Give reasons and examples.

114

FCE Speaking Part 3: Collaborative task

💬 Work in pairs. There is going to be a series of TV programmes about different stages of life. Talk to each other about the advantages and disadvantages of being at the different stages of life shown in the photographs on these two pages. Then decide which programme might be the most interesting.

- What are the advantages and disadvantages of being at these stages of life?
- Which programme might be the most interesting?

Useful language

- Use contrast linkers when talking about the advantages and disadvantages:

e.g. on the one hand/on the other hand/however/although/but/whereas

- Further useful expressions:

One advantage/disadvantage of being a teenager is ...

A good/bad point about being a preteen is ...

A positive thing about being middle-aged is ...

Something that's not so good about being a toddler is ...

It can be difficult when you're retired because ...

FCE Speaking Part 4: Further discussion

💬 Discuss the following questions with your partner. Give reasons for your views.

1 Which stage of life do you think most people look forward to?

2 Some people say that school days are the best time of our lives. How far do you agree?

3 Is it important to have a lot of life experience before having children of your own?

4 Should elderly people live with their children?

5 Teenagers often disagree with their parents. Why do you think this is?

6 What do you think is a good age for young people to leave home?

Useful language

- When you give your opinion use expressions such as:

In my opinion ... /Personally, I think that ... /Actually, I completely disagree ... /I would certainly go along with that ... /My feeling is that ...

- In a discussion you should ask for the other person's opinion too. Use expressions like:

What do you think?/How do you feel about it?/Do you agree?/What's your view on ... ?/How about you?

Language focus: *Wish, if only* and *hope*

1 We use *wish* and *if only* when we talk about things we would like to be different in the present, future or past. Read the following comments from a young adult.

   a *I wish I hadn't argued so much with my parents when I lived at home.*

   b *If only I were eighteen again! There are so many things I'd like to do.*

   c *I wish my parents would move closer to where I live but I know they won't.*

   d *I wish I could go to my school reunion, but I'm going to be busy on that date.*

2 Match each comment **a–d** to a reason 1–4. Then <u>underline</u> the correct alternative in *italics* to complete the rules. The first one has been done for you.

   1 The speaker is expressing a wish about the present which is clearly impossible.

   wish/if only + present/<u>past tense</u>   *b*

   2 The speaker wants to do something him/herself in the future that is not possible.

   wish/if only + could/would

   3 The speaker wants someone else to do something now or in the future that is unlikely.

   wish/if only + will/would

   4 The speaker expresses regret about something that happened in the past.

   wish/if only + past simple/past perfect tense

3 Explain the difference in meaning between these two sentences.

   1 I wish/If only it would stop raining.

   2 I hope it stops raining.

   (www) Read more about *wish*, *if only* and *hope* in the Grammar Reference.

4 Correct the mistakes in the following sentences.

   1 I wish I would get higher marks for the essays we do at the end of term.

   2 We all wish it is warmer today because we're going swimming in the river.

   3 I wish Jack would win his race tomorrow afternoon. He's trained really hard for it.

   4 If only I had ask you to help when I had that problem with my car yesterday.

   5 Clare wishes they will stop building new houses on the edge of her village.

   6 If only I hadn't got car sick every time I travel. It makes my journeys so miserable.

5 Rewrite these sentences about things you 'regret' or 'would like to be different' using *wish*.

   Example:

   I argued a lot with my mum when I was younger.

   I wish I hadn't argued with my mum a lot when I was younger.

   1 I never listened to my parents when I was a teenager.

   2 I'm not old enough to take my driving test.

   3 I'm sorry but I can't come to your birthday celebration on Saturday.

   4 My parents refuse to let me go abroad with my friends this summer.

   5 I was horrible to my brother when I was younger.

   6 I have to go to school early for an exam tomorrow.

'Should have/ought to have'

1 We can also use *should/shouldn't have done* and *ought to have/ought not to have done* to express regret about the past.

   I should have worked much harder.
   I shouldn't have thrown her coat away.
   I ought to have tried to be more independent.

   Find sentences that you wrote in exercises 4 and 5 that show regret and rewrite them beginning with *I should have/shouldn't have* or *I ought to have/ought not to have*.

   Example:

   I wish I hadn't argued a lot with my mum when I was younger.

   I shouldn't have argued with my mum so much when I was younger.

2 (speech) Work in pairs. A reporter is interviewing a woman who is 102 years old. Decide what wishes and regrets you think she has.

   Example:

   I wish I had better eyesight.

   I should have travelled more when I was younger.

FCE Use of English Part 1: Multiple-choice cloze

1 Discuss these questions with a partner.

What factors do you think enable some people to live to more than a hundred years of age?

2 Read the text below, ignoring the gaps. Does it mention any of the ideas you discussed in exercise 1?

Eternal Youth?

What is the secret **(0)** .... long life? That is the big question that scientists have been trying to **(1)** .... for centuries. Some are convinced that they are getting very close but not all researchers are approaching **(2)** .... the same direction.

For a long time it has been thought that **(3)** .... calorie intake by 30% can result in a longer lifespan, but for most people this means **(4)** .... a starvation-like diet. Scientists are now developing a drug which they believe can switch on a particular gene that has the **(5)** .... effect without the pain.

Another approach has been to **(6)** .... centenarians and to analyse their lifestyles. Surprisingly, it seems that **(7)** .... most people's lifespans are 80% determined by environmental factors and 20% by their genetic make-up, with centenarians it is the other way round. Many in the over 100 age **(8)** .... had led unhealthy lifestyles with some of them smoking over 40 cigarettes a day for a long **(9)** .... of their lives. For these people a long life is the result of a longevity gene and scientists say that within three years they will have developed a drug that can imitate this gene.

Or is it all down to the mind? Some scientists believe that if we 'think' younger our bodies will follow. Studies have shown that by **(10)** .... people imagine they are twenty years younger many of the signs of ageing actually reverse.

So, what is the answer? **(11)** .... of the scientists involved are testing their own theories and are convinced that 125 is a good age for them to **(12)** .... for! Let's see.

3 Read the text again and decide which answer (**A, B, C** or **D**) best fits each gap. There is an example at the beginning **(0)**.

0	**A**	<u>of</u>	**B**	at	**C**	on	**D**	in
1	**A**	respond	**B**	reply	**C**	find	**D**	answer
2	**A**	to	**B**	from	**C**	by	**D**	at
3	**A**	falling	**B**	reducing	**C**	holding	**D**	stopping
4	**A**	following	**B**	doing	**C**	leading	**D**	going
5	**A**	compared	**B**	same	**C**	similar	**D**	like
6	**A**	look	**B**	search	**C**	study	**D**	learn
7	**A**	however	**B**	whereas	**C**	despite	**D**	but
8	**A**	group	**B**	level	**C**	class	**D**	section
9	**A**	time	**B**	decade	**C**	period	**D**	stage
10	**A**	allowing	**B**	getting	**C**	forcing	**D**	making
11	**A**	Several	**B**	Various	**C**	Couple	**D**	Group
12	**A**	predict	**B**	direct	**C**	point	**D**	aim

4 Would you like to live to be over a hundred if you were still fit and healthy? Why/Why not?

FCE Speaking Part 2: Talking about photos

1 🗨 These photographs show people facing new experiences.

Student A: Compare the photographs, and say what challenges you think these people are going to face.

Student B: When your partner has finished, answer the following question.

Which situation do you think will be the most exciting?

2 🗨 Change roles and follow the instructions on page 136.

FCE Listening Part 1: Multiple choice

1 🎧 2.31–2.46 You will hear people talking in eight different situations. For questions 1–8, choose the best answer (A, B or C).

1 You hear two friends talking about an unexpected inheritance.
Why did Sue inherit the money?
A She had a very good relationship with her great aunt.
B There was no other family member.
C Her great aunt had been close to Sue's father.

2 You hear a woman talking about her family's reaction to moving to the countryside.
Whose reaction to the move causes her most concern?
A her daughter's
B her son's
C her husband's

3 You hear a man talking on the radio about being homeless. Why is he in this situation?
A His wife fell for someone else.
B He was in debt to his boss.
C He did something illegal.

4 You hear a woman talking about her experiences of using Twitter, the social networking site. How does she feel about her new hobby?
A She wishes she had known about it before.
B She sometimes gets confused by the technology.
C She enjoys the mental challenge.

5 You hear a new writer being interviewed on the radio.
What does he think about his decision to give up his old job?
A It was a little rushed.
B He might regret it later.
C He knew at the time it was right.

6 You hear part of a news bulletin.
Why are some people living in caravans?
A They have been evacuated from their homes because of flooding in recent days.
B They are worried about the safety of their homes.
C They do not have the money to repair their homes.

7 You hear two people talking about a man called Steve who has just come out of prison.
How is Steve feeling?
A relieved
B ashamed
C worried

8 You hear a woman talking about dealing with being famous.
What is she?
A an actor
B a model
C a sportsman's wife

2 🗨 Has anything important changed in your life recently? Tell your partner about it.

FCE Writing Part 1: Email

1 🗨 Read the following Part 1 task. Would it more appropriate to write the reply to Mr Harrison in a formal or an informal style?

A famous author is coming to visit your school to give a talk to the students. You have been asked to help organise the visit. Read the email you have received from Mr. Harrison, the author, and the notes you have made. Then write an email to Mr. Harrison using **all** your notes.

From: David Harrison
Sent: 15th February
Subject: Talk at Masters School

I'm arriving on the 9.30 train from London. Could you arrange for a taxi to meet me? — *Pick up myself – say where*

I intend to talk about how my life has changed since I became a writer. Is there anything else you would like me to include? — *Yes – say what*

I would like to have a short discussion with some of the students on the creative writing course at your school. Is this possible? — *Good idea – read some of their work?*

Do you have anything else arranged following the talk? I have to catch the 4.15 return train. — *Make suggestions*

I look forward to meeting everyone.

Yours sincerely

David Harrison

Write your email in **120–150** words. You must use grammatically correct sentences with accurate spelling and punctuation in a style appropriate for the situation.

2 Read the following reply to Mr Harrison's email. <u>Underline</u> the correct alternatives in 1–12 to ensure the style is consistently appropriate. The first one has been done for you.

(1) <u>Dear</u>/Hi Mr. Harrison,

(2) Thanks/Thank you very much for your email. It is (3) great/very kind of you to give us a talk.

(4) Regarding/About the arrangements for the day, I will meet you myself at the station. If you take the West Road exit, I shall be at the entrance.

Anything you can tell us about your life as a professional writer will be (5) of interest/really brilliant to the group. (6) Perhaps you could also tell us a little/How about telling us a bit about the difficulties you faced when you were starting out.

The students would definitely enjoy meeting you after the talk and if you (7) 've got time/could find time to look at some of their work too, they (8) would be very grateful/'d be very happy.

(9) I haven't sorted out anything else yet/Nothing else has been arranged so far, but if you (10) would like/fancy to visit the new town library, I could take you there on our way back to the station.

(11) I can't wait to meet you/I look forward to meeting you.

(12) Cheers /Yours sincerely

Paul Olsen

3 Now do the task on page 137. Use formal words and expressions from the email in exercise 2 where appropriate.

Vocabulary: Relationships

1 <u>Underline</u> the correct word in *italics* in these dialogues.

1 **A:** You and Tom have been together for a long time. When did you first **fall *for/at*** him?

B: When I saw him at a school dance two years ago. He **chatted me *on/up*** and we **went *to/on* a couple of dates**. The rest is history!

2 **A:** How long have you been **going *out/off*** with Lucy?

B: Well, I first **asked her *out/up*** in January last year. Then we **split *up/out*** at the beginning of the summer after some silly row. We **got *back/out* together** again in August. So, I suppose, on and off, it's been about 18 months.

3 **A:** I haven't seen you and Dave together for a while. Have you **fallen *off/out*** with him?

B: Yes. I just don't **get *in/on* with** his brother and we argued about it. We **broke *out/up*** about a week ago.

A: You'll **make *up/on*** soon I'm sure. You two are **made *for/at*** each other!

2  Discuss the following questions with a partner.

1 If someone asked you out on a date, where would you like to go? Why?

2 Who do you get on best with at school, college or work?

3 Have you fallen out with anyone recently? Why?

4 What do you think is the best way to make up after an argument with a good friend?

5 Which celebrity couple have split up recently?

FCE Reading Part 3: Multiple matching

1 Complete each gap with a word from the box below.

bridesmaid	vicar	reception	bride	married
bouquet	groom	speeches	best man	attended

Wedding of the week

Pamela Dean married Martin Westbrook on Saturday 19th May. Over a hundred people **(1)** .... the simple ceremony, which took place in the couple's local village church. The **(2)** .... wore a lovely dress of white silk and the **(3)** .... looked very smart in a grey silk suit. The couple chose a country hotel for the **(4)** .... and a lot of good food and champagne was eaten and drunk during the afternoon. Both the **(5)** .... who married them in the church and the **(6)** .... , James Hillman who was Martin's oldest friend, made short **(7)** .... and when Pam followed the tradition of throwing the **(8)** .... of flowers over her shoulder, it was caught by the youngest **(9)** .... , Angela, aged seven. She was thrilled but says she probably won't be getting **(10)** .... any time soon!

2  Work in pairs. Look at the photographs on this page and on page 121 and then answer questions 1–3.

1 What is similar and what is different about the photographs?

2 Why do you think the people in the photographs decided to get married in these places?

3 Where do people usually get married in your country? Are there any special traditions?

3 You are going to read a magazine article about people's different wedding locations. For questions **1–15**, choose from the people **(A–E)**. The people may be chosen more than once. When more than one answer is required, these may be given in any order.

Which person or people state the following?

We did not fully consider the consequences of choosing this venue. 1 [ ]

I didn't wear exactly what my partner wanted me to. 2 [ ]

I received a number of different reactions to my plans. 3 [ ]

We did not think of the idea ourselves. 4 [ ] 5 [ ]

Cost was a factor when deciding on the venue. 6 [ ]

I love the architecture of the venue we chose. 7 [ ]

I chose the venue because I had good memories of this place from my childhood. 8 [ ]

We liked the venue because we began our relationship there. 9 [ ]

We didn't have good weather on the day. 10 [ ]

We didn't immediately agree on the idea. 11 [ ] 12 [ ]

My health was temporarily affected by the ceremony. 13 [ ]

We weren't restricted by how many people we could invite. 14 [ ]

My partner's reaction to my idea was not what I had imagined. 15 [ ]

A strange place to get married?

More and more people are choosing to get married in unusual places these days. We asked five people about their wedding locations.

A MARIA

When I first suggested the venue some of my friends thought it was a great idea and others thought it was just plain silly! And my mum seemed quite disappointed while my dad just thought I was joking. The reason I thought of it was because I'd been to Disneyworld as a kid and it was the best holiday I'd ever been on. When it came to deciding where we wanted to get married and I realised that Disney world was an option I thought it would be perfect. Dan took a bit of persuading – dressing up as Mickey Mouse on his wedding day wasn't exactly what he'd had in mind! But he's got a terrific sense of fun and he agreed in the end. It wasn't a cheap wedding but it was quite an amazing experience and the wedding photos are hilarious!

B JOHNNY

My best man, Brian, knew that Jan and I were looking for a really special way to celebrate our marriage but we hadn't come up with anything and he mentioned this air company that arranged wing walking weddings. That's where you get married on the plane – not in it! Well, Jan and I are quite adventurous and we had been wing walking in the past but we had no idea that you could actually get married doing it! I put it to Jan, fully expecting her to think it was a ridiculous idea but she agreed

immediately. Quite honestly, if we'd thought it through properly we'd probably never have gone ahead. There were so many things that could have gone wrong. Suppose it had rained? In actual fact it was very exciting in spite of the discomfort. I had a sore throat for three days after the wedding because of shouting through the microphone to make my vows!

C NIKKI

MacDonalds™ seemed the obvious place for Pete and me to get married because it's where we got together ten years ago when we were both working there. So when our previous boss suggested we get married and have the reception there we both jumped at the chance. Neither Pete nor I wanted a traditional wedding. We wanted something a bit different and somewhere that had a meaning for us both. Also, it was nowhere as expensive as a normal wedding and that was important to us too. My parents were a bit surprised but they came round in the end. It was a great day and I'll never forget the faces of people passing by and looking in at this amazing fast food wedding reception!

D DON

I suppose it's not the most glamorous wedding location in the world but as soon as I read on the internet that the National History Museum in London organised

wedding ceremonies in its Central Hall I knew that was where Penny and I were going to get married. We both love museums and spend a lot of our free time going round them so it seemed logical to be getting married in one of the best! The design of the building is amazing and it was a very powerful and solemn event for us. However, it took a lot of organising as we live in Edinburgh and had to arrange transport and accommodation for our guests. But it was definitely worth it.

E SUSIE

I definitely wasn't impressed when my husband-to-be suggested getting married on the pitch of his favourite football club! However, I gradually warmed to the idea. He's been a fan of the club since he was six and is passionate about them. So, although it wasn't exactly what I'd been planning for my wedding day I knew it meant a lot to him. I even agreed to wearing the club colours – yellow and blue instead of white but I drew the line at football shorts and shirt! The good thing was that we could invite as many guests as we wanted – there was plenty of room. If it hadn't rained it would have been perfect! The best moment was when everyone threw their football scarves in the air when the vicar pronounced us man and wife!

4 ◯ Which wedding location do you think was the best? Why?

FCE Listening Part 4: Multiple choice

1 🗨 Have you read any stories in the news recently about how medical progress or an operation has completely changed a person's life?

2 🗨 Read the following definitions and then discuss questions 1–3 with a partner.

> **hiccup** *noun*: a short repeated sound that you make in your throat without intending to, usually because you have been eating or drinking too quickly
>
> **PHRASE** **get/have (the) hiccups:** to start making hiccup sounds and not be able to stop

1 Do you often get the hiccups? Do you know the reason why?

2 Have you ever had hiccups for a long period of time? How long did they last for?

3 What do you think is the best way to stop hiccups?

3 Read this headline from a newspaper article about the man in the photograph. How do you think hiccups saved his life?

> ## I had hiccups for three years but it saved my life

4 🎧 2.47 You will hear an interview about an interesting news story. For questions 1–7, choose the best answer (**A, B or C**).

1 What does Andy say about the story?
- **A** It is amusing.
- **B** It is difficult to believe.
- **C** It is unusual.

2 What was Chris' life like when he had hiccups?
- **A** The hiccups prevented him from sleeping.
- **B** The hiccups affected his social life.
- **C** The hiccups stopped for a short time each day.

3 What action did doctors initially take to deal with the problem?
- **A** They performed unsuccessful surgery on Chris.
- **B** They advised Chris to use alternative therapies.
- **C** They gave Chris medicine for depression.

4 Chris went to Japan
- **A** to appear on a TV show.
- **B** to study traditional Japanese remedies.
- **C** to have a medical examination.

5 It was discovered that
- **A** Chris also had problems with his eyesight.
- **B** Chris needed surgery that carried a lot of risk.
- **C** Chris had a cancerous growth in the brain.

6 What was the result of the operation?
- **A** Chris cannot walk easily.
- **B** Chris cannot do a lot of sport.
- **C** Chris can only use one arm well.

7 If Chris hadn't had the operation he
- **A** would have worse hiccups than before.
- **B** would have a much shorter life expectancy.
- **C** would not be able to see now.

5 🗨 Work in pairs.

1 Were your ideas for exercise 2 correct?

2 In the interview Andy says *'It's difficult to list all the ways his life is better now.'* In what ways might Chris' daily life have changed for the better since the hiccups stopped?

Vocabulary: Health

1 Complete each gap with one of these words from the listening.

therapy	illness	side-effects	cure	symptoms
operations	pain	passed out	sick	

1 I once .... after an injury because of the **intense** .... **I suffered**.
2 I've never **suffered** any .... **from medication** I've been prescribed.
3 I would definitely use an **alternative** .... if I were very ill.
4 The smell of petrol used to **make me feel** .... when I was a child.
5 I'm not sure what the .... **of depression** actually are.
6 Soon **surgeons will be able to perform** .... to replace any part of our bodies.
7 I don't know anyone who has never been away from school because of ....
8 I believe that one day they'll **find a** .... **for** everything and then we'll live forever.

2 🗣 How true are these statements for you?

Language focus: Causative passive with *have*

1 We use the causative passive when the subject arranges for something to be done by someone else. Look at these sentences about Chris's story. <u>Underline</u> the **subject**, **all the parts of the verb** and the **object** in the sentences. Then complete the rule.

Last year Chris had the tumour removed.

Next month he'll have some X-rays taken to check that the tumour hasn't returned.

The Japanese doctor has had several articles on hiccups published in medical journals.

The causative passive is formed by using subject + correct form of ___ + object + ___ participle.

🌐 Read more about causative passive with *have* in the Grammar Reference.

2 Complete the first gap in each sentence with the correct form of *have* and the second gap with the past participle of a verb from the box.

restyle	whiten	redecorate	service	check

1 My mum always .... her blood pressure .... every six months because of her condition. The local chemist does it for her.
2 I .... my bedroom .... last week. It looks awful and I'm going to do it myself next time.
3 I'm going to .... my hair .... on my next visit. I'm getting really bored with the way it looks.
4 My dad usually .... his car .... once a year. It keeps the engine running well.
5 It's not the first time Delia .... her teeth .... .I think it cost her a fortune!

3 🗣 Work in pairs. Tell your partner about something:

• you have done regularly
  e.g. *I have my teeth checked every six months.*

• you would like to have done

• you would never have done

• you need to have done.

Review

For questions **1–8**, complete the second sentence so that it has a similar meaning to the first sentence, using the word given. **Do not change the word given.** You must use between **two** and **five** words, including the word given.

1 Dave and Roxy regret getting married abroad.

   WISH

   Dave and Roxy .... married abroad.

2 It was wrong of you to stop taking the tablets without asking the doctor.

   SHOULD

   You .... the tablets without asking the doctor.

3 I would really like to hear from Gary.

   WISH

   I .... phone me.

4 It's a pity we can't afford the car we looked at.

   ONLY

   If .... the car we looked at.

5 I'm not happy about having to get up at 5.30 in the morning for this new job.

   WISH

   I .... to get up at 5.30 in the morning for this new job.

6 A top hairdresser did Sarah's hair for the wedding.

   HAD

   Sarah .... a top hairdresser for the wedding.

7 The best heart surgeon will perform Russell's operation.

   PERFORMED

   Russell will .... by the best heart surgeon.

8 The council rejected our planning application.

   HAD

   We .... by the council.

Vocabulary

a Complete each gap in exercises **a** and **b** with one word.

1 A specially arranged bunch of flowers for a celebration is a ....

2 A child who is 11 is not yet a teenager but a ....

3 Something wrong with your body that is a sign of an illness is a ....

4 The man who is getting married is the ....

5 A young child who has just learned to walk is a ....

b

1 Keep these old toy cars – don't **get rid** .... them. They might be worth a lot of money one day.

2 It's almost worth having a row so that you can **make** .... afterwards!

3 I first **fell** .... my future husband when we were at secondary school but he was three years older than me and completely ignored me.

4 All boys **go** .... a stage when they can't stand girls. It doesn't last long.

5 Helen's mum doesn't **approve** .... all her friends at university. She says they're not serious enough about their studies!

6 Every time Jenna has an injection she **passes** .... and has to lie down for half an hour.

FCE Use of English Part 3: Word formation

For questions **1–10**, read the text below. Use the word given in capitals at the end of some of the lines to form a word that fits in the gap **in the same line**. There is an example at the beginning **(0)**. Write your answers **IN CAPITAL LETTERS**.

Let's celebrate ... our divorce!

Divorce rates today are **(0)** APPARENTLY the lowest in the UK since the 1970s,	**APPARENT**
but the number is still high and provides an income for a very **(1)**	**LIKELY**
industry – cake-making. Everyone is aware of the **(2)** .... of the wedding	**IMPORTANT**
cake when couples get married but today, the occasion of a couple's divorce	
is also being seen as a **(3)** .... Many have special parties and together	**CELEBRATE**
cut a **(4)** .... divorce cake to show that the time has come to move on.	**COMIC**
Cake-maker Fay Miller accepts that some people might think her cakes are	
rather insensitive but she insists that her **(5)** .... bring humour to the	**CREATE**
occasion and can encourage a positive attitude to a failed marriage. There	
are obviously those who disapprove but she has received a **(6)** .... small	**RELATIVE**
number of actual **(7)** .... The demand for Fay's cakes in recent months	**COMPLAIN**
has been **(8)** .... high. She is extremely encouraged by this growth in	**SURPRISE**
her business. 'I have a lot of **(9)** .... in what I have achieved,' says Fay.	**PROUD**
'This started off as a small family business and I certainly had no	
(10) .... of expanding so quickly, but it looks as though I might have to!'	**INTEND**

FCE Writing Part 2

Write an answer to one of the following. Write your answer in **120–180** words in an appropriate style.

1 You have seen this announcement in a popular magazine.

> **Article Competition**
>
> Have you ever thought about what might have happened if you'd sent a particular email? Write an article entitled **The email I wish I'd sent!** and we will choose the best to publish in next month's edition of the magazine.

Write your **article.**

2 Your teacher has asked you to write an essay giving your opinions on the following statement.

Having hopes and dreams is one of the most important things in our lives.

Write your **essay**.

3 You see this notice in your college magazine.

> **Write us your review!**
>
> Have you seen any interesting films recently about people who have lived through big life changing events? Write a review for us, saying what it was about, why it was interesting and whether you would recommend it to other people.

Write your **review**.

4 Your teacher has asked you to write a story for an international magazine. The story must **begin** with the following words:

I should never have opened the letter.

Write your **story**.

 Help For information on writing articles, essays, reviews and stories see pages 142–145 in the Writing Bank.

Additional material

Unit 1

Help

- There are several reasons why only one of the four options fits the gap. For example:
  1. It is the only word with the correct meaning.
     Several trees blew down during the recent ....
     A gales √   B blows   C draughts   D bursts
  2. It is part of a collocation.
     A .... breeze caused the high grass to move from side to side.
     A narrow   B slim   C light √   D pale
  3. It is the correct preposition or part of a phrasal verb.
     My role model and the person I look .... most is my father.
     A down on   B up to √   C back on   D forward to
  4. It is the only word which fits grammatically.
     My parents always .... me to do sport, but I was never very good.
     A suggested   B said   C tried   D encouraged √
- Recording new vocabulary in context enables you to see how it is used in combination with other words.

Speaking Part 1: Personal questions Page 13

Student A

Write one more question for each subject. Then ask your partner the questions.

ADVERTS
1. What's your favourite advert at the moment? Why?
2. Do you like watching commercials on TV? Why/Why not?
3. Can you remember a really annoying advertisement that you saw on TV when you were younger?
4. _____ ?

CELEBRITIES
1. Tell us about a celebrity from your country.
2. Do you like to read about celebrities' lives? Why/Why not?
3. Would you like to be famous? Why/Why not?
4. _____

Unit 2

Writing Part 2: Articles Page 27

A way to keep fit ... and much more

Can you think of a better way of keeping in shape than taking part in a team sport? Last year I took up volleyball, and as well as being the fittest I've ever been, I'm also a lot happier.

In the past I'd tried going to the gym and I'd also been running, but I lost interest and gave them both up. Why? Because I was always on my own, and it wasn't nearly as enjoyable as doing something together with other people. Now I have a great time during practice sessions, and I've made lots of new friends.

Playing volleyball has helped me with my exams, too. It gives me a break from my studies, clears my mind and makes me feel good. So after a game I'm much more able to sit at my desk and carry on with my revision.

If you don't do any team sports, then sign up for one now – as well as keeping you physically and mentally fit, it's great fun and wonderful for your social life. What could be better?

A Read the model answer again and match features **1–3** below to their functions **a–c**.

1	The title	**a**	to leave the reader with something to think about
2	The opening question	**b**	to attract the reader's attention and give an idea of the article's general content
3	The closing question	**c**	to involve the reader from the start

B a Is the article written in a formal or informal style?
  b Find examples of the following features in the model:

  1 Contractions: e.g. *I've*

  2 Phrasal verbs: e.g. *took up*

  3 Conjunctions at the beginning of sentences e.g. *Because*

C The writer of the model answer has used a good range of vocabulary and structures. <u>Underline</u> the structures which are used to make comparisons, similar to those you saw on page 25 in this unit.

Example:

Can you think of <u>a better way</u> of keeping in shape <u>than</u> taking part in a team sport?

Unit 3

FCE Speaking Part 3: Collaborative task Page 37

Help

- This is an interactive task so make sure that you talk to your partner (not the examiner) and respond to his or her comments as well as giving your own opinion.
- Don't just describe the photos and what you can see in them. Remember there is a task, which is written in the form of a question above the pictures. Look at the question again if necessary to make sure you are answering it.
- There are always two parts to the task. First you have to talk about the pictures and then make some sort of decision. Don't make the decision at the beginning or too quickly because then you will finish early. It's better to spend longer discussing the pictures even if you don't manage to talk about them all.
- Don't worry if the examiner has to stop you. This means that you have a lot to say, which is good.
- You don't have to agree with your partner about which jobs would be the most difficult.

Unit 4

Word Formation: Prefixes Page 47

3 In 1–6, one of the four words in **bold** has been given the wrong prefix. Find the words and correct them.

1 Paul's teacher said she was growing **impatient** with his behaviour problems. According to her, he is extremely **impolite** and **impleasant** in the classroom, and she is finding him increasingly **impossible** to teach.

2 **Unfortunately**, Chris is still **unemployed**. He was arrested for driving while drunk last June and **unqualified** from driving for two years. So he lost his job with the delivery company and he's **unlikely** to find work as a driver again.

3 Most youngsters who start work with us at 16 are **incapable** of making decisions for themselves. Helen's **independence** and ability to work on her own is **inusual** in someone so **inexperienced**.

4 The safety measures at this funfair have been introduced to **enable** you to enjoy yourself without **endangering** your own life or that of others. Furthermore, in order to **ensure** that everyone has the best time possible, we **encourage** adults from allowing children to go on any ride they consider inappropriate.

5 Jake's **irregular** attendance at football practices annoyed his teammates, who considered him to be an **irresponsible** and **irreliable** member of the team. They felt it was **irrelevant** that he was going through a bad time with his girlfriend.

6 Chris maintained that scientists had been **dishonest** in their attempts to persuade the public of the seriousness of global warming, which he said was not as bad as they made it out to be. I **disagreed** strongly, pointing to the **disappearing** Arctic ice as proof of the problem, but was **disable** to convince him.

Vocabulary: Verb collocations Page 50

3 For **a–f** write each verb from exercise 1 next to the three items of vocabulary with which it forms common collocations. The first one has been done for you.

a _make_

sure

an effort

sense

b _____

ages to

a close look at

a break

c _____

in touch with

better

rid of

d _____

as a surprise

to an end

to the conclusion that

e _____

calm

a promise

an eye on

f _____

a record

the law

into (a building)

4 Rewrite the sentences replacing the words in **bold** with an appropriate collocation from exercise 3.

Example: Could you please **try** to be nice to your brother?

Could you please make an effort to be nice to your brother?

1 The doctor **carefully examined** the injury.
2 The news of their divorce **was unexpected**.
3 When arrested, Smith said he hadn't **done anything illegal**.
4 Can we **throw away** all your old toys?
5 In the event of a fire, **do not panic**.

5 Choose four of the collocations from exercise 3 and write sentences like those in exercise 4. Then give your sentences to your partner, who will rewrite them using the appropriate collocations.

Unit 2

Speaking Part 1: Personal questions Page 13

Student B

Write one more question for each subject. Then ask your partner.

THE WEATHER
1 What sort of weather do you dislike? Why?
2 Tell us about the weather on your last holiday.
3 Do you think the climate of your country affects the people? Why/not?
4 _____ ?

SHOPPING
1 Tell us about something interesting you've bought recently.
2 Do you prefer to go shopping alone or with friends?
3 Do you do a lot of shopping online? Why/not?
4 _____ ?

Unit 5

1 For questions **1–10**, read the text below. Use the word given in capitals at the end of some of the lines to form a word that fits in the gap **in the same line**. There is an example at the beginning **(0)**.

> ## Remember
>
> Check your spelling. An incorrectly spelled word will receive no marks at all in the First Certificate examination.

Ring-necked parakeets

Originally from India, the ring-necked parakeet has become a common

(0) _sight_ in recent years in a number of European cities, including   **SEE**

London, Paris, Amsterdam, Cologne and Barcelona. In the UK there are

now more than 50,000 individuals and the numbers are growing. Three

factors have contributed to the **(1)** _____ of this exotic outsider: **SURVIVE**

a **(2)** _____ food supply, a tolerable climate and a distinct lack of   **RELY**

(3) _____ from other species. Parakeets feed on a wide variety of   **COMPETE**

seeds, berries, fruit and nuts, which are all **(4)** _____ available in   **FREE**

urban parks and gardens. As a native of the Himalayan foothills, they

can live **(5)** _____ in the cold winters of northern Europe, where   **COMFORT**

they have been breeding in the wild for over forty years. And as they

begin nesting in holes in trees as early as January, they normally get

first choice of nesting sites. These **(6)** _____ but very noisy birds   **COLOUR**

receive mixed **(7)** _____ in those countries where they settle: **REACT**

loved by some, they are considered **(8)** _____ visitors by others,   **WELCOME**

who see them as a threat to native species of birds that share similar

habitats. So far, however, there has been little **(9)** _____ of this,   **EVIDENT**

though there are fears that parakeets could become a problem for fruit-

growers and other farmers if they continue to breed at the current rate.

In Britain they enjoy a high level of **(10)** _____ under wildlife   **PROTECT**

legislation, but it is now possible to obtain a licence to control their

numbers in exceptional circumstances.

2 From your answers for **1–10** in exercise 1 add the nouns to the appropriate column of the noun list in your notebook.

3 💬 What reaction do/would parakeets receive where you live?
How easily would these animals adapt to living in the wild in your area? Give reasons.

giraffe   camel   crocodile   bear

Unit 5

FCE Speaking Part 4: Further discussion Page 61

💬 Discuss the following questions with your partner.

Do you think it would be interesting to work in an isolated place? Why?/Why not?

How important is it to be happy in your job?

Some people would prefer not to have to work. Why do you think that is?

How well do you think schools prepare young people for the world of work?

Some people think that all young people should work in the summer holidays to earn money? What do you think?

How difficult is it for young people in your area to find work?

Unit 6

FCE Writing Part 1: Email Page 75

Help

- When you have finished writing, check your email. Answer these questions about it:

  Have I used and developed all the notes appropriately?

  Have I organized the email into logical paragraphs?

  Are the grammatical structures and vocabulary appropriate and accurate?

  Have I included some linking devices?

  Is the spelling correct?

  Is the style of the email appropriate and consistent?

- What do you think is the best way to improve your vocabulary?

Unit 7

Vocabulary: Prepositions Page 83

4 a Choose five of the **verb + preposition** or **preposition + noun phrases** from exercise 2 which were not used in exercise 3. Write a sentence for each, leaving a gap where the verb or noun should be, as in exercise 3.

Example:

The other driver crashed into the back of my car so he's the one who's at _____, not me. [Answer: fault]

b Give your sentences to another student to complete.

FCE Writing Part 2: Reports Page 87

Help

- Underline key words in the question to ensure that you answer it correctly.
- Plan what you are going to write. You might consider the following places:

  fast food restaurants with healthy options   salad bars   cheap seafood restaurants

  restaurants with healthy national dishes   foreign restaurants

  Remember, you can invent information for your report if you want to.
- Organize your ideas into paragraphs, including a brief introduction and conclusion.
- Give the report and each of the paragraphs a heading.
- Use some of the language from the model.
- When you have finished, check your answer for grammar and spelling mistakes.
- See page 146 for more information on writing reports.

Unit 8

Speaking Part 2: Talking about photos Page 92

Help

The question Student B is asked after Student A has finished speaking is sometimes about which job/sport/ activity etc. you would prefer. Say which you would prefer and give a reason.

Useful language

For me, being a tour guide would be better because …

I'd much prefer to be a tour guide because …

I'd like … a lot more than … because …

I'd rather be a … than a …

These photographs show people who need to remember things for their work.

Student A: Compare the photographs and say what sort of things they need to remember.

Student B: When your partner has finished, answer the following question.

Which job would you prefer to have?

Language focus: Passive of reporting verbs Page 98

a Rewrite these sentences using the two passive structures from exercise 1 on page 98. The first one has been done for you.

1 People expect that video games will become even more complex in the future.

> *It is expected that video games will become even more complex in the future.*
> *Video games are expected to become even more complex in the future.*

2 People expect that climate change will get much worse over the next couple of years.

3 People say that eating fish improves brain performance.

4 People think that social networking has made people more isolated.

5 People believe that English and Spanish are easy languages to learn.

6 People say that daily life is getting much faster for most of us.

b Work in pairs. Do you agree with the statements?

Unit 9

Language focus 1: Conditionals Page 104

Student A

a Look at the sentence beginnings below. Consider the work and daily routines of the speakers in bold and complete each sentence in an appropriate way. Include one or two clues which will help your partner guess the profession of each speaker.

Example:

1 **Footballer:** I often go to a night club on Tuesday, unless ...

1 we have a cup match on Wednesday night.

2 **Long-distance lorry driver:** I'd better stop for a rest soon, otherwise ...

3 **Firefighter:** If I didn't use the gym at work every day, ...

4 **Teacher:** I'd enjoy this job more if ...

5 **Model:** It's a great life. If I hadn't chosen this as a career, ...

6 **Golfer:** I might have won if ...

b ⬭ Read out your completed sentences to Student B who will try to guess the profession of the speaker.

Unit 9

Language focus: Relative clauses Page 110

Student A

a Write definitions for words **a–f** using relative clauses, but **without mentioning the words in your definitions**. The numbers in brackets refer to the units of this book in which the words appeared. All the words can be found in one of the Vocabulary sections in the relevant unit.

Example: referee

(8) This noun is a person whose job it is to ensure that players in games such as football and basketball obey the rules.

a   downpour (1)

b   gale (1)

c   wrinkled (3)

d   tubby (3)

e   package holiday (4)

f   demonstration (6)

b Read out the definitions you have written to Student B, who will tell you which words you have defined.

> **Useful language**
>
> This **adjective** describes a person *who/that/whose* ... / a thing *which/that* ...
>
> This **noun** is a place *where* ... /a type of ... *which/that* ... /a group of people *who* ...

Writing Part 2: Set books Page 106

Write an answer to one of the following in **120–180 words** with reference to the set book you have read.

1 Here is an extract from a letter you have received from your English penfriend, Chris.

> and that's why I like her so much. Who is your favourite character from the book and why? Write and tell me.
>
> Chris

Write a **letter** to Chris giving your opinion. Do not write any postal addresses.

2 You see this notice in your college magazine.

> ### The film of the book – Reviews wanted
>
> Have you seen a film version of a book you have read? If so, write us a review saying which you preferred, the film or the book, and why.

Write your **review**.

3 Your English teacher has given you this essay for homework:

In your opinion, which character changes the most in the book?

Write your **essay** explaining your views.

4 Your English teacher is thinking of using the set book again with another group of students she is preparing for the First Certificate exam. She has asked your class to write a report explaining the positive and negative points about using the set book you have read and saying whether you would recommend her to use it again.

Write your **report**.

5 You see this notice in your college magazine.

> ### The Wrong Ending – Articles wanted!
>
> We would like you to send us your articles on books whose endings you didn't like. Write us an article telling us:
> - how your book ended
> - why you weren't happy with it
> - how you would change it.

Write your **article**.

Help

Once you have chosen the question you want to answer:
- <u>underline</u> key words in the question e.g. *classic novel, article, why, still popular today.*
- write down ideas which are relevant to the question.
- select those ideas you will include and organise them into paragraphs.
- write your answer, if possible including one or two relevant short quotations from the book.
- check your answer for mistakes.

Unit 9

Word formation: Nouns 2 Page 107

Use the word given in capitals at the end of each line to form a noun that fits in the gap in the same line. The noun required may be:

- formed using an uncommon suffix   e.g. *behave → behaviour*
- the result of a spelling change   e.g. *think → thought*
- a compound noun   e.g. *net → network*

There is an example at the beginning **(0)**.

When he finished his exams, Paolo felt a huge sense of **(0)** _relief_   **RELIEVE**

as if an enormous **(1)** _____ had been lifted from his shoulders. It was   **WEIGH**

the **(2)** _____ of summer, of course, so he'd only been able to work   **HIGH**

in the evenings, as the midday **(3)** _____ slowed him down and made   **HOT**

studying virtually impossible. In **(4)** _____ to his teacher's advice, he   **RESPOND**

had made himself a revision **(5)** _____ , which he'd kept to, and he   **TIME**

had worked hard to commit the **(6)** _____ of the past year to memory.   **KNOW**

This course had not been his first **(7)** _____ and he had found it   **CHOOSE**

difficult, **(8)** _____ of which were the low marks he had received for   **PROVE**

much of his coursework. There could be no **(9)** _____ , however, if   **COMPLAIN**

he failed; he had done his best. Now the holidays were in **(10)** _____   **SEE**

and he could look forward to a well-deserved rest.

b 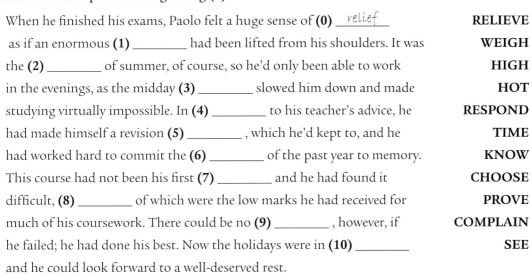 Do you plan your revision when studying for exams? Why/Why not?

Unit 9

Language focus: Conditionals Page 104

Student B

a Look at the sentence beginnings below. Consider the work and daily routines of the speakers in bold and complete each sentence in an appropriate way. Include one or two clues which will help your partner guess the profession of each speaker.

Example:

1   **Dustman:** I'd better have a shower now, otherwise …

1   *I'll smell of rotten food and other rubbish.*

2   **Novelist:** I'll never finish this book unless …
3   **Farmer:** If I went on holiday, …
4   **Tourist guide:** I'd enjoy this job more if …
5   **Soldier:** It's a great life. If I hadn't chosen this as a career, …
6   **Tennis player:** I might have won if …

b Read out your completed sentences to Student A who will try to guess the profession of the speaker.

Unit 9

Language focus: Relative clauses   Page 110

Student B

a Write definitions for words **a–f** using relative clauses, **but without mentioning the words in your definitions.** The numbers in brackets refer to the units of this book in which the words appeared. All the words can be found in one of the Vocabulary sections in the relevant unit.

Example: referee

(8) This noun is a person whose job it is to ensure that players in games such as football and basketball obey the rules.

a pitch (2)

b goggles (2)

c forgery (3)

d fussy (5)

e even-tempered (5)

f cast (8)

b Read out the definitions you have written to Student A, who will tell you which words you have defined.

> **Useful language**
>
> This **adjective** describes a person *who/that/whose …* / a thing *which/that …*
>
> This **noun** is a place *where …* / a type of … *which/that …* / a group of people *who …*

Unit 10

Speaking Part 2: Talking about photos Page 118

These photographs show people whose lives are soon going to change.

Student A: Compare the photographs, and say what sort of changes they can expect.

Student B: When your partner has finished, answer the following question.

Which person's life do you think will change the most?

Unit 10

Writing Part 1: Email Page 119

A computer expert is coming to your school to give a talk and demonstration about the latest changes and advances in computer technology. You have been asked to help organise the visit. Read the email you have received from Mr. Richards, the computer expert, and the notes you have made. Then write an email to Mr. Harrison using all your notes.

---

email

From: Sean Richards
Sent: 18th November
Subject: Talk at Masters School

I shall be travelling to your school by car and plan to arrive at about 10.30. Could you arrange parking for me?

Could you also tell me how much computer experience the students in the group already have?

I shall be talking about recent developments in fighting online fraud. Are there any other aspects of computer technology you would like me to talk about?

My schedule shows that my talk finishes at 12.30. Could you confirm that please?

I look forward to meeting you all.

Yours sincerely

Sean Richards

Yes, organized – give details

Mixed experience - explain

Yes – say what

Confirm 12.30 – suggest lunch in ...

Write your email in **120–150** words. You must use grammatically correct sentences with accurate spelling and punctuation in a style appropriate for the situation.

Writing bank

Part 1: Formal letters and emails

Your family is renting a cottage in England for one week this summer. Read the letter which the owner, Mrs Williams, has written to you and the notes you have made. Then write a letter to Mrs Williams, using **all** your notes.

I have reserved **Dove Cottage** for you and your family from Friday 29th July to Friday 5th August.

If you would like to stay for two further nights, this is also possible as the cottage is free until midday on Sunday 7th August. *— No, because ...*

Tell Mrs Taylor — You can pick up the keys at my house in the town centre or I can meet you at the cottage. Which would you prefer? *— Say which and why*

Could you give me an idea of what time you will be arriving?

The cottage is well equipped and very comfortable and I am sure you will enjoy your stay here.

Has it got ...?

Yours sincerely

Mrs J. Williams

Model answer

relevant beginning

organizing points into logical paragraphs

consistently formal style

appropriate ending

appropriate use of linking words and phrases

where possible, avoid copying language from input material

relevant expansion of notes

Dear Mrs Williams

Thank you for your letter confirming our reservation. Unfortunately, we will not be able to extend our stay in the cottage until Sunday 7th August, because my father has to return to work on the Saturday.

If you do not mind, we would rather collect the keys from you at Dove Cottage, so that we do not have to spend time driving through the busy town centre looking for somewhere to park. We hope to be there between five and six o'clock. However, we will phone you after lunch on July 29th in order to give you a more exact time of arrival.

I would be grateful if you could tell me whether there is a washing machine in the cottage, as this will help us decide how much clothing to take with us.

We look forward to meeting you in July.

Yours sincerely

Karl Maier

Write your **letter** in 120–150 words. You must use grammatically correct sentences with accurate spelling and punctuation in a style appropriate to the situation.

Useful language for formal letters and emails

Beginnings and endings

Dear Sir or Madam & Yours faithfully

Dear Ms Bentley & Yours sincerely

Asking for information

Could you tell me/explain …

I would be grateful/I was wondering if you could tell me …

I would like/be interested to know …

Expressing preferences

We would prefer to (cycle) rather than (walk).

I would rather (stay in a hotel) than (sleep in a tent).

I feel it would be better to (travel on Friday) than (Saturday).

Making suggestions and recommendations

I suggest you (take a taxi to the station).

I strongly advise you to (buy tickets in advance).

I recommend (hiring a car at the airport).

Closing remarks

I look forward to your reply/hearing from you/meeting you.

Thank you in anticipation for your help.

Task

Your family wants to rent a seaside apartment for one week this summer. Read the letter which the owner, Mrs Jones, has written to you and the notes you have made. Then write a letter to Mrs Jones, using **all** your notes.

Yes, because …

Ask Mrs Jones about …

Say which and why

Tell Mrs Jones

I have two apartments available from Friday 24ᵗʰ June to Saturday 2ⁿᵈ July. You would have to leave the apartment at 9.30 on Saturday morning. Is this convenient to you?

One of the apartments is on the fourth floor with a view of the sea, the other is on the ground floor with direct access to the swimming pool. Which would you prefer?

Bathroom towels are provided. For a small extra charge I can also provide towels for the beach and swimming pool. Would you require these?

Is there anything else you would like to know about the cottage or the area?

Yours sincerely

Mrs G Jones

Write your **letter** in **120–150** words. You must use grammatically correct sentences with accurate spelling and punctuation in a style appropriate to the situation.

Part 1: Informal letters and emails

You will soon be going to visit your English-speaking friend Peter for a weekend. Read Peter's email to you, and the notes you have made. Then write an email to Peter, using **all** your notes.

> **From:** Peter
> **Sent:** 12th May
> **Subject:** Nature Day
>
> Here's something that might interest you. The local Natural History Society is holding its annual 'Nature Day' the weekend you come to visit me. Do you fancy going to it?
>
> There's a guided nature walk on Saturday afternoon, and in the evening there's a choice of two illustrated talks: 'Interesting Insects' or 'The Mysteries of Bird Migration'. Which would you prefer?
>
> There's a meeting of the Society tomorrow night, so if there's anything you want me to ask the organisers about the event, let me know.
>
> And is there anything special you'd like to do on the Sunday you're here? I haven't made any plans yet.
>
> Peter

Yes!

Ask Peter to find out …

Say which and why

How about …?

Write your **email** in 120–150 words. You must use grammatically correct sentences with accurate spelling and punctuation in a style appropriate for the situation.

Model answer

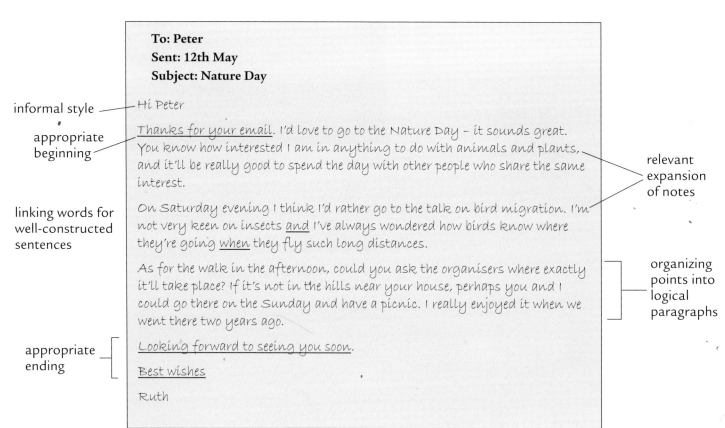

> **To: Peter**
> **Sent: 12th May**
> **Subject: Nature Day**
>
> Hi Peter
>
> Thanks for your email. I'd love to go to the Nature Day – it sounds great. You know how interested I am in anything to do with animals and plants, and it'll be really good to spend the day with other people who share the same interest.
>
> On Saturday evening I think I'd rather go to the talk on bird migration. I'm not very keen on insects <u>and</u> I've always wondered how birds know where they're going <u>when</u> they fly such long distances.
>
> As for the walk in the afternoon, could you ask the organisers where exactly it'll take place? If it's not in the hills near your house, perhaps you and I could go there on the Sunday and have a picnic. I really enjoyed it when we went there two years ago.
>
> Looking forward to seeing you soon.
>
> Best wishes
>
> Ruth

informal style

appropriate beginning

linking words for well-constructed sentences

appropriate ending

relevant expansion of notes

organizing points into logical paragraphs

Useful language for informal letters and emails

Beginnings and opening remarks

Hi Alex/Dear Jo

Thanks for you email/letter.

It was great/lovely/nice to hear from you.

Expressing enthusiasm

I'd love to/I'd be delighted to (go to the festival).

That sounds great/fantastic/ marvellous/fascinating etc.

What an excellent/a great/a wonderful etc idea!

Preferences

I'd prefer to (have a picnic) rather than (eat in a restaurant).

I'd rather (play tennis) than (go swimming).

I think it'd be better to (phone Chris) than (text him).

Making suggestions

Perhaps we could (go to the cinema).

Why don't we/you (buy Sara a watch)?

How about (spending the day on the beach)?

I think we/you should (walk there).

Closing remarks and endings

(I'm) looking forward to seeing you/ hearing from you soon.

(I) can't wait to see you again.

Best wishes/All the best/Bye for now

Task

You have just received an email from your English-speaking friend Ana asking if you'd like to go to an international sporting event. Read Ana's email and the notes you have made. Then write an email to Ana using **all** your notes.

> From: Ana
> Sent: 4 April
> Subject: Universiade
>
> ---
>
> As you know, the World University Games, or 'Universiade', is being held here this summer – it's the most important sports event after the Olympics. Would you like to go?
>
> My dad is on the organizing committee and he can get us free tickets for either swimming on June 30th or basketball on July 5th. Which would you prefer?
>
> You can find out more about the Universiade on the internet – or you can ask me. As my dad's involved, I've become an expert!
>
> You're welcome to stay with us as long as you like. Is there anything special you fancy doing while you're here?
>
> Ana

Yes!

Say which and why

Ask Ana about ...

How about ...?

Write your **email** in 120–150 words. You must use grammatically correct sentences with accurate spelling and punctuation in a style appropriate for the situation.

Part 2: Articles

You see this announcement in *Technology Today* magazine:

> **Life without a computer?**
> How different would your life be if you did not have a computer at home?
> Write and tell us and we will publish the best articles.

Write your **article**.

Model answer

interesting title to attract reader's attention

informal linking devices

opening sentence relevant to title

A computer-free home? Yes, please!

What a pleasure that would be! For one thing, it would be much easier to move in our house if we got rid of our three PCs and two laptops. And with no printers, speakers, keyboards or wires, there'd be less dust everywhere.

for this particular question type use comparatives and *would, might* and *could*

Can you imagine, too, how family relations would improve? My brother might come out of his bedroom more often, and my dad could look at me rather than the computer screen when we're having one or our rare conversations. We would have more time to play games together, cook real food or even talk to each other.

direct questions and statements addressed to the reader

Naturally, homework might be more difficult – I'd have to use books to find information, and write everything with a pen instead of typing it. But at least I'd be able to concentrate more without interruptions from emails and online chat messages.

a lively informal style throughout the article

an amusing comment to finish

Last but not least, just think of the benefits to my health. My eyesight might improve and my back wouldn't ache from sitting down all the time. Would anyone like to buy a computer?

Useful language for articles

Involving the reader

Can you imagine ...?

Just think ...

Have you ever ...?

How would you feel if ...?

Did you know that ...?

Introducing points

Firstly ... Secondly ... Finally ...

For one thing ... For another thing ...

First of all ... What's more ...

Last but not least ...

Attitude adverbs

Naturally, ... (Not) surprisingly, ...

Interestingly, ... Worryingly, ...

Personally, ... (Un)fortunately, ...

Task

Either write your own answer to the task above or write an answer to the following question in **120–180** words:

You see this announcement in *Music plus* magazine:

> **Life without music?**
> How different would your life be if you could not listen to music?
> Write and tell us and we will publish the best articles.

Write your **article**.

Part 2: Essays

Your teacher has asked you to write an essay giving your opinions on the following statement:

> *It is better to have a low-paid job you enjoy than a highly-paid job you dislike.*

Write your **essay**.

Model answer

possible,
void repetition
f language
sed in the title

se of formal
nking devices

appropriately
formal style

It is better to have a low-paid job you enjoy than a highly-paid job you dislike. Many of us would like to have a job which is both well paid and enjoyable. Unfortunately, however, monotonous and badly-paid work is the reality for most people. Nevertheless, it is interesting to reflect on which is more important to us: job satisfaction or money.

On the one hand, earning a high salary allows you to do the things you want. It enables you to have holidays in exotic places, own the house of your dreams and buy the latest technology. Even if you do not like your job, at least you will be happy in your free time.

On the other hand, a well-paid job would mean working long hours, with little free time to enjoy your wealth. By contrast, a satisfying job may not make you rich, but it might give you more control over your time and make you more contented with your life.

In my opinion, the ideal solution would be to spend several years earning a large salary, then find a job you really want to do and live on your savings.

introduction explaining the issue

arguments in favour of one point of view

arguments in favour of a different point of view

conclusion expressing your opinion

Useful language for essays

Saying what people think

Some/Many people feel that …

Others argue that …

One/Another point of view is that …

It is sometimes said/claimed that …

It is widely believed that …

It is generally agreed that …

Expressing your opinion

I personally feel that …

I firmly believe that …

I partly/fully agree that …

In my opinion …

Expressing contrast

On the other hand …

However, …

… whereas …

Having said that, …

Making additional points

In addition (to this), …

Furthermore, …

Moreover, …

What is more, …

(See pages 71 and 99 for further linking words and phrases.)

Task

Either write your own answer to the task above or write an answer to the following question in **120-180** words.

You have had a class discussion about holidays. Now your teacher has asked you to write an essay, giving your opinion on the following statement:

> *Holidays in the countryside are much more enjoyable than holidays at the beach.*

Write your **essay**.

Part 2: Reviews

You have seen this notice in your school library:

REVIEWS NEEDED

We want to buy some new books for the library. Have you read a good book in English recently?

Write us a review of a book you enjoyed, explaining why you liked it and why you think it would be a good choice for the school library.

We will use your reviews to help us decide which books to buy.

Write your **review**.

Model answer

The Thieves of Ostia

introducing the book

'The Thieves of Ostia' by Caroline Lawrence is the first in a series of books entitled 'The Roman Mysteries' and I think it's <u>an absolute must</u> for the school library.

persuading the library to buy the book

information about plot and characters, and reasons why you liked the book

The book is set in the Roman port of Ostia nearly two thousand years ago. It tells the story of Flavia and her three friends, and their attempts to discover who has been killing the dogs of Ostia and why. It's full of mystery and excitement, and the plot has many twists and turns, which make you want to keep reading.

reasons why the book would be a good choice for the library

The book is aimed at ten- to twelve-year-old native English speakers, but it is very popular with older children and <u>would be ideal for</u> teenagers studying English. <u>What's more</u>, it <u>gives a fascinating insight into</u> life in Roman times, so readers learn about history as well as improving their language skills.

use of linking words and phrases

concluding comments

<u>After</u> finishing 'The Thieves of Ostia', students will want to borrow further books from the series. <u>By buying it, then</u>, the library would be doing a lot to encourage students to read more in English.

Useful language for reviews

Giving information about a film, book, musical or play

It is set in (France) in (the nineteenth century).

It tells the story of (Gemma) …

It is based on a novel/a true story.

The film stars (Angelina Jolie) as (Lara Croft).

The main character is (Flavia Gemina).

Expressing an opinion

It is full of mystery/suspense/humour/action/twists and turns.

It gives a fascinating insight into (life in the last century).

The plot is straightforward/predictable/complicated/gripping.

The acting/soundtrack/direction is impressive/disappointing.

I particularly enjoyed … /I didn't particularly like …

Giving a recommendation

This (book) would be ideal for (teenagers)

It is a must/an absolute must for (the film club).

I'd recommend this (hotel) to (families with young children).

It is certainly/not worth reading/watching/going to see/buying.

Task

Either write your own answer to the task above or write an answer to the following question in **120-180** words:

You have seen this notice in your school's English-language magazine:

Animation films - reviews needed

Have you seen an animation film recently?

If so, send us a review of the film, saying what you did and did not like about it. Include information on the characters and the story, and say whether you would recommend the film to other people.

We will publish the best reviews.

Write your **review**.

Part 2: Stories

Your English teacher has asked you to write a story for an international magazine. The story must **begin** with the following words:

When my mobile phone rang and I saw it was Alex, I knew something was wrong.

Write your **story**.

Model answer

use of phrasal verbs

Background

a range of tenses and verb patterns

Development

Outcome

> When my mobile phone rang and I saw it was Alex, I knew something was wrong. I'd <u>dropped her off</u> at the station ten minutes earlier and I was just <u>putting my motorbike away</u>. "<u>The trains aren't running</u>," she said. "The drivers are on strike!" Alex, my ex-girlfriend, hadn't seen her parents for a long time and was planning to pay them a surprise visit during the Easter holidays. She never used to get upset about anything, but this time she was nearly in tears, so I offered to take her on my motorbike.
>
> The two-hundred-kilometre journey to her parents' village took us through some <u>truly</u> <u>spectacular</u> scenery, but it was <u>incredibly</u> cold and we both froze on the motorbike. To make matters worse, we had a problem with the engine on the way and had to stop at a garage to get it repaired.
>
> <u>By the time</u> we arrived we were fed up and looking forward to relaxing at Alex's parents' house. Imagine our disappointment, then, <u>when</u> we found out they'd gone away for the weekend and the house was empty. Alex and I rode home in silence. We split up <u>soon afterwards</u>.

some use of direct speech

include adjectives and adverbs

a range of time linkers

Useful language for stories

Time linkers

(ten) minutes earlier

for a long time

during the Easter/summer/Christmas holidays

soon afterwards

(See also the Grammar reference.)

Experiencing problems

Imagine (my/our) surprise/shock/horror/disappointment when …

To make matters worse …

On top of that/everything else …

(I/She/Tim) could have cried when …

(I/He/Sue) was close to tears/nearly in tears

Happy endings

It was such a relief/pleasant surprise to see/find/discover …

(We/They) were relieved/surprised/delighted/thrilled to see/find/discover …

Just as things were starting to look bad/desperate/hopeless, (something positive happened)

(I) couldn't believe (my) luck when …

Task

Either write your own answer to the task above or write an answer to the following question in **120–180** words.

Your English teacher has asked you to write a story for the college magazine. The story must **begin** with the following words:

That evening Jo rushed home to see if there was any news.

Write your **story**.

Part 2: Reports

You are now reaching the end of your studies for the First Certificate in English examination. Your teacher has asked you to write a report for new students at your school, explaining what resources are available in the school to help students prepare for the examination. You should include information on the resources in your school and advice on how to use them.

Write your **report**.

Model answer

a suitable heading for each section of the report

a range of language for giving advice

a consistent style, in this case formal

summarise the aim of the report without copying the wording of the question

a variety of words and phrases to describe amounts and quantities

conclude with summarising comment and/or final recommendation

Introduction

The purpose of this report is to describe the resources on offer in the school for students preparing for the First Certificate examination and consider ways to make the best use of them.

Books

The library contains a wide selection of readers and novels suitable for students at this level. It is a good idea to read at least one book a month in order to become familiar with a range of vocabulary and structures. There are also a number of FCE grammar practice books, which should be consulted if you are having problems with a specific feature of the language.

Computers

Students are also advised to spend thirty minutes or so a day doing computer-based practice tests. The multimedia room has sixteen computers for study use, with several FCE practice exams installed on each. Internet access also enables students to listen to podcasts and read online newspapers, an excellent way to improve listening and reading skills.

Conclusion

A daily visit to the school's library and multimedia room is recommended to help ensure success in the First Certificate examination.

Useful language for reports

Giving advice and making suggestions

I would recommend/advise (them to go to a seafood restaurant).

I suggest you/they (shop for clothes at 'Brown's').

The best place for (DVDs) is 'The Film Shop'.

You/They should/really must/are advised to (try a salad bar).

(A visit to the cathedral) is an option worth considering.

(A boat trip) is a must/to be recommended.

It is advisable/a good idea to (wear a raincoat).

Talking about facilities

The shopping/sports/cultural/leisure/restaurant etc facilities are …

… excellent/outstanding/second to none.

… adequate/quite good.

Task

Write an answer to the following question in **120–180** words.

A group of teenage students is going to be staying in your town for a week. You have been asked to write a report for the group leader about shopping in your town. Give information on the shopping facilities available in your town and make recommendations on where the students should go.

Write your **report**.

Part 2: Informal letters

This is part of a letter from an English pen friend, Lee.

> My sister Amy will be seven next month. I was thinking of getting her a pet for her birthday. <u>You</u> know a lot about animals – what would you recommend for a child of her age? If you could give me some information on how to look after it, that would be great too.
>
> Thanks, Lee

Write your **letter** to Lee. Do not write any postal addresses.

Model answer

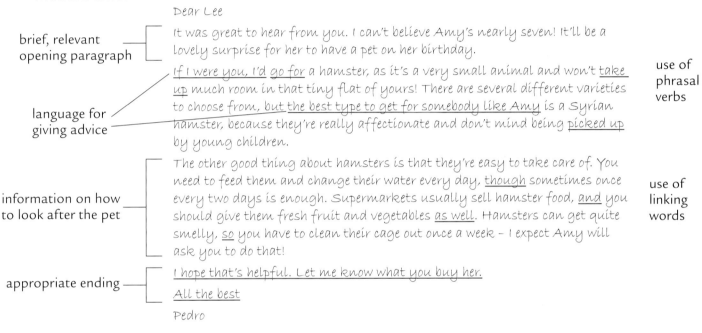

brief, relevant opening paragraph

Dear Lee

It was great to hear from you. I can't believe Amy's nearly seven! It'll be a lovely surprise for her to have a pet on her birthday.

language for giving advice

If I were you, I'd go for a hamster, as it's a very small animal and won't take up much room in that tiny flat of yours! There are several different varieties to choose from, but the best type to get for somebody like Amy is a Syrian hamster, because they're really affectionate and don't mind being picked up by young children.

use of phrasal verbs

information on how to look after the pet

The other good thing about hamsters is that they're easy to take care of. You need to feed them and change their water every day, though sometimes once every two days is enough. Supermarkets usually sell hamster food, and you should give them fresh fruit and vegetables as well. Hamsters can get quite smelly, so you have to clean their cage out once a week – I expect Amy will ask you to do that!

use of linking words

appropriate ending

I hope that's helpful. Let me know what you buy her.

All the best

Pedro

Useful language for informal letters

Beginning the letter

It was great/lovely to hear from you.

Thanks for your letter.

I'm pleased/delighted to hear that …

Sorry to hear about your …

Giving advice

It's (not) a good idea to …

It's best (not) to …

You should/shouldn't …

If I were you, I would/wouldn't …

Whatever you do, make sure you (don't) …

Try to ensure you (don't) …

One thing that works for me is to …

Ending the letter

I hope that's useful/helpful.

Write back soon and let me know …

Give my love/regards/best wishes to …

Looking forward to hearing from you.

Hope to see you soon.

Closing phrase

All the best Best wishes

Bye for now (Lots of) love

Task

Either write your own answer to the task above or write an answer to the following question in **120 – 180** words:

This is part of a letter from an English pen friend, Chris.

> My grandmother lives on her own and she's thinking of getting a pet to keep her company. <u>You</u> know a lot about animals – what would you recommend for someone like her? If you could give me some information on how to look after it, I'd appreciate that too.
>
> Thanks, Chris

Write your **letter** to Chris. Do not write any postal addresses.

Part 2: Letters of application

You see this newspaper advertisement while studying in Britain:

VOLUNTEERS REQUIRED FOR SUMMER WORK

We are looking for people to spend afternoons and Saturdays with groups of young children who have learning or physical disabilities and want to have fun. As well as accompanying the children to the swimming pool and on trips to the countryside, volunteers will be asked to organize further activities of their choice.

Write to Mr Brent and explain why you would be suitable.

Write your **letter of application**.

Model answer

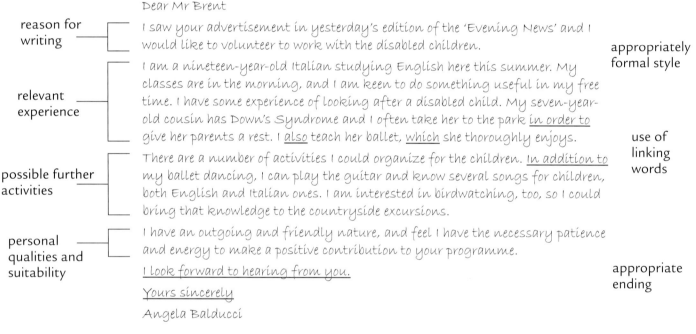

reason for writing

Dear Mr Brent

I saw your advertisement in yesterday's edition of the 'Evening News' and I would like to volunteer to work with the disabled children.

appropriately formal style

relevant experience

I am a nineteen-year-old Italian studying English here this summer. My classes are in the morning, and I am keen to do something useful in my free time. I have some experience of looking after a disabled child. My seven-year-old cousin has Down's Syndrome and I often take her to the park in order to give her parents a rest. I also teach her ballet, which she thoroughly enjoys.

use of linking words

possible further activities

There are a number of activities I could organize for the children. In addition to my ballet dancing, I can play the guitar and know several songs for children, both English and Italian ones. I am interested in birdwatching, too, so I could bring that knowledge to the countryside excursions.

personal qualities and suitability

I have an outgoing and friendly nature, and feel I have the necessary patience and energy to make a positive contribution to your programme.

I look forward to hearing from you.

appropriate ending

Yours sincerely

Angela Balducci

Task

Write an answer to the following question in **120–180** words.

You see this advertisement in an international magazine:

VOLUNTEERS REQUIRED

If you want to work with elderly people, why not spend this summer at the Wildflowers Nursing Home? Food and accommodation are provided. Duties include:

- playing cards and board games and going for walks with residents
- teaching basic computer skills
- organizing further activities of your choice

Write to Mrs Redman and explain why you would be suitable.

Write your **letter of application**.

Useful language for letters of application

Beginnings and endings

Dear Sir or Madam & Yours faithfully

Dear Ms Bentley & Yours sincerely

Reason for writing

I saw/have seen your advertisement in …

I am writing to apply for the job as (a waiter) …

I would like to apply for a grant to study/for …

I would like to volunteer to work with (disabled children) …

Describing skills and experience

I have experience of (looking after children).

I spent (three months) working as (an au pair).

I have excellent communication/computer/organisational skills.

I have a good knowledge of (history/English/computers).

Personal qualities and suitability

I have a/an friendly/sensitive/easy-going/enthusiastic nature.

I feel I have the necessary (patience) and (energy) for the job.

I am confident I would be well suited to the job.

I believe I am an ideal candidate for a grant/the job.

Closing remarks

I enclose my curriculum vitae.

I hope you will consider my application.

Listening scripts

Listening scripts which do not appear on pages 150–157 can be found on the *Direct to FCE* website.

1 Influence

Listening Part 2: Sentence completion

 1.1

(I = Interviewer; S = Summers)

I: Good morning. Now, our topic today is advertising. But it's a particular type of advertising isn't it Professor Summers?

S: Yes. We're looking at product placement.

I: Some people may not know the term 'product placement', so if you could just explain?

S: Of course. It's where certain products are put or as they say 'placed' in TV programmes for commercial reasons. For example, when a company pays a TV programme to show a person drinking a particular brand of bottled water, or eating a chocolate bar. The idea is that we'll watch it and think 'oh yes' I'd like one of those!

I: But hasn't this been going on for years? It's surely not that new?

S: You're right, it has been going on for quite a while, but only in films. You've probably seen it over and over again. It's become a really big, organised form of advertising. Think of some films you've seen this year. Did you recognise any famous brands, especially of soft drinks like Coke or Pepsi? Well, next time you're in the cinema, look out for brands and once you've seen one, watch how often it comes up in the movie. You'll probably see that the actor holds the cup or package just right, so that the name can be easily seen!

I: You've got me thinking now! For me, perhaps the most obvious are the cars – in the James Bond and Back to the Future series, even Tomb Raider.

S: Yes. And a really interesting example of a car is one that they created specially for a film. The Audi RSQ. Did you ever see it in I, Robot? Audi and the directors worked together on that. Very special. But that's film.

When we think about TV, of course, the USA is way ahead of Europe in advertising – they've had product placement in TV shows for quite a while too. You've probably seen American Idol. There, the product placement is very obvious, in fact you can't miss it! The judges have enormous cups of Coca Cola® in front of them throughout the show.

I: Now you come to mention it, yes, it's obvious. But on the similar shows in the UK it doesn't happen, does it?

S: No. But now that the European Parliament has made it legal in most types of programmes, you could soon see product placement on TV right across Europe.

I: Will it always be as obvious as in the American shows?

S: No. Reality shows are good for obvious product placement. But with other types of shows, like dramas, the point is that it should be in the background, but definitely not the centre of attention.

I: I suppose if it's too obvious it has the opposite effect.

S: Exactly. People will switch off. When they watch dramas people have to believe that the people and the story are real! They don't want to think that their favourite actor in a soap opera is actually advertising a particular brand of washing powder!

I: So why are some people against it?

S: A lot of people feel, and rightly so in my opinion, that if advertisers can say what happens in the programme, the quality will get worse.

I: So why is this happening more often these days Professor?

S: Interestingly, it's because we, the people, are beginning to use new technology better! Today, many of us record programmes from TV to watch later and when we do, what happens when we get to a commercial break?

I: We fast forward!

S: Exactly! We don't watch the commercials any more.

I: And how do you feel personally about this?

S: Advertisers will always find new and cleverer ways to influence what we buy. The only thing we can do is to make sure that we continue to keep the important controls we have of not using product placement on Kid's TV or the news.

I: So, if for some reason I start eating the same breakfast cereal as my favourite soap star then it's all because of product placement.

S: I'm afraid so!

2 Success!

Listening Part 3: Multiple matching

 1.2–1.6

Speaker 1

My career on the pitch lasted twenty years, and during that time I was lucky enough to play for three of the biggest clubs in the country. So I had plenty of valuable experience. But of course, working with some of the players nowadays requires an additional kind of skill. They earn a lot of money and some of them have a very high opinion of themselves and their abilities. Dealing with that can be difficult, so when I started out, <u>I'd often pick up the phone and talk to my old bosses, ask them for a few tips.</u> They were my teachers when I was a player, but <u>they were also a great help to me in my early years as a manager.</u> I owe a lot of my success to them.

Speaker 2

Experience has taught me not to listen too closely to what other people say. Theatre critics have written some rather nasty things about me over the years. As I'll be explaining in my autobiography, when I eventually find the time, and the patience, to write it. But, no, you just have to ignore everyone else and get on with it. The key to success is to believe in yourself, to convince yourself you can do it every time you go on stage. I usually spend five minutes before a performance, looking in my dressing room mirror telling myself how good I am. Terribly vain, I know, but it works.

Speaker 3

Young people nowadays think that success is all about being on the telly and having loads of money. For me, success is just deciding what you want from life, what your aims are, and then achieving what you set out to do – doesn't matter how much you earn or how famous or important you become. Not everyone can make it to the top, can they? As a matter of fact, when I left school I started training to be a chef – could have worked in some of the best restaurants if I'd qualified. But I decided early on that I'd be much happier running my own store and selling kitchen equipment. I've actually got two now – so I'm doubly successful!

Speaker 4

Success didn't come overnight for me. Indeed, it was several years before I actually had anything published. During the day I taught English in a private language school – for not very much money, I have to say – and by night I would scribble away in my flat until the early hours of the morning. Essays, short stories, novels – you name it, I had it rejected by publishers. But I was quietly determined and prepared to wait. I knew that it was just a question of time. Then sure enough, one bright young editor read some of my work, liked what I was doing and gave me an opportunity. And I gave up the day job.

Speaker 5

It's never just one thing, is it? I mean, to begin with, luck often comes into it – like bringing out your product at the right time, just when people need it, or think they do, anyway. You can't always plan for that. And then there's skill, of course – knowing how to manage people, for example, or understanding how the market works. But in my book, success mostly comes down to hard work. You have to be prepared to spend seven days a week at the office and work maybe fourteen or fifteen hours a day. That's always my advice to budding entrepreneurs.

Listening Part 4: Multiple choice

 1.7

(I = Interviewer; M = Mark Jacobs)

I: With me today is local man, Mark Jacobs, who spent the last eight months travelling round the world. Nothing particularly unusual about that, you may say, except that Mark successfully completed the 18,000 miles … on his bike. Mark, why did you do that? Were you hoping to break a record?

M: If I was, I failed miserably. The record stands at 175 days and it took me quite a lot longer than that. No, my aim was to raise funds through sponsorship for the Alzheimer Care Trust. My grandfather received a lot of support from them, and as he was the one who encouraged me to take up cycling when I was a teenager, I thought this would be a good way to repay them for all their help. I hope to give the charity a cheque very soon for four hundred thousand pounds.

I: Very impressive. And how do you feel now that you've achieved your goal?

M: Exhausted! No, naturally I'm delighted to have completed the journey and to be in a position to make such a large donation to the Trust. And I have to say I got very emotional last Sunday when I saw all the people who turned out to meet me at the finishing line. I had to get my handkerchief out to dry the tears. It was actually quite funny, though, to see the look of shock on a lot of people's faces when they saw my beard. Shaving wasn't part of my daily routine while I was cycling, so I wasn't quite as handsome as when I started out!

I: You mention daily routine. Tell us about that Mark. What was a typical day like for you?

M: Well, I tried to spend about twelve hours a day in the **saddle**, so I'd usually get up fairly early, somewhere between five and half past, maybe a bit later, do a few stretching exercises and listen to some relaxing music on my phone, just to ease myself into the day. Then it was breakfast. I don't normally eat very much in the morning but that had to change for this trip. I always made sure every night that I had plenty of food for when I got up. And then after I'd eaten, I'd clear away and start cycling.

I: And didn't you ever get bored of it all? I mean twelve hours a day is a lot, isn't it, especially on your own.

M: I went through 23 different countries, most of which I'd never been to before, so I couldn't very well get bored. And I met so many friendly people on the way that I was hardly ever conscious of the fact I was doing it alone. I also had my music to entertain me, of course – and keep me awake. It was often a struggle at the end of the day to keep my eyes open and concentrate on the road.

I: Hm, dangerous. Did you ever have any accidents?

M: I didn't, fortunately. I nearly got blown off my bike once or twice, though. In fact the wind was by far the most difficult thing I had to deal with during the whole trip – particularly in south-east Asia, where strong headwinds tore at my face and were really quite painful. It seemed as if the harder I pedalled, the stronger the wind decided to blow, which wasn't the case of course. But I did lose a bit of time and I got to Australia a little later than I'd intended.

I: Right, now, a lot of listeners were able to follow your progress via your blog. Did you have to take a lot of technological gadgets with you for this kind of thing?

M: Well, I wrote the blog on my phone, which I also used to send texts and listen to music. And phone people as well of course. Then, on the **handlebars** I had a GPS, to show my position. And to power them I had a solar panel fixed to the top of the **pannier** rack at the back. But none of it weighed very much and it didn't take up too much space, so apart from worrying about getting it stolen, it wasn't really a problem.

I: And did anyone ever steal anything?

M: On the contrary. Everyone kept trying to give me things! I was amazed. In some places, people would come up to me and offer me small gifts. Or they'd invite me into their homes, and refuse to accept any money for the food they gave me. It was very heartwarming.

I: Mark, we're going to take a break for news. Don't go away just yet, though. After the news summary, we'll be opening up the phone lines for listeners' questions. So if you want to ask Mark … .

3 It's an illusion

Listening Part 3: Multiple matching

🎧 1.8–1.12

1

It's part of our lives today, isn't it. No one's really hiding anything – people know it's happening. When I buy a magazine and look at the photos of celebs and models I know full well that they've been touched up. People can't look that perfect, can they! And surely, it's not just me. Everyone knows that airbrushing goes on, so there's nothing dishonest about it. As far as I'm concerned, it's fine. People should moan about something else!

2

If I were one of those people on the cover of a magazine I'm sure I'd want a bit of airbrushing to look fit and healthy – particularly when you're getting on a bit! Quite honestly, I think it's only fair. Famous people have their photos everywhere and we're looking at them all the time. I know people say that if they want the publicity then they have to accept everything that goes with it. But we've all got a job to do. If theirs is to look good in magazines then the more help they get the better!

3

I know we're seen as the bad guys here but really, we're only doing what our readers want. We're producing the best looking pictures that we can because that's what people expect to see. So, if anyone, they're the ones to blame. Our readers don't want to see models with black bags under their eyes because they had a late night! Or a spotty face! And if we make an actor's face a little slimmer, that's not going to hurt anyone is it? People have always liked to look at good looking people – think of all the film stars in the past. And quite honestly, if we're talking about making people look good, maybe we should be talking about banning make up!

4

Sometimes you just have to laugh! I look at some of these photos and think – you must be joking! No one has a neck that long or legs that skinny! It gets a bit ridiculous at times. Personally, I don't object to a bit of touching up here and there but when you see some of the pictures….It's unrealistic and the pictures have to be believable, don't they? And it's getting worse! These magazine artists have to limit themselves and accept that they can't go into fantasy land.

5

For me, it's all about the obsession most people have with appearance today and how we and other people look. There's something in the newspapers nearly every day about all the eating disorders that young kids are suffering from. And why is that? Because many of them want to look like the people they see in the magazines. Airbrushing simply makes it all worse and puts young people at risk. I am well aware that the magazines want to sell more copies – it's a business for them. But I think they should take more responsibility. Really.

Listening Part 1: Multiple choice

🎧 1.13–1.28

1

You hear a man talking on a radio phone-in about a quiz programme he saw on TV. Why is he phoning?

A He thinks the topic is not good for the quiz.

B He doesn't enjoy this quiz show.

C He disagrees with a few answers.

I felt I had to phone in because I was really surprised at some of the answers given on the Challenge Quiz on Thursday evening. I'm no car enthusiast but even I know that the correct answers given to the contestants weren't always right. On at least three occasions the car makes weren't what was shown in the pictures. I'm usually impressed by the standard of this particular quiz and it was therefore a bit of a shock. The programme researchers really need to check their facts when planning to ask questions like these because I'm sure I'm not the only person who noticed this.

2

You overhear two friends talking about a film they've just seen. What sort of film was it?

A a horror film

B an action film

C a comedy film

A: Did you enjoy it? I loved the film. Harrison Ford is definitely one of my all time heroes.

B: It's odd, I'm so used to him playing the hero in adventure movies. They suit his style of acting. You know the fast moving stories with lots of clever stunts and the love interest too.

A: I think it was good to see him trying something else. I mean, I've seen him in funny films before but not quite like this. I thought it was hilarious!

B: He's so talented, I reckon he could do nearly anything and do it well. How about Harrison Ford as a vampire – that would be worth seeing!

3

You hear someone leaving a voicemail message. What does he want to do?

A change an arrangement

B ask for some advice

C make a complaint

I'm just phoning to say I won't be able to come round this afternoon because I've got an audition at 3.30! I couldn't believe it – it's ages since I last went for a part but this could be big. You said I should keep trying and you were right! I'm going for a part in 'Together', you know, the soap opera on Channel 6? I think I'm up against some stiff competition and I didn't sleep at all last night. We couldn't meet up somewhere this morning, could we? You always manage to calm me down! I'll buy you the biggest cappuccino and if I get the part you can come along and watch the filming? OK? Give me a ring soon.

4

You hear two mothers talking about their children's birthday parties. What did the magician do at both parties?

A card tricks

B an animal trick

C an egg trick

A: How was the party yesterday? Did Maisie have a good time, and more importantly, did everything go smoothly?

B: It was fantastic. And thanks for giving me the name of that magician. He was terrific. Maisie was thrilled when he pulled an egg from behind her ear!

A: That's a new one! Tommy's friends loved him when we had him last year. I still don't understand how he does those card tricks. Did the kids like those?

B: I think he ran out of time. Maybe we'll get those next year. The high spot of the afternoon was when the rabbit came out of the hat!

A: At our party it was a pigeon! The kids just love that sort of thing, don't they?

5

You hear part of a TV review programme. What is the reviewer's opinion of the first episode of the new series?

A It made a good impression.

B It was disappointing.

C It showed promise.

On paper, the new detective series on Channel 4 last week should have been a huge success. It had everything it needed to succeed – a lot of big names always help a new show. Also they had one of the best script writers in the business who's written over a dozen successful crime series in his career. Somehow it didn't work and I think a lot of people felt let down by the first episode. To be honest, the story line wasn't that strong and some of the acting could have been better. However, it was only the first episode and perhaps next week's instalment will be an improvement.

6

You hear Dave phoning his friend Greta. Why is he phoning her?

A to invite her to a live concert.

B to make travel arrangements.

C to check whether she's going to see the new film.

A; Hi! Are you going to see Coldplay in London next Friday? I know you're a great fan.

B: Yeah. I am so looking forward to it. I've never seen them on stage before. I was really lucky and got tickets at the last moment. How about you?

A: You must have got the last ticket then. When I managed to get through they were sold out. I was hoping you might be able to take me into London, because I'm going to the premier of the new James Bond film and I know the train will be packed.

B: I really wanted to see that too. But you can't do everything! Sure, no problem.

7

You hear a newscaster talking about an art exhibition at a local gallery. Why won't one painting be in the exhibition?

A It might be a fake.

B It has been stolen.

C It wasn't allowed out of the USA.

Some advice for all you art lovers planning a visit to the Walker exhibition at the Main Gallery this week. Don't expect to see Walker's painting of London Bridge. It won't be there. Visitors yesterday afternoon were shocked to see a space where the great canvas should be and there were worries that the painting had been stolen. There have been a lot of thefts from art exhibitions in the recent past as we all know. In fact the work has been withdrawn because art experts are concerned that this may not be the original painting. They believe the colours lack the warmth of a genuine Walker. The owners of the London Bridge were reluctant to allow the painting to come to England from New York and this may have been the reason.

8

You hear a writer talking about her work. What does she feel about writing?

A It is lonely.

B It is unpredictable.

C It is tiring.

There are times when inspiration refuses to come and however long you stare at the paper ideas are simply not there. For me, I can't sit on my own and wait. I need to get on with other things, talk to other people, in a way distract my brain and more often than not inspiration comes while I'm concentrating on another task entirely! The most intriguing part of the creative process is that once I've started to write, the characters quickly take on a life of their own. It's true that often I have no idea what they're going to do or say!

Many writers I speak to say the same thing however they also say that writing leaves them quite tired but I'm very different. I usually feel excited and ready to start something else!

4 Going away

Listening Part 2: Sentence completion

 1.29

1

Presenter

There has been a great deal of debate in the media recently about the distances travelled by the food we eat. Here to talk us through it all is environment correspondent, Mark Mitchell.

Mark Mitchell

Thanks mainly to concerns about climate change, the term 'food miles' has entered our vocabulary. Food miles tell us how far food travels between the place where it is grown or produced and the place where it is eaten - in other words, the distance from 'field to **fork**'. Go into any British supermarket nowadays and you might find pears from Argentina, grapes from Chile, strawberries from Spain or tomatoes from Saudi Arabia. In fact, around fifty per cent of the vegetables and **ninety five** per cent of the fruit eaten in the UK comes from abroad. These figures are a cause for concern to those consumers who want to reduce the negative effect of their everyday lives on the environment. Why? Well, because much of our imported produce arrives by plane. And air travel is responsible for giving off large quantities of gases such as carbon dioxide, which, as we know, is a major cause of rising **global temperatures**. So, in response to consumer demand, and in order to warn shoppers of the possible environmental impact of what they were buying, some supermarkets began labelling produce flown in from abroad with a sticker showing **an aeroplane**. Many people would refuse to put food with these stickers into their shopping basket, particularly so-called 'locavores', who avoid, if possible, any produce which has been imported, preferring instead to buy **locally grown** fruit and vegetables, and meat from nearby farms. As well as doing their bit for the environment, locavores will tell you that locally grown food is much healthier than imported food, which can lose important vitamins on long journeys.

But do we really need to be quite so worried about the distance our food travels? Some experts now say that the whole idea of food miles is too **simplistic** and therefore unhelpful to environmentally conscious consumers. Take apples for example. British apples are picked from September to October. Some are sold fresh and the rest are kept in cold storage for use throughout the year. This is fine, initially, but keeping apples cold uses a lot of energy, and this of course creates those carbon emissions which are so bad for our planet. From June onwards, then, it becomes kinder to the environment to start shipping apples from New Zealand. Similarly, in summer, you can eat British lettuces with a clear conscience. But in winter, the energy needed to grow lettuces in heated greenhouses in Britain is greater than the environmental cost of importing them from Spain.

So it's not only a question of how far food travels but when it travels. And also, of course, how it travels, because the **form of transport** used makes a big difference. For example, food transported by sea is considered by some experts to be better than that which is flown in, because sea transport produces fewer carbon dioxide emissions.

Quite apart from environmental considerations, though, there's also the fact that one million people living in Africa are employed in the trade supplying fresh fruit and vegetables to the UK, a business which is worth several million pounds. If that business came to an end, many people in a number of African countries would be affected. This includes Kenya, which exports green beans to the UK at times when these are no longer in season here. 'Environmentally unfriendly,' say some. 'Not at all,' say others, because Kenyan farmers do not use **tractors**, and they use natural rather than chemical fertilizers, so their growing methods are far less polluting than in Britain.

The concept of food miles, then, is not wrong; it is simply incomplete as it does not consider the total energy used during the growing, transportation, production, storage and distribution of what we eat.

5 Fitting in

Listening Part 3: Multiple matching

 1.30–1.34

Speaker 1

I often laugh about it now, but at the time it was quite hurtful. I felt I was being **left out**. I was the new girl in the department and they'd all been working together for years. Whenever someone had a birthday, they would all go out for a drink after work, but they'd never ask me if I wanted to go. They were the best of friends and I was an unwelcome outsider – that's what it felt like, anyway. And this went on for ages. I never thought about leaving, though – which is just as well because things are really good now. But it wasn't until I'd been in the job for about nine months that I began to feel like I was one of the crowd.

Speaker 2

When my dad got promotion, we had to move to a different part of the country. And of course that meant me having to change schools, which I got a bit stressed out about. I thought everyone would make fun of my accent and I'd have trouble making new friends and everything. It wasn't long before I'd **settled in**, though. By the end of the first week I'd **got in with** a group of lads from my class who all played football at break time. We always had a good laugh, and we used to **hang around together** outside of school as well. I'm still in touch with some of them, even after all this time.

Speaker 3

When we first moved over here I had a pretty strong accent, which some of the other kids seemed to think was quite humorous. They had a bit of a joke about it, trying to imitate me and everything. It was all good-natured, but at first it used to get me down, and made me wish I was back in Australia. My parents **found out** fairly early on what was happening, and they told me just to ignore them all. So I did. And actually, the accent thing probably made it easier for me to get accepted. I was a novelty, almost like some kind of exotic creature from a faraway land that they could **show off** to their mates.

Speaker 4

Many moons ago, when I was about eleven, my parents wanted me to join the scouts. My dad had been in a group when he was younger and he kept telling me what a great time he'd had, camping and tying knots and all that sort of stuff. He even managed to convince me I might enjoy it. But I never really **took to** it like he had – mainly because there was no one there I particularly liked or **got on with**. I was very shy and I didn't mix well with other kids. I **stuck with** it for a while, but I left eventually – not long after my mum and dad had bought the uniform. They were fed up about that.

Speaker 5

I couldn't wait to move out to the countryside. I hated my job and I couldn't **put up with** the noise and the stress any longer. Some of my friends advised me against it - they said I'd miss the people, the energy and the hustle and bustle of the city. But they were wrong. I loved the peace and quiet, and the pace of life. And almost as soon as I'd moved in, I made a really good group of friends. But not long ago, while I was sleeping upstairs, someone broke into my cottage and stole a few things. It's been great living here, but I don't feel safe now on my own and I probably won't stay much longer.

Listening Part 1: Multiple choice

 1.35–1.50

1

You hear a teenager talking to a friend about becoming a firefighter. What has prevented her from making an application?

A her age

B her eyesight

C her height

M: So how come you're still working in the supermarket? I thought you were going to apply to be a firefighter. Aren't you tall enough or something?

F: Cheeky thing! I'm not that short. And anyway, it doesn't matter how tall or short you are, as long as you pass the fitness tests. No, I've still got to wait another six months – till my eighteenth. I'll be old enough to start training then.

M: And what about your glasses. You never see firefighters wearing specs, do you?

F: Yeah, I was a bit worried about that. But I checked it out on their webpage, and I don't think it'll be a problem. You can be a firefighter with worse vision than I have.

2

You hear a wildlife cameraman talking on the radio about his work. What aspect of his work does he particularly enjoy?

A the solitude

B the danger

C the unpredictability

Obviously, there's an element of risk involved. I often spend long periods on my own in some very isolated places, and if I'm attacked by a bear or bitten by a snake there's no one there to help me. But I value my personal safety and take precautions to prevent that kind of thing happening. Actually, to be honest, it's a rather dull and monotonous existence much of the time. Last year I spent six weeks alone in a Himalayan hut for just five minutes' footage of snow leopards. Next month I'll be trying to film pumas in the Andes. Of course, I may not succeed, but that's the attraction for me. Never knowing if you'll get what you want. Because when you do, it's priceless.

3

You hear a woman talking about a walking holiday she is going on soon with some friends. Why are they going without a guide?

A They will have more freedom to do what they want.

B They cannot find a guide for the place they are going to.

C They have had a bad experience with a guide in the past.

We're spending another week in the Lake District next month. Just a small group of us. I have to say I'm looking forward to not having someone telling me what to do every day. We had a guide the last two times we went. Steve his name was. Nice chap – very competent. Not like these guides you hear about that get lost or make you walk further than you really want to. In fact, he

phoned Julie up to see if we'd be needing him again. But we're going to do it without him this year. We'll be able to get up when we decide and we can plan our own walks. It should be fun.

4

You hear a commercial fisherman being interviewed on the radio. How does he feel about life at sea?

A He often misses his family.

B He dislikes the lack of privacy.

C He doesn't get on with the crew.

F: Is it hard being away from home for so long?

M: It would be really tough if I was married, and had kids, like some of the other guys. But in my case I guess you could say the crew is my family. We live, work, eat and breathe together for weeks on end.

F: Do you ever get fed up with each other?

M: Sure, we have arguments from time to time. Just like families do. But we talk together and sort things out. You have to. The thing is that living conditions are cramped, even on the larger boats, and it's difficult to get away from each other. Sometimes I'd do anything for a bit of space to myself.

5

You hear a British woman talking about travelling to Mongolia. What advice does she give to tourists who visit Mongolia?

A They should be tolerant of discomfort.

B They should avoid some of the local food.

C They should take gifts for the nomads.

The whole reason for going to a place like Mongolia is to experience a different way of life. And to do that you need to be prepared to put up with conditions you might complain about on a holiday at home. Let's face it, you aren't likely to get much of a feel for the country if you stay in a five-star hotel. Spending a week with the nomads on the other hand gives you a wonderful insight into life in Mongolia. OK, so you might not sleep so well in a tent, and maybe yoghurt and fermented horse's milk are not your favourite things to eat and drink. But it's a real

privilege to spend time in the presence of these warm and fascinating people.

6

You hear an elderly man talking about retirement. How does he say he sometimes feels now that he has retired?

A isolated

B bad-tempered

C anxious

I'm still very active, so I can't complain. Not like some people I know who've retired. You see it with some of my neighbours – they're grumpy, irritable and they spend half their time moaning. Probably because they never do anything. The couple who live next door to me just sit in front of the telly all day – you never see them. You can't cut yourself off like that, you've got to get out and do things. If I'm not up in the hills walking, I'm in the local library or playing bowls. I never stop. I just get a bit worried now and then that one day I won't have my health and I won't be able to do all the things I do now. I wouldn't like that.

7

You overhear a woman talking about her husband. What is her husband's job?

A an army officer

B a prison officer

C a police officer

Jim likes what he does. He seems to get on well with everyone, especially the young lads who are in there for long sentences. Some of the officers act as if they're in the army – they're good at giving orders but they don't talk much to the prisoners. Jim's different, though – he's just naturally friendly. You know, some of the inmates don't get a lot of visits, so they tell all their problems to him. He's a really good listener. Actually, next month he'll have been working there for ten years. He's never stayed in a job for as long as that before. He used to be in the police force, of course, but he never really took to it. It was too stressful, so he left after a couple of years.

8

You hear an extract from a radio play. What is the man's relationship with the teenage girl?

A He is her father.

B He is her employer.

C He is one of her teachers.

M: Here's a good job for you - in the hotel business.

F: Yeah, I saw that one. I'm not going to apply for it, though.

M: Why not? You got some decent qualifications at school, and you've had a bit of experience here. I think you've got a good chance.

F: There's no point. It says you need two years' experience – like every other job that's going. I don't know how people like me are supposed to find work. Age discrimination, my dad calls it.

M: Bah, don't worry about that. They say that so they don't get millions of applications. I'll write you a good reference. You've been a real help to me working here. I'm just sorry I've got to sell the café.

7 Survival

Listening Part 2: Sentence completion

 2.18

(I = Interviewer; J = John)

I: Now for our Out and About section of the programme, here's John with information about an interesting new exhibition down at the Maritime Museum.

J: Hello, Susie. Yes, the curators at the Maritime Museum have done it again! This latest exhibition, entitled Endurance and Survival, promises to be just as successful as last year's **enormously popular** Surf's Up event. If you enjoy tales of endurance and survival against the odds, then you **really must go along** and see it. The centrepiece is the James Caird, the small lifeboat in which Antarctic explorer Ernest Shackleton and five of his 27-man crew sailed an incredible 800 miles to South Georgia across some of the most dangerous waters in the world. They had **had to** leave the rest of the crew behind on a small island in order to go and look for help. That was in April 1916. Shackleton's ship, Endurance, had got stuck in the Antarctic ice almost a year and a half before that in January 1915, and their long battle for survival is surely one of the most epic adventures of all time.

I: And did everyone **get back safely**?

J: Yes. **Incredibly**, Shackleton and all those who'd sailed on the Endurance lived to tell the tale. And **remarkably**, so did all five members of the Robertson family and a friend after their yacht was attacked and sunk by whales in the Pacific Ocean. The disaster occurred in the summer of 1972, about 200 miles from the Galápagos islands. They spent the next five weeks fighting for their lives, first in a life raft, and when that deflated, a small open dinghy. The only food they had was a tin of biscuits, half a pound of sweets, ten oranges, six lemons, and a bag of onions! And there was enough water for just ten days.

I: And they still managed to survive!

J: Yes, they did. They had to collect rainwater and catch fish to supplement their provisions. And they also caught turtles which bumped into their dinghy.

I: And how were they rescued?

J: Well, they were **eventually picked up** 300 miles west of Costa Rica by a Japanese fishing boat. And from there they were taken to Panama. You can see the small dinghy in the exhibition, as well as some of the objects that the Robertsons sailed with. Many other survival stories are featured, and there's also a fascinating look at the skills and personal qualities you need to have if you want to sail round the world. [Laughs] It left me in no doubt at all that I would be **extremely foolish** even to think of doing it!

I: And do you think children would enjoy this exhibition, John?

J: Oh yes, certainly. Some sections **specifically cater** for kids. This is not one of those museums where you **mustn't** touch anything. There are loads of interactive exhibits, with buttons to push and things to do. And you can climb into the different boats on display and imagine what conditions must have been like for those who sailed in them. **Surprisingly**, though, what my 12-year-old boy found most interesting was the display of navigation equipment. I think he was fascinated by how it's developed over the centuries, and the exhibition gives you a real sense of how important it is for survival at sea.

I: It all sounds **absolutely fascinating**, John.

J: Yeah, Susie, you're a sailing enthusiast. You'd love it - you **ought** to pay a visit.

I: Yes, I probably will. And how much will I **have to** pay to get in?

J: Right, well, I have the prices in front of me. It's nine pounds fifty for adults, seven pounds seventy-five for senior citizens, and six pounds fifty for students and children aged six and over. Children under six **don't have to** pay. Students **need to** show their student card, of course, and senior citizens **should** take some proof of their age, just in case they're asked to provide it.

I: Thanks, John. Well, there you have it. The exhibition is on until January of next year ...

9 Slave to routine

Listening Part 2: Sentence completion

 2.25

(I = Interviewer; G = Greg Chandler)

I: With us today on 'The Chat Show' is bestselling author Greg Chandler, whose second novel, "Fast and furious" sold over a million copies in its first year alone. He's here to tell us about his most recent offering, a non-fiction work this time, entitled Take it slowly. Greg, tell us about the book. What inspired you to write it?

G: Well, it came out of a realization that we never seem to take pleasure in the moment. We spend all our time nowadays running around, always in a hurry, thinking about what we've got to do next, and not what we're doing now. As soon as we wake up we check the time: it's the first thing we do every day. And then throughout the rest of the day it's the clock that determines our **behaviour**, that dictates what we do and when we do it. And we rush around, in this mad, non-stop race against time doing everything as quickly as we possibly can.

I: We have a kind of obsession with speed, don't we?

G: Yes, that's right. It's become an addiction. We need to have the fastest possible internet connection, we want to know the quickest route from A to B, we eat fast food, we speed-read and we even look for a partner through speed-dating.

I: So you're basically saying we need to slow down.

G: Yes, slow down and enjoy life. It's as simple as that. But we seem to have forgotten how to do it. And that's what this book is about – helping people learn to do something which should really be second nature.

I: So what's the key? What's your main **advice**?

G: Well, it's a whole way of thinking, so before anything else, it's important to embrace the **belief** that your life would be better if you took things more slowly. That's the key. And once you've accepted that, then my number one tip is always 'Don't wear a watch'. The first step to taking control of your time is to pay less attention to it. I don't wear a watch, and I still get to meetings on time, I'm still aware of time, but it doesn't dominate my life, and I'm not glancing at my wrist every five minutes worrying about what time it is.

I: Interesting. And what else would you recommend?

G: Well, there's the whole area of eating; taking time over your food, not rushing it. For example, don't eat your breakfast standing up. It's an important meal, perhaps the most important one of the day, so set aside enough time in the morning to sit down and enjoy it. Also, chew your food, don't swallow it before you've had time to take in the flavour. And it's worth sitting quietly for a few moments before eating a meal – it'll slow you right down and help you appreciate your food.

I: Food for **thought** there, indeed. Actually, while we're on the subject, tell us about the Slow Food movement, Greg. You mention that in your book.

G: Yeah, this is a non-profit organisation that promotes food which is good, clean and fair; that is, food which tastes good, which uses clean production methods that respect the environment, and whose producers are paid a fair wage. It's a reaction to food produced on an industrial scale which is often none of these things – fast food, readymade meals, that kind of thing.

I: It's not particularly healthy, either.

G: Exactly. Of course, Slow Food is not the only organisation in the 'slow' movement. You may have heard about the Cittaslow.

I: Is that Slow Cities?

G: That's right. Slow Cities. Well, towns mainly, because they all have under fifty thousand inhabitants. There are more than one hundred and twenty towns in the **network** now, and that's in eighteen different countries. To become members they all have to agree to a set of over fifty goals and principles, which aim to improve the quality of life there, to enable people to live at a slower, healthier, more relaxed pace.

I: And what sorts of things do they do to achieve this?

G: Anything from planting flowers in the high street to promoting healthy eating or improving the traffic system. They value local traditions and more traditional ways of doing things, they prefer bikes to cars, peace and quiet to noise. It's about celebrating diversity and rejecting the fast-lane, homogenized world you see in so many cities across the globe.

I: Sounds great, Greg. I only wish this city could become a member …

Phrasal verb list

Phrasal verb	Meaning
ask someone out (10)	invite someone to go with you to a cinema, restaurant etc because you want to start a romantic relationship with them
break into something (4)	enter a building by force, especially in order to steal things
break up (with someone) (10)	if two people break up, they end their relationship
bring something back (8)	cause ideas, feelings, or memories to be in your mind again
carry on with/doing something (2)	continue doing something
catch on (5)	become popular or fashionable
catch up (8)	talk to someone you have not seen for some time and find out what they have been doing
chat someone up (10)	start a conversation with someone because you want to start a romantic relationship with them
check someone/something out (3)	examine someone or something in order to be certain that everything is correct, true or satisfactory
come up with something (2)	think of an idea or a plan
cover something up (1)	hide the truth about something
cram something into something (9)	do a lot of activities in a short time
draw up (9)	if a vehicle draws up, it arrives at a place and stops
drop someone off (4)	take someone to a place in a car, usually without getting out of the car yourself
end up (1)	be in a particular place or state after doing something or because of doing something
fall for something (3)	believe that a trick or joke is true
fall for someone (10)	fall in love with someone
fall out (with someone) (10)	stop being friendly with someone because you have had an argument or a disagreement with them
find something out (5)	discover a fact or piece of information
fish something out (9)	pull something out of a bag or other container
get something across (6)	make people understand something
get back together (with someone) (10)	if two people who ended their romantic relationship get back together, they start having a relationship with each other again
get by (on/with) something (7)	have just enough of something such as money or knowledge to be able to do what you need to do
get in with someone (5)	begin to be involved with a particular person or group
get on (2)	be successful in life or at work
get on with someone (5)	have a friendly relationship with someone
get through something (7)	manage to deal with a difficult situation
give something up (1)	stop doing something that you do regularly
go away (4)	leave your home for a period of time, especially for a holiday
go back on something (6)	fail to do something that you have promised or agreed to do
go for something (1)	choose a particular thing
go off (6)	happen in the way that had been planned
go on to do something (2)	do something after you have finished doing something else
go out (4)	leave your house and go somewhere, especially in order to do something enjoyable
go out with someone (10)	have a romantic relationship with someone and spend a lot of time with them
grow up (2)	change from being a child to being an adult
hang around together (5)	spend time with each other
lash out at someone (9)	try to hit someone suddenly
leak out (6)	if private or secret information leaks out, it becomes known by the public
leave someone/something out (5)	not include someone or something
let someone down (1)	make someone disappointed by not doing something that they are expecting you to do

lie in (9)	stay in bed in the morning for longer than usual	sort something out (10)	make arrangements for something to happen
live on something (7)	have a particular amount of money to buy the things that you need to live	split up (with someone) (10)	end a marriage or romantic relationship
look back on something (1)	think about a time or event in the past	stand out (5)	be easy to see or notice because of being different
look forward to (doing) something (5)	feel happy and excited about something that is going to happen	stay out (10)	not return to your home, especially when it is late
look up to someone (1)	admire and respect someone	stick with something (5)	continue to do something
make out (that) (3)	pretend that something is true	take someone in (3)	trick someone into believing something that is not true
make something up (4)	invent a story, poem etc	take off (4)	if an aircraft takes off, it leaves the ground and starts flying
make up (with someone) (10)	become friendly with someone again after having had an argument	take someone on (2)	start to employ someone
move on to something (3)	stop discussing or doing something and begin discussing or doing something different	take something on (8)	accept some work or responsibility
		take to someone/something (5)	begin to like someone or something
		take something up (2)	start doing something new as a habit, job or interest
pass out (10)	suddenly become unconscious	take something up (Writing Bank)	fill a particular amount of space or time
pick someone up (4)	go and meet someone, usually in a vehicle	talk someone into (doing) something (1)	persuade someone to do something
pick someone/something up (Writing Bank)	lift someone or something up from a surface	talk something through (1)	discuss a plan or situation in a detailed way
put something away (Writing Bank)	put something in the place where you usually keep it when you are not using it	throw something away (4)	get rid of something that you no longer want, for example by putting it in a dustbin
put someone up (4)	let someone stay in your house		
put up with someone/ something (5)	accept an annoying situation without complaining, even though you do not like it	touch down (4)	if an aircraft touches down, it lands
rub off on someone (1)	if a quality that someone has rubs off, it begins to affect another person so that they begin to have that quality too	tune out (1)	stop paying attention
		turn away from something (6)	refuse to accept or use something any longer
		turn out (2)	develop in a particular way or have a particular result
see someone off (4)	go somewhere such as a station or airport with someone in order to say goodbye to them	turn up (9)	come somewhere unexpectedly
		weigh something up (6)	consider the good and bad aspects of something in order to reach a decision about it
set time aside (9)	reserve time		
set something up (2)	start a business or an organization	work something out (2)	calculate
settle in (5)	become familiar with a new way of life, place, or job		
show something off to someone (5)	show people something you are very proud of so they will admire it		
sign up for something (2)	join a course or organization		
sleep in (9)	continue sleeping after the time you usually get up		
sort something out (5)	do what is necessary to deal with a problem, disagreement, or difficult situation successfully		

Answer key

Unit 1 Influences

Vocabulary: Influences page 6

2a
1 do, have
2 admire, encourage
3 talk
4 shape
5 look, copy

2b
1 A   2 C   3 no match   4 D   5 B

Reading Part 3:
Multiple matching page 6

2
1 D   2 A   3 B   4 D   5 B
6 B   7 C   8 D   9 C   10 A
11 B   12 D   13 B   14 A   15 D

3a
1 end
2 rub
3 look
4 talked
5 cover
6 let
7 given

Language focus: Past tenses page 8

1
1 took
2 had, wanted; had, been
3 was going
4 had/'d been covering

2 a
a 2   b 1   c 3   d 4

2 b
1 past perfect continuous
2 past continuous
3 past simple
4 past perfect simple

3
1 affected, had/was having
2 walked, was imitating
3 passed, had encouraged/encouraged
4 had, had been exercising
5 was, looked up to
6 wanted, had eaten

Speaking and vocabulary:
The weather page 8

2
1 heavy
2 drop
3 high
4 hard
5 gale
6 wave
7 spell
8 light

Use of English Part 1:
Multiple-choice cloze page 9

2
1 C   2 B   3 A   4 B   5 A
6 B   7 A   8 C   9 A   10 C
11 A   12 C

Speaking and reading:
the influence of advertising page 10

1
billboard **E**   junk mail **D**   commercial **F**
jingle **B**   cold calling **A**   poster **C**

3
1 B   Something I absolutely hate is cold calling. I get really ratty with them.
2 A   If I want something new I usually ask a friend who knows more about it than I do!
3 C   If it's simple .... it often sticks in people's minds. All these clever adverts ... I'm sure they can't be very successful.
4 E   They can be quite dangerous ... it can make you lose concentration.
5 D   There are ways of asking to go on a list so that you don't get junk mail.

Listening Part 2:
Sentence completion page 11

4
1   chocolate bar
2   films
3   soft
4   name
5   Robot
6   American
7   centre of attention
8   get worse
9   commercials/commercial break
10   the news

Language focus:
Present perfect simple and continuous page 12

Present perfect simple

1a
1 no   2 no   3 yes   4 there will be more product placement in TV shows across Europe

1b
a 4   b 1+2   c 2   d 3

2
1 b   2 a   3 d   4 c   5 d   6 a

3
1 already/so far this month
2 already/never/just
3 since 2009
4 never
5 yet/this morning
6 ever

Present perfect continuous

1
a 2   b 3   c 1

2
1 Have you seen (before now – no specific time)
2 have been talking (repeated action in recent past)
3 have even been (recently/unspecified time or place)
4 I've been drinking (recent repeated activity)
5 drunk (completed activity before now – no specific time)
6 I've been (state continuing up to present)
7 wasn't (completed activity)
8 had (state up to present – stative verb 'have')

Speaking Part 1:
Personal questions page 13

1
1 a   2 b   3 b

Writing Part 1: Email page 14

2 The informal style of punctuation, the use of contractions and colloquial phrases and missing words indicate that this is an informal email.

You would use an informal style to reply to the email.

3
a exclamation mark, dash
b I'm, you've, I'm, haven't, I've, you've, I'm, don't know, Money's, I've
c (I) left it
(it was) great to get your email
(I) bet you've never done that!
d great, typical me, bet

Review page 16

Use of English Part 4: Transformations

1 since I last watched
2 not/n't been to France for
3 have/'ve known Gary since
4 we have/'ve been playing
5 best meal I have/'ve ever
6 were you playing
7 have/'ve been feeling
8 have/'ve never been to/travelled to/ visited

Language focus

1 was coming
2 noticed
3 picked
4 realised
5 belonged
6 had written
7 phoned

8 was walking
9 went
10 had found
11 'd been worrying
12 had
13 'd dropped
14 had chosen

Use of English Part 2: Open cloze

1 been **2** The **3** on **4** was
5 no **6** up **7** have **8** of
9 Since **10** and **11** its **12** ago

Vocabulary

1

1 up **2** down **3** up **4** for
5 into **6** back **7** off

2

1 downpour
2 spell
3 heat
4 high breeze
5 dropped

Unit 2 Success!

Vocabulary and Speaking: Success page 18

1 do
2 make
3 be
4 get
5 going
6 achieved
7 go, turn
8 did, got

Listening Part 3: Multiple matching page 18

1

1 C **2** F **3** D **4** A **5** E
B not used

2

Speaker 1 C I listened to the advice of other experts.
... so when I started out, I'd often pick up the phone and talk to my old bosses, ask them for a few tips.
... they were also a great help to me in my early years as a manager.

Speaker 2 F You need to have confidence in your own ability.
The key to success is to believe in yourself, to convince yourself you can do it every time you go on stage. I usually spend five minutes before a performance, looking in my dressing room mirror telling myself how good I am.

Speaker 3 D A successful person is someone who accomplishes their goals.
For me, success is just deciding what you want from life, what your aims are, and then achieving what you set out to do ...

But I decided early on that I'd be much happier running my own store and selling kitchen equipment. I've actually got two now – so I'm doubly successful!

Speaker 4 A I had to be patient for success to come.
Success didn't come overnight for me. Indeed, it was several years before I actually had anything published.
But I was quietly determined and prepared to wait. I knew that it was just a question of time.

Speaker 5 E A combination of factors is required to become successful.
It's never just one thing, is it?
... to begin with, luck often comes into it
And then there's skill, of course ...
But in my book, success mostly comes down to hard work.

3

Speaker 1

B I enjoy the wealth associated with success.
They earn a lot of money...

F You need to have confidence in your own ability.
... some of them have a very high opinion of themselves and their abilities.

D A successful person is someone who accomplishes their goals.
[The connection between 'goals' and the football career of the speaker.]

Speaker 2

C I listened to the advice of other experts.
Experience has taught me not to listen too closely to what other people say.

A I had to be patient for success to come.
As I'll be explaining in my autobiography – when I eventually find the time, and the patience, to write it.

Speaker 3

B I enjoy the wealth associated with success.
Young people nowadays think that success is all about being on the telly and having loads of money.

Speaker 4

B I enjoy the wealth associated with success.
During the day I taught English in a private language school – for not very much money, I have to say...

Speaker 5

C I listened to the advice of other experts.
That's always my advice to budding entrepreneurs.

Reading Part 2: Gapped text page 20

3
The article mentions the following general points:

- *His career before he set up his online sweet business*

- *How and when he came up with his idea*
- *How he started the business*
- *The early days*
- *A problem which was solved*
- *How the business has grown*
- *His criteria for choosing the sweets he sells*
- *Advice to would-be entrepreneurs*

4

1 F **2** H **3** E **4** A **5** C **6** G
7 B D not used

5

1 c **2** f **3** e **4** a **5** d **6** b

Language focus: Ability page 22

1a

1 couldn't **2** can't **3** managed
4 succeeded

b

2 "... <u>we are not able to talk</u> to you."
3 In the end, <u>they were able to send out</u> all the orders.
4 Fortunately, <u>Parker was able to persuade</u> them to continue production ...

2 a
could is possible when we talk about general ability in the past (as in 1) but not when we talk about ability to do something on one occasion in the past (as in 2).

2 b
*My dog ran away last night but **we managed to find him and bring** him home.*
*My dog ran away last night but **we succeeded in finding him and bringing** him home.*
*My dog ran away last night but **we were able to find him and bring** him home.*

3

1 *can* – there is no infinitive form of modal verbs such as 'can'
2 *didn't succeed in* – the preposition *in* has to be followed by a gerund (*getting to sleep*)
3 *could* – there is no past participle form of modals such as 'can'
4 *was incapable* – *be capable/be incapable* are followed by *of* and a gerund (*incapable of riding a bike*)
5 *could* – as this is one occasion in the past, *could* is not possible.
6 *unable* – the correct way to use this would be *I am unable to lend ...*

5

1 capable
2 able
3 managed
4 how
5 succeeded
6 can
7 could
8 unable
9 was
10 impossible

Word formation: Adjectives page 23

1

b lucky **c** traditional **d** fixed
e interesting

2

2 poisonous dangerous humorous
3 professional emotional natural
4 wealthy cloudy sunny
5 careful harmful beautiful
6 reasonable comfortable reliable
7 frightening worrying surprising
8 dependent insistent apparent

3

1 healthy **2** uncomfortable **3** worrying
4 exhausted **5** spectator **6** viewers
7 harmful **8** careless **9** dangerously
10 humorous

Listening Part 4: Multiple choice page 24

2

1 C

... my aim was to raise funds through sponsorship for the Alzheimer Care Trust.

I hope to give the charity a cheque very soon for four hundred thousand pounds.

3

A *My grandfather ... encouraged me to take up cycling when I was a teenager*

B **Interviewer:** *Were you hoping to break a record?*

Mark: *If I was, I failed miserably. The record stands at 175 days and it took me quite a lot longer than that.*

4 & 5

2 B **3** B **4** C **5** A **6** A **7** B

2 **What does Mark say about the people who came to welcome him home?**

A Some of them were crying.
It was Mark who was crying: *I got very emotional ... I had to get my handkerchief out to dry the tears.*

B Many were surprised by his appearance.
Correct answer: *It was actually quite funny, though, to see the look of shock on a lot of people's faces when they saw my beard.*

C There were not as many as he had expected.
Not stated. There were probably more than he expected: *I got very emotional last Sunday when I saw all the people who turned out to meet me at the finishing line.*

3 **It was important for Mark each morning to**

A get up at exactly the same time.
He got up early but not always at exactly the same time: *I'd usually get up fairly early, somewhere between five and half past, maybe a bit later*

B have a large breakfast.
Correct answer: *I don't normally eat very much in the morning but that had to change for this trip. I always made sure every night that I had plenty of food for when I got up.*

C phone home.
Not stated: *and listen to some relaxing music on my phone.*

4 **While he was cycling, Mark frequently felt**

A fed up.
Not stated: *I went through 23 different countries, most of which I'd never been to before, so I couldn't very well get bored.*

B lonely.
Not stated: *I met so many friendly people on the way that I was hardly ever conscious of the fact I was doing it alone.*

C tired.
Correct answer: *I also had my music to ... keep me awake. It was often a struggle at the end of the day to keep my eyes open and concentrate on the road.*

5 **Mark says that high winds caused him to**

A progress more slowly than planned.
Correct answer: *But I did lose a bit of time and I got to Australia a little later than I'd intended.*

B lose confidence in his cycling ability.
Not stated; he lost time, not confidence: *I did lose a lot of time...*

C fall off his bicycle and injure himself.
He says he nearly did: Interviewer: *Hm, dangerous. Did you ever have any accidents?*
Mark: *I didn't, fortunately. I nearly got blown off my bike once or twice, though.*

6 **What does Mark say about the technological equipment he took?**

A It wasn't very heavy.
Correct answer: *But none of it weighed very much ...*

B There was too much.
Not stated; he simply lists the equipment and its functions.

C Some of it was stolen.
He had to be careful, but none was stolen:
Mark: *apart from worrying about getting it stolen, it wasn't really a problem.*
Interviewer: *And did anyone ever steal anything?*
Mark: *On the contrary. Everyone kept trying to give me things!*

7 **In some countries he visited, Mark was impressed with**

A the quality of the food.
Not stated; he mentions food but not the quality: ... *they'd invite me into their homes, and refuse to accept any money for the food they gave me.*

B the generosity of the people.
Correct answer: this is explained in the whole of Mark's last turn.
He says *I was amazed* **and** *It was very heartwarming.*

C the size of the houses.
Not stated; he mentions homes but not the size: *they'd invite me into their homes ...*

Language focus: Comparisons page 25

1

The words given are those that appeared in the recording: the bracketed words are also grammatically possible.

1 than
2 as (so)
3 most (least)
4 the, the
5 little (bit, lot)

2

Adjective/Adverb	Comparative	Superlative
fast	*faster*	*the fastest*
wet	*wetter*	*the wettest*
white	*whiter*	*the whitest*
early	*earlier*	*the earliest*
slowly	*more slowly*	*the most slowly*
gentle	*gentler/ more gentle*	*the gentlest/ most gentle*
reliable	*more reliable*	*the most reliable*
good	*better*	*the best*
bad	*worse*	*the worst*
far	*farther/further*	*the farthest/ furthest*

3a

1 d **2** c **3** e **4** b **5** a

3b

1 c **2** d **3** e **4** a **5** d

4a

1 Books are <u>much</u> more interesting than films

2 It's better to try and fail <u>than</u> never try at all.

3 The people in my country are among the friendliest <u>in</u> the world.

4 The more qualifications you have, the <u>more easily</u> you will find a job.

5 The Harry Potter films are by far the most entertaining films that have <u>ever</u> been made.

6 Cats are not <u>quite</u> as sociable as dogs.

7 English is probably the <u>most</u> difficult language of all to learn.

8 Many of the mistakes in this exercise are the same <u>as</u> the ones that I often make.

Answer key

Vocabulary: Sport page 26

2a & b

Underlined word	Normally associated with
a track	athletics
b pitch	football
c goggles	swimming, skiing
d court	tennis, basketball
e vest	basketball, athletics
f helmet	skating, skiing
g hole	golf
h trunks	swimming

Sport	Place	Clothes & Equipment	Other words
Football	pitch	boots	referee, match
Tennis	court	racket, net	umpire
Basketball	court	vest	time out, referee
Athletics	track	vest, starting blocks	field event, meeting
Golf	course	clubs	tournament, hole
Swimming	pool	goggles, trunks, costume	lane
Skiing	slope	goggles, sticks, helmet	slalom
Skating	rink	Rollerblades™, helmet, knee pads	

3

a taken up, take part, takes place
b silver, second, runner-up
c viewers, spectators, crowd
d beat, drew, won
e gone, playing, practise

Writing Part 2: Articles (Additional material) page 127

A
1 b   2 c   3 a

B
a more informal
b Contractions: *I've, I'm, I'd (x2), wasn't, I've, I'm, don't, it's*
   Phrasal verbs: *took up, gave up, carry on with, sign up for*
   Conjunctions at the beginning of sentences *Because, So*

C
*Can you think of **a better way** of keeping in shape **than** taking part in a team sport?*
*as well as being **the fittest I've ever been**, I'm also **a lot happier***
*... it **wasn't nearly as enjoyable as** doing something together with other people.*
*I'm **much more able** to sit at my desk and carry on with my revision.*
*What could be **better**?*

Review page 28

Language focus
1 least, in, a, by
2 not, as, as, bit/little
3 many, as, such, less
4 more, the, ever, quite
5 many, worse, fewer

Use of English Part 4: Transformations

1 didn't/did not **succeed** in finding
2 is/will be **impossible** for me
3 not **capable** of looking
4 **managed** to get
5 is not/isn't **quite** as/so old
6 dirtiest beach I have/I've **ever**
7 **longer** you sleep, the better
8 are not/aren't **as** many students

Use of English Part 3: Word formation

1 different   2 easily   3 employment
4 length   5 original   6 unchanged
7 successful   8 owners   9 production
10 surprised

Unit 3 It's an illusion

Vocabulary: Fakes page 30

2
1 into   2 taken   3 check   4 tell
5 imitation   6 genuine   7 fallen
8 out   9 coming   10 forgery
11 cloning   12 guard   13 cheating
14 copying   15 tell

Listening Part 3: Multiple matching page 31

2
1 C   2 D   3 B   4 F   5 A

Vocabulary: Appearance page 31

1
1 clear   2 wrinkled   3 slim
4 straight   5 thick   6 full
7 narrow   8 dull

2
1 b   2 d   3 a   4 e   5 c

Language focus: Modals of speculation and deduction page 32

1
must be, can't have grown
could be
must have had
must be wearing

2a
1 *could*
2 *must*
3 *can't*
   may and *might* can be used in place of *could*

2b
1 perfect infinitive
2 continuous infinitive
3 simple infinitive

3

1 Jack **can't** have gone
2 This can't **be** Winchester already
3 he **might/may/could** be there.
4 I must have been **doing** something else when she told you.
5 it **might/may** not be – it's difficult to tell.

Vocabulary: Expressions with *take* page 32

1
1 c   2 f   3 b   4 a   5 d   6 e

Use of English Part 4: Transformations page 33

1 might have met while/when
2 must have been tired because
3 is capable of passing
4 tell the difference between
5 had done the shopping
6 might not have remembered to
7 a possibility (that) Phil gave
8 take into account

Reading Part 1: Multiple choice page 34

2a animation film
2b possible types of films: crime thriller, courtroom drama, western, romance, romantic comedy, musical, historical film, biopic, disaster film, political thriller
4 It is mainly about Pixar
5 1 D   2 A   3 C   4 C   5 B
    6 A   7 C   8 D

Language focus: Present simple and continuous page 36

1
1 *Pixar never sits still.*
2 *The major studios are putting a lot of money into their own 3D titles.*
3 *Pixar makes cartoons that both children and adults adore.*
4 *There's something in the newspapers about all the eating disorders young kids are suffering from today.*
5 *People are always moaning about something!*

6 And it's getting worse!

7 'Carl, our main character, <u>goes</u> on an emotional journey.'

2

a continuous (sentence 5)
b simple (sentence 3)
c continuous (sentences 2 & 4)
d continuous (sentence 6)
e continuous (sentence 2)
f simple (sentence 1)
g simple (sentence 7)

3

1 a simple – regular action
  b continuous – annoying
2 a continuous – action in progress
  b continuous – temporary activity
3 a simple continuous – regular
  b continuous – in process of change

4

1 are selling
2 'm only working
3 don't understand, 're saying
4 don't usually take
5 is going
6 are always popping up

Listening Part 1:
Multiple choice page 36

1 1 C 2 C 3 A 4 B 5 B
  6 B 7 A 8 B

Writing Part 2: Reviews page 38

3

Plot: the story of Merlin the wizard and King Arthur when they were both young. Each week they have a new adventure, often fighting magical monsters/ characters from the old legends

Actors: newcomers Bradley James and Colin Morgan

Setting: location in a spectacular French castle and the Welsh forests,

Special effects: excellent use of special effects to create the monsters.

Writer's opinion: I was really impressed by the first few episodes of this series

4 1 c 2 e 3 d 4 b 5 a
5 2 4 3 1

Review page 40

Language focus

1 must have invited
2 can't be, must be
3 can't have spent
4 might/could/may have phoned
5 must speak

Vocabulary

1 tell
2 made
3 cheating
4 take
5 crooked

6 in
7 risk
8 clear

Use of English Part 2: Open cloze

1 being
2 could/did
3 managed
4 more
5 had
6 do/can
7 have
8 always/forever
9 must
10 never
11 makes
12 to

Use of English Part 1:
Multiple-choice cloze

1 C **2** A **3** C **4** A **5** D
6 C **7** D **8** B **9** D **10** B
11 A **12** B

Unit 4 Going Away

Reading Part 3:
Multiple matching page 42

1 B **2** C **3** E **4** C **5** A **6** D
7 B **8** E **9** D **10** C **11** D
12 B **13** A **14** C/E **15** E/C

Language focus:
Gerunds and infinitives page 44

1

1 not having
2 Reading
3 letting, watch
4 To prevent
5 looking
6 to get
7 to calm, restore
8 afford, to have

2

1 c
2 a
3 b, i
4 d
5 c
6 e
7 f, i
8 h, g

3

1 **to** protect
2 before **going**
3 need to **put**
4 Avoid **going** out
5 do not let your skin ~~to~~ **burn**.
6 don't forget **to drink**
7 **Correct**
8 get used to **wearing**
9 **Correct**
10 **Spending** time

Vocabulary: Travel page 45

1 C taxied, B took off
2 D give you a lift, C pick you up
3 D rest, B enjoy
4 A delayed, C boarded
5 B put, D stayed
6 C went away, A went on
7 C change, B get
8 D trip, C tour

Use of English Part 2:
Open cloze page 46

1

1 up **2** on **3** it **4** who/that
5 because/as **6** have/'ve **7** not
8 the **9** little **10** all

2

Samantha Lazarris went to Puerto Rico instead of Costa Rica.

The travel agent had used the wrong booking code.

She had to spend £800 on three extra flights.

3

1 up
2 of
3 until
4 had
5 in
6 the
7 As
8 to
9 It
10 instead
11 other
12 would/will

4

1 phrasal verb
2 preposition/set phrase
3 conjunction
4 auxiliary verb
5 preposition
6 article
7 set phrase/preposition
8 preposition
9 pronoun
10 *instead of* is a preposition
11 pronoun
12 auxiliary verb

Listening Part 2:
Sentence completion page 47

1

food mile noun [C] a measure of the distance travelled by foods between the place where they are produced and the place where they are eaten.

Source: *Macmillan English Dictionary*

2

1 fork
2 ninety five/95
3 global temperatures
4 (an) aeroplane/airplane

5 locally grown
6 simplistic
7 June (onwards)
8 (form/method/means/mode of) transport
9 one
10 tractors

Word formation: Prefixes page 47

1
a unhelpful   b unfriendly   c incomplete

2
1 dishonest   2 unlucky   3 illegal
4 impractical   5 incorrect
6 irrational

3 (Additional material page 128)
1 unpleasant
2 disqualified
3 unusual
4 discourage
5 unreliable
6 unable

Reading Part 2: Gapped text page 48

1
Her father, Dardie, left first: 'I was sad to see Dardie go', she says. Then her mother, Marmie, announced she was going. This was 'unthinkable' to the author. She was also separated from four of her five siblings and had to go and live with her godparents. She describes the two who went with their mother as 'the lucky two' and says 'This was the day when a veil of unhappiness came down on my life.'

2 1 D   2 H   3 C   4 F   5 A
6 E   7 G   B not used

Vocabulary:
Verb collocations page 50

1 1 made (took)   2 take   3 made
4 get, make   5 kept   6 break
7 come   8 took

2
Possible answers
3 invented stories/tales
4 have an opportunity to, get rich
5 didn't say anything
6 not do what she said she would
7 become a reality
8 look after

3 (Additional material page 128)
b take   c get   d come   e keep
f break

4
1 took a close look at
2 came as a surprise
3 broken the law
4 get rid of
5 keep calm

Writing Part 1: Letter page 50

1
Ian Webster's letter is written in a formal style.

Features
No contractions: _We are_ delighted _you have chosen_
More formal language: _I hope you are happy with this arrangement /if you require any further information / Yours sincerely_

No phrasal verbs or informal punctuation.

A formal style would be appropriate for the reply. Ian Webster is a College Director, who you have probably not met, since the style of his letter is also formal.

4a
She begins by thanking Mr Webster for his letter.
Her ending is suitably formal: _I look forward to hearing from you. Yours sincerely_, followed by her full name.

4b

Yes, because ...	First of all
Say which and why	With regard to (the public holiday)
Tell Mr Webster	In answer to your question about (our level)
Ask him about ...	Finally, (we would be interested to know ..)

4c As, since

4d
Familys – families, becuase –because, custums – customs, takeing – taking, confidente – confident, preffer – prefer, imediately – immediately, oportunity – opportunity, intrested – interested, programe – programme/program

Review page 52

Use of English Part 3: Word formation
1 extraordinary   2 attractive
3 directly   4 visitors
5 entertainment(s)   6 choice
7 incomplete   8 jewellery/jewelry
9 residence   10 enable

Vocabulary
1 an eye   2 as   3 close   4 sense
5 came   6 a chance   7 get   8 sure

Language focus
1 visiting
2 to go
3 to do
4 looking/to look
5 to go (or go)
6 seeing
7 to miss
8 having
9 to buy

10 leaving
11 Travelling
12 not walk
13 to get
14 to cycle
15 imagine
16 going
17 having
18 to get
19 getting
20 to see

Phrasal verbs revision
1 came, gave, set, ended
2 see, dropped, took, touched
3 making, made, talk, taken, fall
4 look, let, growing, looked, breaking

Unit 5 Fitting in

Listening Part 3:
Multiple matching page 55
1 1 D   2 F   3 C   4 A   5 E

Language focus:
Time linkers with past tenses page 56

1   Students are required to write the same word that the speaker used. However, the words in brackets show alternatives that would be possible in the context.
2   for
3   Whenever (When)
4   until, for
5   When (After)
6   before (until)
7   By (At, although the past simple rather than the past perfect would be more likely to follow _at the end_)
8   At
9   for, eventually, after
10   soon
11   While (When)

2
2   _They'd all been working_
past perfect continuous
3   _someone had_
past simple
they would all go out
would + infinitive
without _to_
4   _It wasn't_
past simple
I'd been
past perfect simple
I began to feel
past simple, infinitive
with _to_
I was
past simple

5 *my dad got*
past simple

we had to move
past simple, infinitive
with *to*

6 *It wasn't*
past simple

I'd settled in
past perfect simple

7 *I'd got in with*
past perfect simple

8 *it used to get me down*
used to + infinitive

9 *I stuck with it*
past simple

I left
past simple

my mum and dad had bought
past perfect simple

10 *I'd moved in*
past perfect simple

I made
past simple

11 *I was sleeping*
past continuous

someone broke into
past simple

3
1 Not long ~~time~~ after I ...
2 It wasn't until I **had** been studying ...
3 .... before ~~of~~ leaving the house ...
4 ... attention **while/when** I was reading ...
5 As soon as I **(had) got** up
6 ... my friends **for** over half an hour ...
7 .... an hour after ~~that~~ I went ...
8 ... but **in the end/eventually** I decided ...

Writing Part 2: Story page 56

1
Answer B would receive a higher mark.

Answer A is poorly planned and organized (eg *I forgot to say why I didn't know anyone*) and would lose marks for not beginning the story with the given words. Of the past tenses, only the past simple is used and there is little evidence of a range of vocabulary and linking words.

The positive features of answer B are drawn out in exercises 2 and 3.

2
Paragraph 1: **Background to events** and introduction to Liam.

Paragraph 2: **Development of events:** problem leading to events of final paragraph and introduction to the uncle.

Paragraph 3: **Outcome of events:** the writer's low expectations for the day and the surprise awaiting him/her.

3
• **a variety of tenses**

Past simple: e.g. *I arrived at the airport, things didn't go, I thought, I ended up, we hardly spoke*

Past continuous: *they were sorting everything out, it was going to be terrible*

Past perfect simple: *Liam had stayed at my house, we'd got on really well, they'd been involved*

Past perfect continuous: *I'd been looking forward to*

• **a wide range of vocabulary**

Collocations: e.g. *go according to plan, be involved in a car accident, spend the rest of the day, we hardly spoke a word, feed the animals, milk the cows, have a wonderful time*

Phrasal verbs: *look forward to, get on with, pick up, end up, sort out, find out*

• **suitable linking words**

when, though, because, but, while, at first, and, (not) until, so, when ... eventually

Reading Part 1:
Multiple choice page 58

Help box

Hurly-burly: a lot of noisy activity. This contrasts with the content of the previous sentence, which *'couldn't be more different'*.

Caught on: became popular. We can assume from the Kastam's lifestyle described earlier in the paragraph, that the innovations mentioned might well not exist or at least be popular on Tanna.

3
1 A 2 B 3 D 4 C 5 D 6 B
7 A 8 B

Word formation: Nouns page 60

1
2 inhabitants 3 visitors
4 viewers, commuters
5 investigation, distance
6 innovations, electricity
7 homelessness 8 living

2a & b

-ist	-ant	-er
tourist	inhabitant	viewer
cyclist	assistant	commuter
scientist	participant	employer
		winner

-or	-ion
visitor	investigation
competitor	innovation
spectator	prediction
	reduction

-ance	-ity
distance	electricity
appearance	ability
performance	generosity

-ness	-ing
homelessness	living
tiredness	building
weakness	meeting

3
a government **b** neighbourhood
c confidence **d** announcement
e patience

4b
growth – grow *violence* – violent
youths – young
neighbourhood – neighbour *safety* – safe

4c
magician – magic
disappointment – disappoint
embarrassment – embarrass
failure – fail *confidence* – confident

4d
childhood – child
adolescence – adolescent
championships – champion
announcement – announce

4e
difficulty – difficult *retirement* – retire
friendships – friend *librarian* – library
presence – present *arrival* – arrive
replacement – replace *warmth* – warm
patience – patient

5

-ure	-al
signature	proposal
failure	arrival

-ment	-ian
unemployment	politician
payment	magician
government	librarian
disappointment	
embarrassment	
retirement	
announcement	
replacement	

-th
growth
youth
warmth

-ence	-hood
violence	neighbourhood
confidence	childhood
adolescence	
presence	
patience	

-y	-ship
difficulty	friendship
safety	championship

Use of English Part 3:
Word formation (Additional material)
page 130

1
1 survival 2 reliable 3 competition
4 freely 5 comfortably 6 colourful
7 reactions 8 unwelcome 9 evidence
10 protection

2

-al	-ion	-ence
survival	competition	evidence
	reaction	
	protection	

Vocabulary: Personality page 61

1

1 **reserved** = shy, unwilling to talk about or show one's feelings; the others all describe someone who enjoys meeting and talking to people.

2 **patient** = able to wait for a long time or deal with a difficult situation without becoming angry or upset; the others describe someone who gets angry easily

3 **considerable** = large in size or amount, and is not the same as *considerate*, which means kind and caring; the others describe a person who can be trusted to do the right thing.

4 **sensitive** = caring about someone and not wanting to hurt their feelings or likely to become angry or upset easily; the others might be used to describe someone who seeks out and/or is capable of dealing with difficult or dangerous situations.

5 **nervous** = worried, afraid, not calm; the others describe someone who remains calm and does not easily get upset or angry.

6 **tolerant** = willing to accept or put up with someone else's behaviour and opinions even if you disagree with them; the others could be used to describe someone who believes in themselves and their own abilities and judgements.

7 **lazy** = not willing to work or make an effort; the others describe someone who thinks about other people and wants to help them.

8 **practical** = making sensible decisions *or* able to do or make useful things; the others are negative and describe someone who is not polite.

Speaking Part 3: Collaborative task page 61

Useful language

Here are some adjectives which might be useful for the jobs in the photographs:

Positive
tough, friendly, self-assured, sociable, outgoing, even-tempered, responsible, adventurous, cheerful, lively, enthusiastic, practical, reliable, patient, sensible, tolerant, decisive, easygoing, brave, confident

Negative (what the people shouldn't be)
fussy, moody, nervous, bad-tempered, grumpy, lazy

Listening Part 1: Multiple choice page 62

1 A   2 C   3 A   4 B   5 A   6 C
7 B   8 B

Language focus: The future page 62

2 I'll be old enough to start training then.

3 (We'll be able to get up) when we decide.

4 I may not succeed.

5 It should be fun.

6 You aren't likely to get much of a feel for the country.

7 I'm not going to apply for it.

8 We're spending another week in the Lake District next month.

9 Next month I'll be trying to film pumas in the Andes.

10 Next month he'll have been working there for ten years.

2

1 going   2 should   3 well
4 are playing   5 has finished   6 likely
7 have been learning   8 hope

Writing Part 2: Letter of application page 63

2

The writer would be suitable for the job. She has had some relevant experience, she has a good knowledge of the types of books which will be available in the library, she speaks languages that the school offers, and as well as having the right personal qualities she is very keen.

3

Paragraph 2: *to give information about herself and knowledge relevant to the job*

Paragraph 3: *to give details of relevant experience*

Paragraph 4: *to describe relevant personal qualities and explain why she thinks she is suitable for the job*

4 Possible answers
Dear

I have seen your advertisement in the latest issue of

I am writing to apply for the job as

I am ...years old

As a result of ... I ...

I have a good knowledge of

I also spent ... working

(computer) skills

In addition to ... I

I have a (patient) and (friendly) nature

... which I think is important for ...

I feel I would be well suited to a job in ...

I look forward to hearing from you.

Yours sincerely

Review page 64

Use of English Part 4: Transformations

1 not long after he had/'d *or* not long after having

2 until I (had/'d) found/worked

3 as soon as you arrive

4 unlikely to win

5 its complete failure to

6 were such a disappointment

7 following (your) payment of

8 during his childhood

Vocabulary

1

1 mannered   2 assured   3 tempered
4 minded   5 going   6 tempered

2

2 **un**sociable   **ir**responsible   **un**reliable

3 **un**friendly   **im**patient   **im**polite

4 thought**less**   **in**tolerant   **in**sensitive

5 **un**kind   **un**caring   **im**practical

Phrasal verbs revision

1 1 d   2 b   3 a   4 h   5 g   6 c
7 e   8 f

Language focus

1 am/'m going (to go) *or* will/'ll be going

2 won't take/doesn't take

3 is coming/is going to come/will be coming

4 gets

5 shall we go (also: can/should we go)

6 am/'m going to stay

7 start/are starting/are going to start

8 will/'ll be revising *or* am/'m going to revise *or* am/'m revising

9 'll phone

10 will/'ll be watching

11 to start

12 setting off

13 to be

14 will/'ll probably get *or* are/'re probably going to get

15 will/'ll give

16 get *or* have/'ve got

Unit 6 A matter of opinion

Vocabulary: Expressing your opinions page 66

3a

1 action
2 complaining
3 across
4 demonstrations
5 strongly
6 far
7 disruption
8 minds

Reading Part 3:
Multiple matching page 66

3

1 D	**2** A	**3** C	**4** B	**5** D
6 A	**7** B	**8** A	**9** D	**10** D
11 C	**12** B	**13** B	**14** A	**15** C

Language Focus:
Reported speech page 68

1 present simple becomes past simple.

2a

2 *must* changes to *had to*
3 *will* changes to *would*
4 present continuous changes to past continuous
5 *can* changes to *could*
6 present perfect changes to past perfect

2b

2, 4 & 5 *we* changes to *they*
4 *our* changes to *their*
5 *here* changes to *there*

Reporting verbs page 68

1

1 reminding   **2** predicting   **3** warning
4 refusing   **5** persuading   **6** ordering
7 offering   **8** advising

2

2 Maria predicted that Roy Green would win the election. (pattern 3)
3 My brother warned me not to be late that evening or our dad would be angry. (pattern 2)
4 The student refused to sign that petition. (pattern 1)
5 My friend persuaded me to take a break. (pattern 2)
6 The teacher ordered the class to sit down. (pattern 2)
7 Mike offered to help me with the research. (pattern 2)
8 My dad advised my brother to compare prices before buying a computer. (pattern 2)

Vocabulary: Making decisions page 69

1

1 consideration   **2** mind, going
3 rush, weigh   **4** make   **5** fence
6 option   **7** rule

Listening Part 4:
Multiple choice page 70

1

It is the House of Commons (one of the two Houses of Parliament) and members of Parliament usually sit there to debate important issues.

2

1 B	**2** C	**3** A	**4** C	**5** B
6 C	**7** A			

4

They chose lowering the voting age.

Writing Part 2: Essay page 71

3

1 however/whilst
2 firstly/secondly
3 as/because
4 such as
5 to conclude
6 personally/in my opinion/I firmly believe that/I fully agree that/I feel that

Language focus:
Reported questions page 72

1

How many members of the Youth Parliament spoke in the debate?

Are you going to campaign for any of the matters you discussed?

Will the Youth Parliament return to the House of Commons at a future date?

2

1 There is no inversion in reported questions.
2 yes
3 They are not used in reported questions.
4 if/whether

3

1 ... if/whether he had enjoyed the experience.
2 ... if/whether anyone had been wearing a suit and tie.
3 ... how long the Youth Parliament had been trying to get to the House of Commons.
4 ... if/whether he was going to stand for election the following year.
5 ... if/whether he thought the MPs had been impressed by the debates.

Use of English Part 1:
Multiple choice cloze page 73

1 B because the article concerns the future of newspapers and the possibility of losing them.

1 C	**2** D	**3** A	**4** C	**5** A
6 B	**7** D	**8** D	**9** C	**10** B
11 B	**12** A			

Reading Part 2: Gapped text page 74

3

1 C	**2** B	**3** H	**4** A	**5** F
6 E	**7** G	Distractor – D		

Review page 76

Language focus

He said he had/'d been expecting to see me on the train but couldn't/hadn't been able to find me.

He asked me if/whether I had/'d gone.

He said it had been amazing.

He said he was sitting there watching the march on TV.

He asked me if/whether I was watching it too.

He said it looked really impressive.

He said it had been a long day so he was going to bed early.

He said he would give me a ring soon.

Vocabulary

1

1 take   **2** make   **3** caused   **4** take
5 goes   **6** get

2

1 minds   **2** line   **3** weighed
4 strongly   **5** demonstration   **6** lead

Phrasal verbs revision

1 a up   b up with
2 a off   b back on
3 a on   b to
4 a for   b after

Use of English Part 2: Open cloze

1 at	**2** be	**3** how	**4** what	**5** on
6 have	**7** it	**8** why	**9** as	

10 able/ready/willing/prepared
11 whether   **12** not/never

Unit 7 Survival

Speaking page 78

1

Possible answers
What aspects of the modern world threaten their survival?

Books: e-readers, television and computer games and other activities which lead to people reading less
Letters: emails, text messages, cheap phone calls, free calls made over the Internet
Small shops: large shopping centres, internet shopping
Tropical rainforests: agriculture which favours the growth of exportable products such as rubber, bananas, coffee and cattle.
Cinemas: DVDs, illegal downloading of films on Internet, television
Whales: whale hunting, fishing nets, oil pollution, habitat destruction
Board games: television and computer games

Vocabulary: Surviving page 79

1

1 get   **2** make   **3** live   **4** stay   **5** get

2

a stay alive   **b** get by with
c live on money
d get through the day
e find it hard to make ends meet

Listening Part 1:
Multiple choice page 79

1 B	**2** B	**3** A	**4** C	**5** A
6 C	**7** B	**8** A		

Language focus: Countable and uncountable nouns page 80

1

1 hypermarkets [C]
2 tigers [C]
3 eBooks [C]
4 schools [C] money. [U]
5 damage [U] street. [C]
6 trees [C]
7 house [C] roof tiles. [C]
8 knowledge [U] research. [U]
9 journalist [C] help [U] advice. [U]
10 problems [C] behaviour. [U]

2

Before [U] nouns

a large amount of   much   a great deal of

Before plural [C] nouns

many   a large number of
very few   several   a couple of   a few

Before [U] and plural [C] nouns

some   a lot of

3a 1 *few*   2 *a few*
3b *little* and *a little*

4

1 in very good health, finding work/a **job**
2 The news ... **is** depressing, it's terrible weather
3 a lot of damage, to the furniture
4 We went on **holiday/a trip** to Italy, three **pieces of** luggage/three bags
5 traffic information, public transport

5

1 Several, number
2 many, plenty
3 Each, few, little, lot
4 amount, much
5 enough, few

Use of English Part 2: Open cloze page 81

1

1 Cardiff   2 three   3 twenty   4 one
5 Rugby   6 choral singing
7 Catherine Zeta-Jones   8 eldest

2

1 in   2 is   3 as   4 both
5 every/each   6 until/till   7 These/The
8 which   9 to   10 few   11 has
12 Although/Though/While/Whilst

Reading Part 2: Gapped text page 82

3

1 F   2 H   3 A   4 E   5 G
6 C   7 B

Vocabulary: Prepositions page 83

1

a on   b about   c at   d in   e at
f at

2a

2 to   3 for   4 on   5 about   6 at

2b

1 on   2 at   3 by   4 out of   5 in

3

1 charge, fire, risk, danger
2 accident, purpose, pay
3 order, complaining, smiles
4 participated, resulted, agree

Listening Part 2: Sentence completion page 84

1 Endurance and Survival
2 five/5
3 January
4 whales
5 bag of onions
6 Japanese
7 round/around the world
8 interactive
9 navigation equipment
10 children under/below 6/six (years old)

Language focus: obligation, prohibition, advice and necessity page 84

1

1 must (*have to* and *should* are also possible)
2 had to   3 mustn't   4 ought
5 have to   6 don't have to   7 need
8 should

2

Advice (present)

She ought to go out.

Lack of necessity (present)

There's no need for her to go out.
She needn't go out.

Prohibition (present)

She isn't allowed to go out.
They won't let her go out.

Prohibition (past)

She wasn't allowed to go out.
They wouldn't let her go out.

Obligation (past)

They made her go out.
She was made to go out.

3

1 you aren't allowed/you won't be allowed
2 We had/'d better
3 He made me stay
4 We don't have to wear
5 I needn't have spent
6 had to/have to buy
7 I have to walk
8 no need for you to bring

4a

Possible answers

It might be ...

1 ... an employee at a petting zoo or a farm speaking to children about the animals.
2 ... one child talking to another about the mess they've made at home and their mother's reaction if she sees it.
3 ... one pupil talking to another about how a teacher punished him or her.
4 ... a bank or shop employee talking to a friend about their dress code at work.
5 ... one examination candidate talking to another about the exam.
6 ... one person talking to another about a pair of binoculars.
7 ... one person talking to another about their car.
8 ... one person talking about towels to a friend who is coming to stay.

Word formation: Adverbs page 86

1a patiently, carefully, fully, dully

1b reasonably, gently, truly, wholly, immediately, bravely

1c happily, noisily

1d automatically, scientifically, publicly

2

2 safely   3 eventually   4 specifically
5 enormously   6 extremely
7 absolutely   8 incredibly
9 remarkably   10 surprisingly

3

1 successfully / extremely
2 critically / initially
3 incredibly / surprisingly

Writing Part 2: Reports page 87

2

1 Introduction
2 Going dancing
3 The sea is free
4 Indoor water fun
5 Conclusion

3

The target reader is the leader of the group of foreign students. The report is written in a formal style.

4a

Words and phrases for showing the amount or number of people and things.

*a **great deal of** money*
*its **large number of** discotheques*
***many** (discotheques)*
***Most** town centre discotheques*
***all** your students*
***plenty of** amusements*
***every** age group*
***several** water slides*

4b

Words and phrases for talking about price.

*do not **involve spending a great deal of money***
*town centre discotheques are **not cheap***
*admission is **inexpensive***
*drinks are **affordably priced***
*The sea is **free***
*There is **no charge for** entry*
*prices are **reasonable***
*there are **generous student discounts***
*without having to **spend a fortune***

4c

Phrases for making recommendations.
I would advise students to go to those on the seafront
the beach (is) *a must for* all your students
I would also *recommend a visit to the indoor Aqua Park*

5

many ... are specifically aimed at under-16s, so are ideally suited to your younger group members.
who will love its fine sand and clean water
which appeal to every age group
it is highly popular with young people

Review page 88

Use of English Part 4: Transformations

1 they should build
2 did not/didn't/would not/wouldn't let her go
3 had/'d better leave
4 made him tidy
5 no need for you to
6 aren't we allowed to *or* are we not allowed to
7 needn't have bought
8 must not be removed

Vocabulary

1 on, for
2 for, at
3 for, at
4 about, at
5 in, at
6 at, by
7 In, in
8 to, on

Language focus

1 each/every, much
2 many, little
3 few, few
4 plenty/lots, couple
5 number, any
6 some, no/little

Use of English Part 3: Word formation

1 truly
2 survival
3 exceptionally
4 successfully
5 dramatically
6 Unable
7 dangerously
8 decision
9 Amazingly
10 hesitation

Unit 8 Strength of mind

Vocabulary: Memory page 90

3

1 unforgettable   2 memorizes
3 photographic   4 long   5 brings
6 memorable   7 from

Listening Part 4 : Multiple choice page 91

2

| 1 B | 2 B | 3 A | 4 B | 5 C |
| 6 C | 7 B | | | |

Vocabulary: Expressions with mind page 92

1

| 1 d | 2 a | 3 c | 4 f | 5 e |
| 6 g | 7 b | | | |

2

| 1 c | 2 d | 3 f | 4 g | 5 a |
| 6 b | 7 e | | | |

Language focus: The passive page 93

1

| a 1 | b 2 | c 3 | d 4 | e 2 |
| f 1 | g 2 | h 4 | i 2 | |

2

a being taken
b are (always) held
c was built
d have (often) been asked
e had been handed in
f be stored
g will be posted
h to be taken
i are being supervised

Present simple: are (always) held
Present continuous: are being supervised
Present perfect: have (often) been asked
Past simple: was built
Past perfect: had been handed in
Future simple: will be posted
Gerund: being taken
Infinitive with *to*: to be taken
Infinitive without *to*: be stored

3

(to) be, past, by

4

| 1 b | 2 a | 3 d | 4 c |

5

1 How to Develop a Perfect Memory was written by Dominic O'Brien in 1993.

2 This artist's work will still be remembered in two hundred years from now.

3 We were being given a vocabulary test when the fire alarm went off.

4 I have been asked by my neighbour not to play my music too loud.

5 Memory competitions are regularly held all round the world.

6 Mobile phones must be switched off before entering the classroom.

6

An expensive laptop has been found in the Sports hall. It was discovered by a cleaner early this morning and must have been left there after yesterday's exam. At the moment it is being kept in the head teacher's office. A notice about the laptop will be put on the main noticeboard asking the owner to go to the head teacher, and students in all classes should be told about it. Students should also be reminded that laptops are not permitted in exam rooms. When the name of the owner is known, the laptop will be confiscated for a period of one month.

Writing Part 1: Letter page 94

2 b

Yes, the style is appropriately and consistently informal.

Contractions

I'd love, You didn't say, I'm out walking, I haven't done, I've got to, doesn't happen when you're

Punctuation

The play sounds great – I'd love to come and see you!

I've got to resit my exams – the ones you asked about. I did terribly!

Language

It was really nice to hear from you and catch up on your news.

The play sounds great

I've got to resit my exams

Good luck and see you on 15th

Best wishes

3

By the way, even when, or, because, As soon as, when

Vocabulary: Arts and culture page 95

2

2 performance: you watch a performance – the others are all places.
3 ballerina: this is one person – the others are all groups
4 exhibition: this is a group of things – the others are all types of art
5 instrument: this is an object – the others are all people
6 lyrics – the others are all types of music
7 sculpture – the others are all people
8 stage – the others involve illustrations of some kind

4

1 stage
2 best-seller
3 graffiti
4 concert hall
5 lyrics

Reading Part 1: Multiple choice page 96

4

a preserve
b reverence

c scarcity
d smash
e the limelight
f tantrums
g demographic
h prosperity

5

| **1** B | **2** C | **3** C | **4** D | **5** B |
| **6** A | **7** B | **8** D | | |

Language focus:
Passive of reporting verbs page 98

1

1 to have appeared
2 to be getting
3 to improve

a to be getting   **b** to improve
c to have appeared

2

It is known that Alfred Hitchcock appeared in most of his films.

It is thought that the human brain is getting bigger.

It is said that memory improves the more often we use it.

Additional material page 132

a

2 It is expected that climate change will get much worse over the next couple of years.
Climate change is expected to get much worse over the next couple of years.

3 It is said that eating fish improves brain performance.
Eating fish is said to improve brain performance.

4 It is thought that social networking has made people more isolated.
Social networking is thought to have made people more isolated.

5 It is believed that English and Spanish are easy languages to learn.
English and Spanish are believed to be easy languages to learn.

6 It is said that daily life is getting much faster for most of us.
Daily life is said to be getting much faster for most of us.

Vocabulary: The senses page 98

1 smell, hearing, taste, sight, touch

2

1 stared   **2** overheard   **3** suck
4 stroked   **5** sniff   **6** yell   **7** gazed
8 rubbed

Listening Part 3:
Multiple matching page 98

1

| **1** D | **2** C | **3** A | **4** F | **5** E |

Writing Part 2: Essay page 99

3

In paragraph 2 he/she gives reasons why people agree with the idea.

In paragraph 3 he/she gives reasons why people disagree with the idea.

In paragraph 4 he/she gives his/her own opinion.

4

1 To support the idea
2 However
3 In addition to this
4 On a personal level
5 I agree that; in my opinion; I personally believe that

5

ideas which support one point of view

On one hand.   There is an argument that ...   Some people feel that ...   One point of view is that ...

ideas which support a contrasting point of view

On the other hand   Whereas   Others argue that ...

an additional point

As well as this   What is more   Moreover

an example from personal experience

From personal experience ...   I know myself that ....

a personal opinion

Having looked at both sides I feel that   My personal view is that ...   On balance, I think

Review page 100

Use of English Part 4: Transformations

1 were given the/our results by
2 should be given to
3 is currently being questioned
4 have just been dropped off
5 is not expected to make
6 are known to be
7 is thought to be getting
8 is believed to have taken

Vocabulary

1 went
2 term
3 unforgettable
4 cast
5 glanced
6 off
7 swallow
8 limelight
9 modest
10 preserve

Language Focus

1 The celebrity was photographed by two members of the paparazzi as he was leaving his house this morning.
2 The tablets should be taken with food.

3 Memory is said to get worse with age.
4 The writer was being interviewed by television presenter, Mervyn Bagg, when the lights suddenly went out in the studio.
5 All films will be made in 3D in the future.
6 Pat had been chosen to join the orchestra so he was celebrating all night.
7 The decorating must be finished before we go on holiday.
8 The play has been given positive reviews by most critics.

Use of English Part 1:
Multiple-choice cloze

1 B	**2** A	**3** B	**4** D	**5** A
6 B	**7** C	**8** C	**9** A	**10** D
11 B	**12** B			

Unit 9 A slave to routine

Reading Part 1:
Multiple choice page 102

2

Polly notices with annoyance that Iryna has not put out his school clothes for him.

'I can't find my school tie,' Polly's son complains. 'Iryna's hidden it.'

'Iryna!' Polly calls up the stairs. The girl is supposed to be down by now.

'Oh, damn and blast!' she says, trying to text Iryna at a traffic light. 'I wonder where she is?'

Possible answer

Iryna could be Tania and Robbie's elder sister, Polly's sister or perhaps the family's live-in au pair.

3

a fish out   **b** lash out   **c** turn up
d draw up   **e** cram into   **f** burrow
g surge   **h** grind   **i** flip   **j** slumber

4

| **1** B | **2** B | **3** D | **4** C | **5** A |
| **6** C | **7** B | **8** A | | |

Language focus: Conditionals page 104

1

b future simple (passive), present simple
c *would* + infinitive (without *to*), past simple
d past perfect, *would* + *have* + past participle (or *would* + perfect infinitive without *to*)
e past perfect, *might not* + infinitive (without *to*)

2

| **1** d | **2** e | **3** c | **4** a | **5** b |

3

a you get good marks
b you get good marks

4

a or   **b** otherwise

5
1 if we are/'re late
2 I'd hate it *or* if I have to work
3 would have walked
4 unless you study *or* if you don't study
5 as long as you look after them
6 If we'd taken

6
2 did not/didn't have, would/'d go
3 will/'ll make
4 had/'d known, would not/wouldn't have brought
5 will/'ll change, shows
6 had/'d had, would not/wouldn't be
7 would/'d stay, were/was

Vocabulary: Time page 105

1a
1 to   2 on   3 in
1b
1 minute   2 fast   3 left

Suggested meanings
1 she is unable to put up with/tolerate it any longer
2 the time on her watch is always five minutes later than the correct time
3 there are only forty-eight seconds remaining for them

2a
a from time to time   b at all times
c Time after time   d at a time
e at the time   f By the time

3a
1 take   2 make   3 have   4 find
5 set   6 spend/waste   7 waste/spend
8 pass

Writing FCE Part 2: Set books page 106

2
It covers many genres (science-fiction, adventure, horror and suspense).

The story is well told, and the writing interests the reader throughout.

The central themes are still relevant today (it is timeless).

It offers the reader a great deal to think and talk about.

3
Features of articles
The first paragraph includes a direct question which catches the reader's attention.

There is a further question in paragraph two and the direct 'you' in the final paragraph.

The final paragraph includes an interesting observation which leaves the reader something to think about.

Quotations
The writer uses quotations to refer to the Morlocks (*'queer little ape-like'* and *'bleached, obscene'*) and to the Eloi (*'exquisite creatures'*). He/She also mentions the 'Haves' and the 'Have-nots', labels used in the novel.

Listening Part 2: Sentence completion page 107

1 Take it slowly
2 check the time
3 speed
4 enjoy life
5 wear a watch
6 standing up
7 (eating) a meal
8 fair
9 fifty/50
10 traditional

Word formation: Nouns 2 page 107

1
a behaviour   b advice   c belief
d thought   e network
2
2 sale   3 loss   4 flight   5 gift
6 laughter

Additional material task page 135

a
1 weight   2 height   3 heat
4 response   5 timetable   6 knowledge
7 choice   8 proof   9 complaint(s)
10 sight

Vocabulary: Sleep page 108

1 get   2 lie, hits   3 getting
4 sleeping, had   5 fallen   6 overslept

Reading Part 2: Gapped text page 108

3
1 F   2 A   3 C   4 E   5 G
6 B   7 H   D not used

Language focus: Relative clauses page 110

1
1 Sentences a, e and g are **non-defining relative clauses**. The information in non-defining relative clauses is not essential to our understanding of who or what is being written or spoken about in the main clause so commas are used to separate the two clauses.

The other sentences are defining relative clauses: these clauses identify, or define, the person (eg *parents* in d) or thing (eg *studies* in b) being talked about and are essential for our understanding of the sentence. Commas are not used in defining relative clauses.

2 *Who* and *which* can be replaced by *that* in defining relative clauses, that is, b (*studies which suggest*) and d (*parents who have*) but not *families in which both partners had*: if a relative pronoun is preceded by a preposition, *who, whom* or *which* can be used (as well as *what* and *whose*) but not *that*.

3 c: the relative pronoun can only be omitted in **defining relative clauses**, and only if it refers to the object of the verb in the relative clause. In this case, *that* refers to the word *something*, which is the object of the verb *do* (*...schools can do something...*). By contrast, in sentence b for example, *which* refers to the word *studies*, which is the subject of the verb *suggest*.

4 e: which refers to the clause *The classrooms are lighter and more spacious*.

5 *what* in sentence f.

2
2 Last Saturday, <u>when</u> she stayed at my house, Sally slept in the attic, <u>which</u> my parents have converted into a guestroom.
3 I got exactly <u>what</u> I wanted for my birthday – a new watch. It was the only thing <u>which</u> I really needed.
4 I don't see any reason *why* my parents won't let me have a sleepover party for my birthday.
5 Our headteacher, <u>who</u> is retiring at the end of the year, has been at this school for over twenty years.
6 An equinox is one of two days during the year on <u>which</u> night and day are of equal length.
7 There's a prize for anyone <u>who</u> can tell me the name of the group <u>whose</u> first hit record was 'Love me do'.
8 I slept until half past nine this morning, <u>which</u> is very unusual for me.
9 The only person <u>who</u> I really get on with at work is leaving next week. She's got a job at The Grand Hotel, <u>where</u> her dad works as a doorman.

3
a **The relative pronoun can be omitted in:**
3 It was the only thing I really needed.
4 I don't see any reason my parents won't let ...
9 The only person I really get on with at work ...

b **The relative pronoun can be replaced by 'that' in:**
3 It was the only thing **that** I really needed.
7 There's a prize for anyone **that** can tell me ...
9 The only person **that** I really get on with at work ...

Writing Part 2:
Informal letters page 111

2

Content: No. A brief general opening paragraph would be appropriate, but a large portion of the first paragraph is devoted to information which is irrelevant to the question.

Organisation: Yes, although a list of numbered points, whilst acceptable, does not enable the writer to use a range of effective linking devices. In addition, the first paragraph, if it were relevant, would be better as two.

Cohesion: No. There is very little evidence of linking in this answer. The first paragraph is a sequence of short sentences and this is followed by a list of imperatives.

Range: Yes. There is some evidence of a range of structures and vocabulary: eg [you're] looking forward to your holiday, it must be [terrible] for you, If it doesn't work, you should go to the doctor's. There is, however, also some repetition (I'm going to, looking forward to, I'm sure, I went), which could be avoided.

Accuracy: Yes. The answer is sufficiently accurate at FCE. There are some spelling mistakes (see exercise 3), but no grammatical errors.

Register: Yes. The letter is consistently informal to neutral throughout.

Format: No. It is not clear that this is a letter. The beginning and ending in particular are not appropriate.

Target reader: Yes, possibly, although it is not clear for example how much exercise Robin should do or when he should do it, what Helena means by 'too late', or which herbal infusions are recommended.

3

I'm **really** looking forward
You're probably looking forward
it will be **beautiful**
a nice **break**
you are finding it **difficult**
I would be very **nervous**
Don't eat **too** late
I hope my **advice** is useful

Review page 112

Use of English Part 2: Open cloze

1 each/every   **2** to   **3** few
4 this/that   **5** if/when/whenever
6 not   **7** what/the   **8** who/that
9 are   **10** which/that   **11** front
12 as

Language focus

1

2 If Rachel's dad hadn't given her a lift, she wouldn't have got to the station on time. *or* Rachel wouldn't have got to the station on time if her dad hadn't given her a lift.

3 I wouldn't know so much about Slow Food if I hadn't read an article about it. *or* If I hadn't read an article about Slow Food, I wouldn't know so much about it.

4 Richard wouldn't have played football last Saturday if the usual goalkeeper hadn't had flu. *or* If the usual goalkeeper hadn't had flu, Richard wouldn't have played football last Saturday.

5 If I'd realized it was Jackie's birthday, I would have bought her a present. *or* I would have bought Jackie a present if I'd realized it was her birthday.

6 You wouldn't have wet feet if you'd worn the right kind of shoes. *or* If you'd worn the right kind of shoes, you wouldn't have wet feet.

2

2 **which** seems quite early
3 **who** was going camping
4 **which/that** had been prescribed
5 **whose** working day
6 for **which** they're not qualified
7 the reason **why** he decided
8 the café **which/that** is next to
9 **when** it snowed all day

Vocabulary

1 lay, get   **2** good   **3** lie-in   **4** took
5 most   **6** all   **7** after   **8** at   **9** fast
10 set

Phrasal verbs revision

1

2 down   **3** in   **4** on   **5** into   **6** out
7 through   **8** for

2

2 touch down = land
let down = disappoint

3 settle in = become familiar with (a new job, house, way of life etc)
take in = deceive/trick

4 go on = do something after finishing something else
catch on = become popular

5 talk into = persuade
break into = enter a building by force, especially to steal things

6 leak out = become known
work out = calculate

7 talk through = discuss in detail
get through = survive

8 go for = choose
fall for = be deceived/tricked by, believe something which is not true

Unit 10 Changes

Vocabulary and speaking: Age

Possible answers

1 toddler
2 adolescent, youngster, teenager
3 preteen

4 newborn, in their twenties *or* past thirty
5 elderly, retired, senior citizen, getting on

Listening Part 3:
Multiple matching page 114

2
1 C   **2** F   **3** B   **4** A   **5** D
4
1 through
2 of
3 of
4 out
5 to

Language focus:
Wish, if only and *hope* page 116

2 2d could, 3c would, 4a past perfect

3 in sentence 1 it is unlikely that it will stop raining whereas in sentence 2 the possibility is 50/50.

4

1 I wish I **could get** *or* **I got** higher marks
2 We all wish it **were/was** warmer today
3 I hope Jack **wins** his race
4 If only I **had asked** you to help
5 Clare wishes they **would** stop building
6 If only I **didn't get** carsick

5 *Possible answers*

1 I wish I had/'d listened to my parents when I was a teenager.
2 I wish I were/was old enough to take my driving test.
3 I wish I could come to your birthday celebration on Saturday.
4 I wish my parents would let me go abroad with my friends this summer.
5 I wish I hadn't been (so) horrible to my brother when I was younger.
6 I wish I didn't have to go to school early for an exam tomorrow.

Should have/Ought to have

1

I ought to/should have asked you to help me when I had that problem with my car yesterday.

1 SPEAKING

a 💬 Work in pairs and follow the instructions.

You are planning a day out with some friends from another country.

1 Think about a city that you know. It can be where you live or a different city.
2 Make a list of interesting places that tourists can visit.
3 Agree on two or three places you'd both like to go to.

2 VOCABULARY

a Read the blog on page 45 quickly and find the adjectives in the box below in the text. Match the words to the definitions (1–6).

| spooky   magical   underground   tiny |
| frightening   thought-provoking |

1 very small _____
2 makes you feel fear _____
3 makes you think a lot about something _____
4 having a very exciting or special quality _____
5 a place can be strange and scary. _____
6 below the surface _____

3 READING

BETTER READING: SCANNING

Sometimes you need to scan a text (look at the text quickly) to find specific information. For example, you may want to know what time a museum opens or what you can see there.

Read the blog on page 2 and match the places (1–4) with descriptions (a–d).

1 ☐ Mail Rail   3 ☐ House of Dreams
2 ☐ Leadenhall Market   4 ☐ Clown Museum

a This is in the artist's house.
b You can ride trains that carried letters.
c You can visit only one day a month.
d It was in a Harry Potter film.

a Read the blog again and answer the questions. Write *L* (Leadenhall Market), *M* (Mail Rail), *C* (Clown Museum), *P* (Platform 9¾) or *H* (House of Dreams Museum).

Which place ... ?
1 has been used in films _____ _____
2 is the oldest _____
3 is not open at normal times _____ _____
4 is not where you think it is _____
5 is made out of things the artist has obtained _____

b Read the blog again. What are/were the following things used for?

1 the Mail Rail before it was open for tourists _____
2 Platform 9¾ in the Harry Potter film _____
3 the artist's house _____
4 the egg faces _____

4 SPEAKING

a 💬 Work in groups and discuss the questions.

1 Which place in the blog would you most like to visit? Why?
2 What are some alternative places for tourists to visit in your country? Tell each other about them. Which of your classmate's places would you most like to visit? Why?

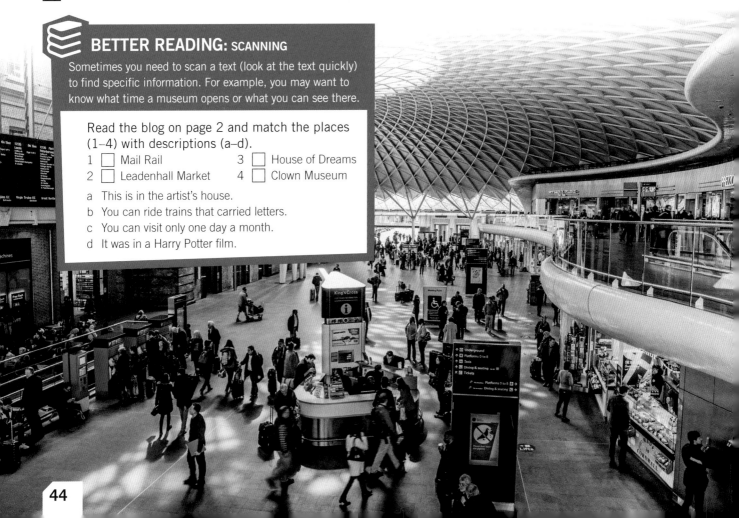

When the bank says 'NO!'

Have you ever tried to get a loan, but the bank said 'No!'? Maybe you can't afford a loan, or you don't have a bank account? People have got loans or borrowed money in different ways for hundreds of years, and not just from banks.

1 Credit unions

In the 1850s, Franz Hermann Schulze-Delitzsch was fed up with banks. He wanted to help other people, and he created a new organisation. People paid a little money each month. If someone wanted to borrow money, they could. The idea was a big success. At around the same time, Ninomiya Sontoku did something similar in his village in Japan. Everyone in the village could borrow money for up to 100 days. If the person couldn't pay back the money, the whole village helped them to repay it.

2 Microcredit

In the 1970s, there were lots of problems in Bangladesh. Many people in villages were poor and hungry, and they couldn't get loans from normal banks. Dr. Muhammad Yunus, a professor of economics, found an answer. He gave very small loans to people (for example, $25), and they started small businesses. For instance, they made furniture or bought animals for farming. Dr. Muhammad Yunus's 'Village Bank' was born. In 2006, Yunus won the Nobel Peace Prize for his work with the poor. In 2015, the bank had 8.81 million borrowers in 81,392 villages. 97% of their customers were women.

3 Crowdfunding

In 2007, a London music group needed money to make an album. They asked their fans for help online. They said that if the fans gave them money, they could have some of the profits later on. They received £26,000 from a thousand fans! Since then, lots of bands have done the same. This is one example of crowdfunding. You ask lots of people to each give a small amount of money to help you to start a business. And if the business makes a profit, you give the people some of it. So they may get some of their money back or not. They could also make some profit!

People have tried to crowdfund lots of strange and interesting things. Hans Fex wanted money for his Mini Museum. He creates tiny 'museums' you can put in your pocket. The museums include rock from the moon, and pieces of dinosaur egg. He raised $1.2m from 5,030 people. He now has his own website and has created three different museums. The first two have sold out.

4 Kiva.org

Kiva.org is a very special crowdfunding website. It is for poor people, or those in developing countries like India. Some of them want to start a business, and others need money to go to school or university.

The idea is very simple. A borrower asks for a loan. It is posted on the Kiva website. Then lenders can then choose to lend money to the borrower. The minimum loan is $25. The borrowers use the money and repay the loans. 97% of loans are repaid. The lenders can then take the money or invest it in someone else.

So far, Kiva has had 2.5 million borrowers in 83 countries. There have been 1.5 million lenders. They have lent 1.02 billion dollars. Oprah Winfrey said: 'Kiva is a simple concept that can change a person's life.'

I ought to/should have listened to my parents when I was a teenager.

I ought not to/shouldn't have been (so) horrible to my brother when I was younger

Use of English Part 1: Multiple-choice cloze page 117

3

1 D	2 B	3 B	4 A	5 B
6 C	7 B	8 A	9 C	10 D
11 A	12 D			

Listening Part 1: Multiple choice cloze page 118

1

1 B	2 A	3 C	4 C	5 A
6 C	7 B	8 A		

Writing Part 1: Email page 119

1

a formal style

2

2 Thank you very much
3 very kind
4 Regarding
5 of interest
6 Perhaps you could also tell us a little
7 could find time
8 would be very grateful.
9 Nothing else has been arranged so far
10 would like
11 I look forward to meeting you
12 Yours sincerely

Vocabulary: Relationships page 120

1

1	for	up	on	
2	out	out	up	back
3	out	on	up	up	for

Reading Part 3: Multiple matching page 120

1

1 attended　2 bride　3 groom
4 reception　5 vicar　6 best man
7 speeches　8 bouquet　9 bridesmaid
10 married

3

1 B	2 E	3 A	4 B/C	5 C/B
6 C	7 D	8 A	9 C	10 E
11 A/E	12 E/A	13 B	14 E	15 B

Listening Part 4: Multiple choice page 122

4

1 C	2 B	3 A	4 C	5 B
6 C	7 B			

Vocabulary: Health page 123

1

1 passed out, pain　2 side-effects
3 therapy　4 sick　5 symptoms
6 operations　7 illness　8 cure

Language focus: Causative passive with *have* page 123

1

have, past

2

1 has　checked
2 had　redecorated
3 have　restyled
4 has　serviced
5 has　had whitened

Review page 124

Use of English Part 4: Transformations

1

1 wish they had not/hadn't got
2 should not/'nt have stopped taking
3 wish Gary would
4 only we could afford
5 wish I did not/didn't have
6 had her hair done by
7 have his/the operation performed
8 had our planning application rejected

Vocabulary

a

1 bouquet　2 preteen　3 symptom
4 groom　5 toddler

b

1 of　2 up　3 for　4 through
5 of　6 out

Use of English Part 3: Word formation

1

1 unlikely　2 importance
3 celebration　4 comical　5 creations
6 relatively　7 complaints
8 surprisingly　9 pride　10 intention

Macmillan Education

Between Towns Road, Oxford OX4 3PP

A division of Macmillan Publishers Limited

Companies and representatives throughout the world

ISBN 9780230409569 (+ key)

ISBN 9780230419223 (- key)

Text © Roy Norris and Lynda Edwards 2011

Design and illustration © Macmillan Publishers Limited 2011

First published 2011

Designed by xen

Illustrated by Russ Cook, Wes Lowe, Laura Martinez, Norbert Sipos, Theresa Tibbetts, Harry Venning, Pablo Velarde.

Cover design by Designers Collective

Authors' acknowledgements

The authors would like to thank Simon Mullan, Lee Williams, David Gorman and Oliver Brunetti for their invaluable help with piloting.

The publishers would like to thank Mark Harrison, Elisabeth Johns and Darina Richter.

The authors and publishers would like to thank the following for permission to reproduce their photographs:

Alamy/ ACE STOCK LIMITED pp54(br), 114(r), Apex News and Pictures Agency p6(d), Nic Cleave Photography p132(r), GeoPic p137(l), Chris Howes/ Wild Places Photography p81(b), INTERFOTO p84(l), paulasfotos p29, Trinity Mirror / Mirrorpix p81(m), Wales p81(t);

Ardea/ Jagdeep Rajput p130, Adrian Warren p78(bm), M. Watson p45(m), Yann Arthus-Bertrand p91;

Corbis/ © A.M.P.A.S.®/ Andrew Ross p19(bl), Paul Barton p19(tl), Sayre Berman p6(b), Randy Faris p43(l), Andrew Fox p19(br), Annie Griffiths Belt p48(b), Nicole Hill/Rubberball p118(t), Mike Kemp/Rubberball p40, Robert Landau p37(tl), Frank Lukasseck p61(tmr), Tim Pannell p19(tr);

Getty/ AFP pp66(b), 69(mr), 72(l), 74(b), 96, Janie Airey p43(br), altrendo images p54(tr), Michael Blann p107, Bloomberg via Getty Images p78(br), Matthew Bresler p46(m), Doug Crouch p78(tm), John Eder p78(bml), Getty Images pp26, 74(tm and bm), 132(l), Daisy Gilardini p61(tr), Tim Graham p61(tml), Daniel Grendon p98(t), IIC/ Axiom p57(b), Image Source p120, imagewerks p57(t), Jupiterimages p54(tl), Izzet Keribar p78(tr), Jonathan Knowles p103, Elyse Lewin p114(l), Stuart McClymont p69(ml), Neil Overy p52, Lisa Peardon p54(bl), Monty Rakusen p42(l), Jeff Rotman p61(b), Manoj Shah p45(t), Paul Simcock p92(t), Kim Steele p37(tr), VisionsofAmerica/Joe Sohm p45(b), Wayne Walton p49(l);

MACMILLAN/ BRAND X pp49(r), 105(ml), ComStock p105(m and mr), CORBIS pp 9, 69(l), 72(m), DIGITAL VISION CORBIS pp98(tm), 137(r), GETTY p105(r), IMAGE SOURCE pp43(tr), 53, 78(tl and bmr), 115(r), MACMILLAN AUSTRALIA p25, BANANASTOCK p6(a), PHOTOALTO p6(c), PHOTODISC p 61(tl), STOCKBYTE pp105(l), 114(m);

Nature Picture Library/ Jose B. Ruiz p86;

Photolibrary/ Sylvester Adams p48(t), Christian Arnal p42(r), Malcolm Brice p69(r), Michel Bussy Photoalto p13, Andoni Canela p46(t), EDWARD CROSS p58, Raymond Forbes p69(m), Tom Grill p115(l), Christian Heinrich p46(b), Hill Street Studio p82, I love images p98(m), Image source pp 109, 118(b), Juice Images p47, Paul Kay p84(r), Mike Kemp p125, Robin Laurance p117, Pixtal Images p72(r), Radius Images p98(bm), Ken Redding p8, SGM SGM p66(m), Paula Solloway p92(b), Travelstock44/ LOOK-foto p121, Michael Weber p98(b), Gerhard Zwerger-Schoner p24;

Reuters/ Daniel Munoz p74(t) ;

Rex Features/ AGF s.r.l./Rex Features p37(tm), c.20thC.Fox/Everett p11, c.W.Disney/Everett p34, Robert Hunt Library p17, ITV/Rex Features p37(br), Rex Features pp37(bl), 66(t), CHARLES SYKES/Rex Features p37(bm), Adam Woolfitt / Robert Harding p70(t) ;

Photo p21 courtesy of Michael Parker.

Photo p39 © 2010 Shine Limited. Licensed by Fremantle Media Enterprises

Photo p70(b) ©Parliamentary copyright. Photography by Terry Moore.

Photo p122 courtesy of Christopher Sands.

Macmillan Reader ©Macmillan p89.

The author and publishers are grateful for permission to reprint the following copyright material:

Material from 'Mindboggling, Meet the memory champ who'll be battling for Britain at tomorrow's world finals – if he can remember where he put his lucky hat!', by Sarah Chalmers copyright © Solo Syndication, first appeared in The Daily Mail 30.08.07, reprinted by permission of the publisher;

Material from 'Pixar: The real toon army' by Guy Adams, copyright © Guy Adams 2009, first appeared in The Independent 23.09.09, reprinted by permission of the publisher;

Material from 'Holidaymaker ends up in wrong country' by Jamie Grierson, copyright © Jamie Grierson 2009, first appeared in The Independent 10.02.09, reprinted by permission of the publisher;

Material from 'Strange island: Pacific tribesmen come to study Britain' by Guy Adams, copyright © Guy Adams 2007, first appeared in The Independent 08.09.07, reprinted by permission of the publisher;

Material from 'Nintendo's biggest brain' by Tim Ingham, copyright © Tim Ingham 2010, first appeared in The Independent 24.03.10, reprinted by permission of the publisher;

Material from 'To sleep, perchance to get better grades' by Richard Garner, copyright © Richard Garner 2009, first appeared in The Independent 10.11.09, reprinted by permission of the publisher;

Material from Hearts and Minds by Amanda Craig. Copyright © 2009, reprinted by permission of Little Brown Book Group and Antony Harwood Limited;

Dictionary definitions taken from 'Macmillan Phrasal Verbs Plus', copyright © Macmillan Publishers Limited 2005;

Dictionary definitions taken from 'Macmillan English Dictionary (online)', copyright © Macmillan Publishers Limited 2010;

Material from 'How I made it: Michael Parker, founder of A Quarter Of' by Rachel Bridge, copyright © Rachel Bridge 2009, first appeared in Times online 06.09.09, reprinted by permission of News International;

Material from 'Anxious toddlers? Grumpy teens? Poor sleeping habits may be to blame' by Tanya Byron, copyright © Tanya Byron 2010, first appeared in Times online 06.02.10, reprinted by permission of News International;

Material from 'I had hiccups for three years but it saved my life' by Kate Jackson, copyright © Kate Jackson 2010, first appeared in The Sun online, reprinted by permission of News International;

Adapted material from 'I'm a Teacher, Get Me Out of Here!' by Francis Gilbert, copyright © Francis Gilbert 2004, reprinted by permission of Short Books Limited;

Text © 1995 Floella Benjamin from 'Coming to England' by Floella Benjamin. Reproduced by permission of Walker Books Limited, London SE11 5HJ, www. walker.co.uk

Printed and bound in Thailand

2017	2016	2015	2014	2013	2012	2011
10	9	8	7	6	5	4 3 2 1